"This book holds the promise of helping the reader understand deeply—more deeply than from superficial descriptions of culture—Native ways of thinking, speaking, and acting."
—*Dr. Robert Leavitt, director, Micmac-Maliseet Institute, University of New Brunswick, Canada*

"Evan Pritchard's *No Word for Time* is a startlingly translucent cultural document. The work is lucid, well written, and offers information on American mytho-poetics that is sorely needed in the field." —Eric A. Huberman, assistant professor in history of religions, Vassar College

"There are fleeting stories and there are eternal stories. Evan Pritchard's eloquent book is about the discovery of this difference. I go back to *No Word for Time* again and again to hear, to read the eternal stories of the Algonquin way of life." —Gioia Timpanelli, author of *Sometimes the Soul: Two Novels of Sicily*

"What makes Evan Pritchard's *No Word for Time* stand out from the Native American books presently in print is the engaging voice of the narrator: informative but never pedantic, personal but never self-absorbed. He never forgets that although he is writing a book, he is also talking to a reader. The book is spiritual in the best sense. If I were to come across this book in a store, I would buy one copy for myself and three for friends, with instructions for them not to return it, but pass it on." —Nancy Willard, author of *Sister Water* and *Telling Time*

No Word FOR Time

THE WAY OF THE ALGONQUIN PEOPLE

EVAN T. PRITCHARD

Council Oak Books
San Francisco/Tulsa

Council Oak Books, LLC

1290 Chestnut Street, Suite 2, San Francicso, CA 94109

1350 East 15th Street, Tulsa, OK 74120

Book design by M. Teresa Valero

Cover design by Yolanda Montijo

Cover image: *River Bluffs, 1320 Miles above St. Louis,* courtesy of the Smithsonian American Art Museum, Gift of Mrs. Joseph Harrison, Jr.

01 02 03 04 05   5 4 3 2 1

Library of Congress Cataloging-in-publication data

Pritchard, Evan T., 1955-

        No word for time: the way of the Algonquin/ Evan T. Pritchard. p.   cm.

        Includes bibliographical references.

        ISBN 1-57178-103-X (alk. paper)

        1. Algonquin Indians—History.

        2. Algonquin mythology.

        3. Algonquin philosophy. I. Title.

Egg.A349P75   1997

970' .004973—dc21

97-7492

CIP

Printed in Canada

Contents

AUTHOR'S NOTE

I have learned much about Native American wisdom through the exploration of Algonquin speech — not only through its words and phrases, but through the context in which they are spoken and the way of seeing the world they convey. Algonquin speech is a fine art, expressing a natural philosophy to which people from all paths and nations can relate. The title *No Word for Time* alludes to the gap between traditional and modern lifestyles, and to the fact that the Algonquin view is not easily expressed in English and vice versa. It is a world view in which time is measured in experiences and "things take as long as they take."

Very little recorded here on the Algonquins is taken from other books. It is what I learned from listening to and observing the elders in day-to-day situations "in the field."[i] Yet when I speak about "the elders" I am also speaking about my own grandfathers and grandmothers of the Miramichi ("Meer-ah-muh-shee") branch of the Micmac Nation. Their ways were handed down to me through the family, through dreams, and through my own blood, and those ways must have been little different from what I describe here. Though I may use the word "they," I do not separate myself from the Algonquin people. I am "they."

I am a descendant of "King" John Julian, chief of the Miramichi branch of the Micmac people, according to my great-aunt Helen Perley, who passed away October 6, 1994, at the age of ninety. [ii] Most of King John's descendants and "the Julian Tribe," as they were called, perished during the fever of 1834.

The area has been reclaimed by other Micmac people, but Helen was the "last real Miramichi" for all she knew, and lived accordingly. Over time, their culture has been absorbed by the great family of seven Wabanaki nations whose diverse people survive in the tens of thousands and who live the traditional way of the Wabanaki, according to their own inclinations and needs. Today there are over 10,000 Micmacs on "reserves" (the Canadian equivalent of reservations), and an estimated 20,000 more living among white society, a good portion of whom still speak the Micmac language with its poetic images. In addition, there are six other Wabanaki tribes whose total population most likely exceeds that of the Micmac.[iii] They too live both on and off reservations in the Northeast and continue to maintain their oral traditions, either openly or in secret.

[x] I am Algonquin by delineation, though family records obscure the fact. More importantly, I am one by inclination, and that is no small matter to a people who care first about a man's spirit and second about his bloodline. When the talking feather, the *galoosawach'n abee*, [iv] comes to me in the circle, strong medicine comes out. Holding the sacred eagle feather in your hand places you in touch with the Creator, and you must speak from the heart or pass the feather on. Some of the following has come to me this way.

Can a book be a talking feather? Perhaps not. The ancestors mistrusted books, but I do feel sometimes that the pencil is my "talking stick," and makes my truth come out, as does the feather.

I don't try to mimic the strong, simple voice of my teachers, as I am often tempted to do. But neither can I write in the formal, unimaginative manner I was taught in public school.

Therefore I must walk in a delicate balance between these two worlds of speech if there is any hope of bridging them both. My aim is to be understood and appreciated both by Algonquin readers "up on the reserves," and in a place such as Columbia (named after you-know-who) University, a place so far removed from the forests and pine barrens of the Wabanaki. As the elders say, "The Great Spirit is so powerful, it can do anything!" Let's wait and see.

Pronounciation Key

For the most part, the spelling of Micmac words used in this text is based on that developed in The Introductory Guide to Micmac Words and Phrases, by Stephen Augustine and me. This spelling system is self-explanatory to English-speaking people, and seems most appropriate for an English text such as this. There are several other spelling systems for Micmac which are widely used, are more "correct," and which use fewer letters; however, they are either more oriented toward French, or require more phonetical study on the part of the reader.

There is considerable controversy concerning these existing systems, which seems worthwhile noting. The Restigouche system, widely used in print, was developed out of the work of a Monsieur Pacifique, a French-speaking person, and is based on French vowels. The Nova Scotia system, widely used in everyday situations, is similar to the Pacifique, but uses *g* instead of *k*, as I have chosen to do here. Another writing system, developed by Mildred Millet of Big Cove, is based on Pacifique's work and is also oriented toward French. Its use is more likely to be found among elders today but not as much in print.

Although not as logical as the Pacifique systems, these spellings indicate the actual speech of the Micmac people I have learned from. I have found that these spellings allow English-only readers to grasp approximate pronunciations intuitively.

In an effort to make the transition as simple as possible for the reader, I will point out a few pronounciation tips:

a   as in call

ah   a longer, more stressed *a*

ay   as in day

bp   as a hard *b* or soft *p*.

ch   as in the Scottish loch, but not too harshly.
The *ch* in Miramichi is like *sh*.

d   as in dog

dj   as in edge

dt   a soft *t* as in water

edtch   as in well-fed chickens

e   as in best

ee   as in eel

eh   at end of word, as it sounds

g   as in good, but at the beginning of a word its harder than the English *g* in go, it is like a soft *k*.

i   as in inch

k   as in luck, at end of word. More forward in the mouth than *q*, harder than *g*.

o   as in know

oo   as in cool (also as aspiration, see note below)

q   is a click in the back of the throat

q(oo)   is a click in the back of the throat while lips are in "oo" shape, followed by an exhaled breath, usually at the end of a word. (Other systems use *W* either before and after a word to indicate the same aspiration.)

tch	as in witch
u	as in but (often appears between consonants)
w	as in wild (ex. Wabanaki). I use *w* where it is hard, and *oo* where it is soft.
'	is a glottal stop. In modern usage (Big Cove dialect) it usually indicates where a middle letter such as *ch*, *q*, or *g* has been dropped but is sometimes found in older dialects.
gh	ending as in Cavanaugh

I have used the older of the currently spoken dialects where possible for the sake of consistency. The new dialect often drops the initial *g*. It also drops the *q(oo)* and *ch* and sometimes *g* in the middle of a word, replaced by a glottal stop.

I have tried to use this spelling consistently except where proper names are involved. Micmac would be pronounced "Mik-mak," Lenape would be "Len-a-pee," and Wabanaki would be "Wa-ba-na-kee."

Many elders feel strongly that Micmac will always be an oral language and that no one logical writing system will ever codify the rich layers of sounds that the language holds, or its variations from place to place. There may even be a fear that a universal writing system (other than the use of heiroglyphs, which is not orthographic) would forever change and limit the way people pronounce and use the language, which is part of an ancient tradition.

I do not intend for anything in this book to be taken as the last word concerning anything. I only hope that it gives the reader an introduction to the world of the Algonquin elders and their language. For a true understanding, and a true grasp of pronounciation, one would have to live and work among the elders and listen to everything that is said with an open mind.

As stated in the introduction to *Micmac Words and Phrases* (with Stephen Augustine, teacher of native literacy on nine Micmac reserves), "Nothing written here is meant to supercede any part of the great oral tradition of the Maritimes, but is merely meant to be an introduction. We hope that this book will encourage those who have access to the elders in the Micmac tradition to listen more carefully to them and learn from what they tell us."

INTRODUCTION

Every culture has a wisdom teaching and a literary tradition, whether oral or written. In some cases, that wisdom is elusive to English translation and that literature is hard to define in Western terms. For the Algonquins, and more specifically for my own Wabanaki people (who are the northeasternmost of all Native Americans), poetry is a constant but invisible force. They don't write in metaphor, they speak it; they don't recite poetry, they live it. The creative act of living is central to their wisdom and the art of speaking is central to the art of living.

But how can you remove poetry from paper and the picture frame which paper imposes? In the postmodern world, every art form needs a boundary, a frame inside of which we can say, "All of this relates; all of this has special meaning." But has this always been necessary?

Each Algonquin society and its worldview can be a frame inside of which life can be art; within that boundary, all things relate and have special meaning. Within that boundary, speech and action can be sacred poetry with layers of special meaning for those ready to enter into it. It is a matter of shared context, something absent in the postmodern world.

A sacred dream, for example, has meaning within the context of your mind. If you act upon it, your actions may or may not make sense in the context of your day-to-day existence, depending on the choices you've made in the past. These actions will convey the same meaning to others only if there is a shared context between you.

A long time ago, our ancestors didn't need "art with a capital A" to express their sacred dream. There were already customs and rituals and expressions in place, including those we would separate from the rest of life as Art. A slight variation on any of these forms could be used to convey new meaning on many levels. At the same time, they realized that other people from other places have different ways, different dreams, and different frames through which they see the world, and that this is to be expected.

Part of Wabanaki poetry lies in their vast and perplexing mythology, while other parts lie in how they speak to one another, in how they interact with one another, and in how they sing to one another. Just as importantly, there is a poetry in the manner in which certain actions are performed which many refer to as "the sacred manner." Each of these is an integral part of the way traditional (and neo-traditional) Wabanaki express their wisdom, their thoughts and emotions, their creativity, their reality. While some may not recognize these as such, poetry is the English term which comes closest to describing their fiery inwardness, their heightened sense of beauty, their way of saying so much with so few words.

Of all the terms we could use to describe this ancient way of speaking and acting, poetry is the one which I feel would be most acceptable to Wabanaki people. Unfortunately, because we have no shared context within which to place nonverbal expression, the greater part of this art does not translate directly into book form. Therefore, I will have to focus on the art of speaking instead, an art that seems to be shared by most Algonquin people. A single Micmac word or phrase can sometimes be approximated by a few paragraphs of English, though not always. I will do my best. It is these elusive, semi-translatable phrases which give us the best hope of catching a glimpse of Algonquin wisdom in its pure form, and a glimpse of that context in which they live so expressively.

How This Book Began

This book grew out of a lecture-discussion I conducted at a Columbia University seminar (as much from the discussion as from the lecture itself) which explored sacred poetry world-wide. I called it "the Way of the Wabanaki." In that the subject was poetry, I focused on my personal insights regarding the way the Wabanaki live and interact. At the same time, I did not consciously divulge any of those teachings given to me as part of my training in what is strictly a Wabanaki oral tradition. I had plenty to say on my own account about what the Wabanaki have preserved in their culture which I felt would be inspirational and useful to the class.

The students themselves, for the most part young and sympathetic to the native situation, and who hailed from every sub-continent (and spiritual discipline) of the globe, seemed amazed at the startling parallels between my descriptions of everyday Wabanaki thought and speech — largely unrecorded by the outside world — and the most ancient sayings and beautiful writings of Asia, which are well known by comparison. Several were moved to tears or angry outbursts at unexpected moments, as one by one they realized what it was that Western expansion had displaced. I had to reassure them that all was not lost for the Native American people by any means — their culture is not dead, but the forces working against it at this time of upheaval are so great that it could well die, and soon.

As I later expanded my notes into a book, the global scope of that forum and the interrelationships we discovered between distant earth-based cultures stayed in my mind. The Wabanaki way of life stresses relationship above all else; it stresses the way each of the seven Wabanaki nations relate to each other like members of a family, how the Wabanaki family circle, or "hoop," as it is called, relates to other Algonquin nations (see appendix), and how the Algonquin hoop of nation families relates to all the native brothers across Turtle Island. Just as importantly, the Wabanaki understand the relationship between Native American people and those of other lands. We all have a part to play in this world, and we all are related. The multipurpose expression *nogomaq* in Micmac means "we are all related," or "all my relations." It is more than a saying, it's a way of life.

Many important genetic, linguistic, and cultural studies in the last few years have strongly indicated that Native Americans and Asians have common ancestry, even as recently as 10,000 years ago. This is a point of contention among many Native Americans (see "Creation as It Really Happened, p.191") but it does confirm the teaching, "We are all related." My own travels in Asia, and my studies with Jamgong Klungtrul Rimpoche and other Tibetan Lamas, have led me to similar suspicions, as the cross-cultural notes in this book suggest.

Therefore, the cross-cultural parallels we uncovered together in that class have been left intact and in some cases, expanded. Yet it remains a personal distillation of the revelations I experienced while living and working among my Wabanaki people, modern-day people with jobs and houses, but who still possess the same pragmatic philosophical bent as their ancestors.

Algonquins in a Global Context

I've heard a number of people remark that Native Americans "must have been an inferior race, because they contributed nothing to world culture — no great novels, no great cities, no great philosophies, no great poems, no great inventions or discoveries" (or something to that effect). Of course, most young people today sense this must be wrong, but are not sure how wrong, or why. I hope to address some of these questions.

First of all, Native Americans are not past tense. Native people today are producing a remarkable quantity and quality of artistic works which reflect the heritage of each individual artist, both overtly and as part of the unconscious process.[vi]

Also keep in mind that most of the culture that existed here in America was erased, debased, altered, or plagiarized so quickly by Europe's "explorers"[vii] that little was left intact to give to the world, even as a memorial. Of course, disease played a major role in the drama, but those who survived the poxes and fevers were usually left without land and lifestyle, in contrast to the European survivors of the plagues who inherited great wealth with which to rebuild.

The richness of Algonquin culture and the story of what became of it has a great deal of significance for Americans today, especially for the thirty percent[viii] who have invisible traces of native ancestry and who may find themselves instinctively continuing this way of life, and perhaps even this way of speaking, and are struggling to find a context in which they still have significance.

The richness of Algonquin philosophy inspired Henry David Thoreau to ponder on the rights of the individual, partly through contact with a Penobscot guide, Joseph Polis.[ix]

It was the richness of the Algonquin philosophy which inspired Thomas Paine, a student of native languages, to lay the foundation for much of what is unique about U.S. government. It is interesting that the U.S. Constitution begins with the common Algonquin expression, "We the People," *ulnuq*. This is no coincidence: Charles Thomson, an honorary Delaware (Lenape) and student of the Lenape language, was the Constitutional Secretary at the time. It was his brilliant appendix to Jefferson's *Notes on the State of Virginia* which became a blueprint for the Constitution.[x] I feel that the U.S. Bill of Rights also shows considerable influence by the Algonquin way of governing a free people.

Today, the ink in the letters "We" in "We the People" is eroding (mysteriously?) on the original document in Washington DC. If those Constitutional rights enscribed are eroding as well (as the ACLU might contest), isn't it a good time to take another look at Algonquin society and reexamine one of democracy's roots?

This native way of life doesn't need to be justified or defended — people who see clearly the wisdom of this way of life will choose it of their own accord and, for those who have no such inclination, nothing will convince them. But in the face of so much misinformation and so many misconceptions about native speech and culture,[xi] it seems worthwhile to present some additional facts. Then let people make up their own minds.

I don't mean to imply that all Algonquin people are philosophers or poets. Far from it (see "Not All Saints"), but I do imply that their oral tradition contains great poetic wisdom, which may come as a shock to readers whose concept of "culture" has been strictly literate and literary until now.

Native American culture shares at least a part of its origins in common with early Asian culture, which in turn shares a common origin with all earth-based cultures around the world.[xii] There is no one on earth without ancestors who honored the earth in a similar way. Traces of this way of life have survived in every culture and, though the Wabanaki understanding of things is unique, beautiful, and full of fresh insight, it's important to put it in its true context, a part of an understanding that men and women around the globe shared at one time. We could call this understanding ecological, holistic, even holographic in nature. It is nonlinear, nontemporal, non-Cartesian. What we call the Australian Aboriginal "dreamtime" isn't "time" to Aborignal people, it's reality! If there are many ancient cultures in which there is no word for time, it leads us to ask; "When was time invented, and for what purpose?"

What happened to that understanding, that "dreamtime"? The same thing that could happen to the way of the Wabanaki, unfortunately. Is it worth holding on to, is it worth saving? The students attending the seminar seemed to think so!

With the rate of clinical depression doubling every five years in America, many alarmed cultural psychologists have studied and written about hunting and gathering societies. It is under these conditions that the human brain evolved, and in hunting and gathering societies depression is (for the most part) nonexistent.

We can't all return to hunting and gathering as a way of life, but we can learn the lessons of that way of life and apply them to the twentieth century. As I hope to show, many Algonquin people have accomplished this difficult feat and bridged these distant worlds, particularly those who "follow the spirit."

But as any "bridge between worlds" will tell you, time is the great barrier. Time=money, money=good is a convincing equation, but it can undermine the art of speaking as well as the art of living. We all have to cope with this equation in our own way, and it's refreshing to enter a world where people still hold other equations in greater esteem.

In the landmark health book *Type A Behavior and Your Heart*, Dr. Meyer Friedman shows how a deadline-oriented lifestyle can lead to a distortion of the perception of time, which in turn leads to an irregular heart beat, eventual heart disease, and death. Dr. Emmett Miller (of Cherokee and African descent) developed the "relaxion tape" concept in part as a resource for those with "type A behavior." Another resource might be a visit to a reservation and the experiencie of "Indian time."

As I shared the beauty and insight of everyday Micmac expressions with the people at the seminar, it became painfully clear to everyone that the Algonquin people who greeted the boats had a philosophy and literary sensibility embedded in their oral tradition that was directly comparable with the celebrated wisdom of China, India, and Japan. If history had taken another turn, Native American wisdom could have been written down and translated into every language in the world, a great contribution to world philosophy; but few of the European settlers took the time to understand or write it down, while it seems clear that some of those who did so purposely maligned its meanings.

The good news is that considerable pockets of this poetic

oral tradition still exist — at least for a few more years, until television comes to each Native American home, dividing each viewer's life into half-hour segments, isolating them from their neighbors (and local dialect), presenting unrealistic standards for self-esteem, and wiping every last vestige of dreamtime away forever. In the meantime, I feel strongly compelled to put what little I know to paper, and hope it finds a friendly reception. Maybe if enough people do the same, there will come a day when no one will make the mistake of saying, "They have contributed nothing to world culture." The Algonquin art of conversation was — and still remains — a form of poetry equal to any in the world.

Waneeshee, "May the way be beautiful for you."[xiii]

BEGINNING –
IT'LL TAKE YOUR WHOLE LIFE

Many years ago, I was hungering so strongly to find my own Micmac roots that I found myself knocking at the door of a perfect stranger on a Micmac reservation deep in the interior of the Canadian Maritimes. This mysterious stranger was rumored to consider himself a "medicine man," although no one knew much about him at the time. There was no clue that this so-called medicine man, Ben Payson (a fictitious name I use to honor his request for anonymity) was even home, but I kept knocking. Yes, I was nervous, but he seemed to be my last chance and I had promised my family I would try to learn the ways from an elder. My throat was dry as cotton.

The door opened and I stood back. There in the doorway was the most amazing looking human being, his big muscular arms crossing his bare chest. I caught my breath. He had the round, sloped face of the Algonquin and his long white hair poured down in rivers over his big shoulders. His barrel chest seemed impenetrable to spears and arrows, and he looked at me with a warrior's clarity and a warrior's wariness of strangers. His mustache softened the look of his face and his mouth, but not the intensity of his gaze. His upper eyelids had the steep curve of full-blooded Native American people, giving his eyes the appearance of being almond-shaped.

It struck me that he was the chief of his own world, possessing total authority over his own affairs. His feet were firmly planted in the doorway as if it were a gate and he were the gatekeeper. He possessed the power of confidence that comes from devotion to his people and total belief in his way of life. "Here is a man of true power," I thought.

"I'm looking for someone...named...Ben...Payson."

"Yure lookin' at 'im!" He tossed the words back at me without uncrossing his arms.

"I thought you could help me. I want to learn about the Micmacs." I figured that my mere interest would win him over.

"Why you wanna learn...about Micmac?" he growled.

My jaw dropped. I had never expected such a question. Why indeed? I thought, "Doesn't he want to share his personal philosophy with the world?"

"Why?" I paused for a long time. I didn't know the answer, and he wasn't about to give me a clue.

"Why?" I answered, stalling. "Because I need to know. I want to learn everything there is to know about the Micmac way of life. I want to learn the language, the ceremonies, the stories...."

He finally stepped forward a little bit. "Ha! You can't just learn about Micmac ways in a few days. That'll take your whole life!"

I had a career, a wife, a family, but at that moment, I couldn't think of anything better to do with my life. I looked him squarely in the eye and said, "I'm not busy."

He responded, "You can't just walk up and say, 'Teach me everything about this Micmac way of life.' What if you're not ready for it?"

An eagle-like power entered me and filled me with fierceness, and I felt as if my feet were to lift from the ground like a raptor's talons. "I am not doing this for myself. I'm doing this for my mother, my sister, my brother, and for all my aunts and uncles.

"I'm doing this for all my relations, every one of them."

What I said next is still a jumble to me now, as it was then. What I wish I'd said was: "This is their way of life, but it has been kept from them. All of them have Micmac ancestors, as I do, and it's time they found a Micmac medicine man to teach them what society has taken away. They need this and sent me to find it for them, and nothing is going to stop me!"

I'd said all of it in one breath of fire. I was shaking and paused to catch my breath for a moment. "...and if you don't teach me, I'll find somebody who will!" I grasped the handrail for balance. Those last words came through me like a freight train. I couldn't stop them.

It looked as if I'd made a mess of everything. I wanted to give up, to leave and run home, having failed in my quest, but something held me there a second longer, a strong inner arm. I felt dizzy.

"You come on inside," he said quietly. I obeyed, and stepped past him through the shadows of the doorway, and into the kitchen. That was the beginning of my training in the ways of "We the People."

WE THE PEOPLE

Thousands of years ago, before the divergence of Algonquin into at least eighty-four variants, there was probably one Algonquin word which meant "We the People." Today there is still a single word in most Algonquin tongues for "We the People," but it is a different word in each case. However you say it, the word refers to a shared frame of reference, a common context in which everything relates and has meaning. The context implied by that original "We the People" of ancient times was definitely one where there was no word for time.

Algonquins constitute one of the largest and most diverse language groups in the world, including Wabanaki, Lenni Lenape, Ojibwa, Shawnee, Mohegan, Cree, Wampanog, Fox, and Massachusetts, to name a few of the eighty-four tongues included. While Algonquin philosophy shares much in common with that of other major native populations, it is also unique unto itself. It is that freedom-loving, timeless Algonquin way of life which is the basis for this book.

Algonquin culture is so diverse in itself, it is dangerous to generalize about anything. There will be exceptions to every rule. My Mesquaki (Fox) brothers in Iowa so enjoy their freedom that they relish being different from other Algonquins in every way. The same could be said about the Maliseet and many other nations in this family. Still, they are Algonquin through and through.

Linguistically, it is even more important to avoid generalizations. Each Algonquin language has its own philosophical bent, each equally valid. I have heard spoken each of the seven languages of the Wabanaki hoop of nations of the Northeast, and even they are as different from each other as brothers of the same father are different. I have listened to the different sounds the mouth makes as it cherishes these ancient utterances. I have asked questions and watched Wabanaki elders and how they deal with problems. Although diverse, they are a cohesive group, philosophically and culturally, and provide me with something to hold on to as I go out onto this limb of what Algonquin people "tend to do." The way of life which I've observed and participated in is specifically that of these people. I call it "the Way of the Wabanaki," but it is a way that seems to be shared by Algonquins from coast to coast.

To give focus to this Wabanaki teaching the way a main character gives focus to a story, I will be using the Micmac language as an illustration of what I am trying to say — the main character in the story. Since the Micmac language and culture seem to sit toward the center of that diverse Wabanaki tent, it will provide us with a core sample of that language and tradition which is in itself central to Algonquin thought.

The Wabanaki are the "People of the Dawn" (some say "children" of the dawn: *waban* means dawn), and this family or great hoop of seven tribes of the Northeast Algonquians consists of the Micmac, the Maliseet (also spelled Malecite), the Passamaquoddy, the Penobscot, the Abenaki, the Montagnais, and the Naskapi nations, plus all the people who are descendants of those tribes. These are the *ulnuq,* "we the people," who are *nogomaugh,* "all related by blood." All seven nations are still in existence today and each of their languages is still spoken.[1]

In my writing here I will focus on the Micmac because they are my own people, and it is what I know. However, each of the seven Wabanaki nations and their respective languages are of equal importance. If any one of them were lost, it would break the great hoop of the Wabanaki family, which has somehow remained intact for thousands of years.

The "People of the Dawn" are the easternmost Native Americans and in the times of the ancestors, their ceremonies assisted the sun each day in its rising. They received the bless-

5

ings of the sun which they so revered, drew in its red energy, and passed those blessings on to the people behind them, who would in turn pass it on to the people of the West. It was an important duty. The Abenaki say, "As long as there is one person to honor the sun each morning, it will rise again." So far, so good.

THE POETICS OF THE SACRED

There are many ways in which the Micmac language reflects the timelessness of Algonquin life. Algonquin culture is very poetic, and very sacred, but it is hard to pin down in European terms what that poetry consists of, or even what is sacred and what is not. Rhyme, rhythm, meter, and verse distinguish European poetry from prose, but with the exception of certain songs, these are absent in Algonquin poetics.

The word poetry comes from the old Greek "to make," derived from a root that means "to pile up or arrange." This ancient understanding of poetry from tribal Europe comes very close to describing the poetics of sacred speech among the Algonquin. Prayer words are not lined up like train cars, they are artistically arranged one by one, piled up like lodge stones, or arranged in a circle like the stones in a medicine wheel design. Artistic intuition replaces strophic structure.

A distinction between spirit and matter pervades European concepts of the sacred, but these sentiments are not shared by most Algonquins. Krishnamurti once said, "If you distinguish between the sacred and the profane, you do the world damage."[2] Though this may overstate the Algonquin point of view, the native way recognizes nature as an expression of spirit, and not an evil force in combat with the divine. There are pure and impure aspects to everything of this world and the next. The native way is not to isolate good or bad from the rest of life, but to heal that which is sick and transform that which is poison. It is all part of the same circle, and to do damage to the earth does spiritual damage as well.

Don't look too closely for familiar structure in our sacred poetry. You may find cyclical patterns of speech typical of oral traditions, but no "formula." The poetry is in what you say and how you say it. Too much structure in speech shows unnaturalness, or worse, insincerity, and that would be against the sacred manner.

Insincerity is the unthinkable thought. Even the ne'er-do-well does what he does with relative sincerity. So, for a holy man, sincerity is an absolute. The *bpoo-oh-in*, a person with extraordinary spiritual powers or a curer — sometimes referred to by English-speaking people as a medicine man — must set the example of sincerity for his people, in his speech as well as his actions. This means maintaining an informality and warmth in his speaking. A curer is a humble position: to cure or heal is the same word as to help in Micmac. So the term medicine man literally translates as *abowchun mach djeenum*, a helper.

A truly sacred gathering should be humbly presented. It's best if it is not too precisely scheduled, but should simply "gather." Spirit does not arrive on a timetable — remember, the Sermon on the Mount was not a publicized event. It simply "fell together."

7

WHAT IS POETRY?

What is poetry in a world without time? A world without writing? A world without verse? We say this. When the people cry when they hear it, it is poetry. When the people work together, it is poetry in motion. This much we know. When the elder performs the ceremony, it is sacred speech made visible.

What is sacred speech? This much I have learned. When tears fill everyone's eyes, the people have been touched by God. When the people fall silent, their minds have been stilled, their hearts opened by the heart of the speaker.

There are sacred stories, such as the Creation stories, which should be told according to sacred tradition, but without dry, memorized monologues. The art of balancing these two is difficult, and so the elders are usually asked to go first. The elders never tell the same story the same way — they update it, make it relevant to people's needs here and now, and the spirit enters into it. Life never repeats itself, but some people always seem to.

"Walk your talk" is an ancient teaching of the Algonquins. The Hindu equivalent might be *satya kriya*, or "right action." Algonquins honor their famous orators and stress speaking from the heart and listening with the soul, but what gets results is action, so practice what you preach. Buddha said, "Talk doesn't cook the rice." The Lenni Lenape say, "Talk won't grow corn." It amounts to the same thing.

The elder really does teach by example, often in ways that are not obvious and are sometimes shocking. For instance, if Someone-Who-Chatters-Too-Much comes to Grandfather

Like-a-Moose for wisdom (to memorize and chatter about later), the elder might agree to teach him wisdom and then sit in silence for three hours, while Someone-Who-Chatters wonders, "What gives?"

Algonquin wisdom is dynamic, it's always in context to the person hearing it and the person speaking. Wisdom honors individual limitations and circumstances and the Algonquin teachers give the teachings according to "what you can handle." The problem is that newcomers don't know who they are speaking to and often don't know who they are themselves, at least not through Algonquin eyes.

When native persons come for teaching for the first time, the first teaching they might get is "honor your ancestors — get prayer ribbons, tobacco, and eagle feathers, and come back later." But when non-natives want to "become Indian," the first teaching they might get is "honor your own ancestors before you go chasing after someone else's." And if the teacher is serious, he might add, "Go make some candles, spin some wool, or learn carpentry. Then come back."

9

SETTING THE STAGE

Although we are distinct spiritual beings equal to any who have ever lived, in this world we are largely defined by the sum total of our relationships, to nature and to each other. It is a humbling thought, and humility is always welcome. In a family-based community, context is usually clear. We know who's older, who's usually wiser, and who has proven himself dependable and strong (and who hasn't!).

Context also encompasses history, myth, and ceremonial tradition. In this context, action alone can have layers of poetic meaning, and speech combined with action can speak volumes. But most modern people have no context, and don't know how to pick up the clues, and would miss much of the poetry of traditional life, not to mention its earthy humor.

Unless one is familiar with the woof and warp of this tradition and its people, the core of native poetics — speech combined with action — will remain elusive and untranslatable.

When I first cornered Grandfather Turtle on his doorstep, I was expecting to learn information about the Micmac way of life the way I would learn it from a book. Context was the farthest thing from my mind. That left it up to him to establish who he was, by his actions and speech, and to find out who I was by forcing me to take action and state my case. Therapists call this "establishing healthy boundaries." It also established a context for both verbal and nonverbal dialogue, and set the stage for the art of speaking. He quickly created the Algonquin picture frame inside which his words and acts would ring true to their meaning.

Through his refusal to enter into my sloppy and ill-defined context, he had shown me whom I was talking to — someone happy to be with his own thoughts — not a man who likes to chat. After I revealed that I had been sent by my Micmac relatives and said "If you don't teach me I'll find someone who will," he knew who he was talking to as well. I too was not there to chat, although I'd take what I could get.

After succeeding in drawing me out of hiding; after establishing himself clearly as a man of knowledge; after showing that this teaching was not for everyone and that this discussion was not casual; then he could share the teachings with me generously, instructing me in the ways of the Wabanaki. We established a shared context for real communication, although that context changed and deepened two days later when he agreed to adopt me as his grandson. Since that time, we have been working together for the good of the people and I have come to learn volumes about the poetry of context, the sacred poetry of action.

NO WORD FOR TIME

There is no word for time in the Micmac language, nor in most Algonquin tongues. You can't say it.

You can ask "*Donn?*" or "When is it?" but your answer may be expressed in images, not numbers. There are words for day, *nagwew*, and night, *depkik*, one for sunrise, sunset, for one lunar cycle, one yearly cycle, youth, adulthood, and old age, but no word for an absolute time which measures the universe from outside of it.

The way time is dealt with in Algonquin speech teaches us that time is relative and elusive in nature, just as Einstein proved, and as quantum researchers are discovering. There is no concept of time outside its embodiments in the things of nature. I've heard Micmac people point to the sky and use the expression, "Where is it now?" meaning, "What is the position of the sun?" I've even agreed to an appointment to meet an elder when the sun sits "there above the trees" but no mention of hours.

The myth that some people are on Indian Time is no myth.

We all come into this world on Indian Time and depart from it the same way. It's just that some native people seem to be able to maintain that natural rhythm during the interceding period called "life" as well.

I can't count the number of Algonquin people I've known who have never worn watches in their lives. This is no small point. Some try for a while and then throw the watch away, or give it away either in ceremony or unceremoniously. It has to do with dignity, perception, and many other less tangible factors such as energy flows and vibrations. Obviously, many native people wear watches to work and have business meetings at three o'clock with their accountants, and show up promptly on time, but there seems to be a profound difference to traditional Algonquin people between wearing a watch and not wearing a watch which goes beyond the obvious symbolism. A watch reminds you of the demands of others. Perhaps it also clouds the perception of real time, which is at the heart of physical reality.

Time separates us from the past and the future, but in Micmac, the emphasis is on the here and now. There is a past tense, and a future tense as well, there are tales of the great past, and prophecies of the future, but it all is related to the now. When anthropology students are upset when Algonquin people use modern conveniences as part of a sacred tradition, such as using a public address system at a powwow or a compound bow to go hunting, it is because they are confused by past and future. Native traditions have been in a process of constant change for 10,000 years yet are always in the now. There is no one point in that story where you can divide old from new.

NO HOLIDAYS OR WEEKENDS

Traditionally, there are no birthdays, no anniversary days, no holidays (and no weekends!), not in the Western sense. Every day is a holiday to those who are interested in finding that sacredness around them right now. Feasts are organized to celebrate things happening now, but anniversaries are not in the now. New Year's Day is the day of the new moon when the creek freezes, the first day of winter, but that is an actual event. You can see it for yourself. It is honored with a feast, and usually falls right about Thanksgiving. Of course, winter starts later in the south and earlier in the north — all woodland people know that. There is no description of time separate from events. The language honors the relationship between time and space in a way that Einstein could appreciate.

Of course, words have more recently been devised for the days of the week, but they are typical Algonquin observations on these European concepts. For example, in Micmac, Saturday becomes *gesspeteq*, literally "sitting on the edge of the week." Friday becomes *gweltamultik*, or "day of feasting."

There's no word for hour, minute, or second in Micmac. There is however a word for now, *neegeh*, which is used constantly in every situation, because one always tries to connect with the here and now.

Ben Payson, whom I call Grandfather Turtle, said, "The Micmac people don't have Sunday. If you're doing the ceremony today, today will be Sunday for you and the rest of the people. Everything you do you are doing directly to the Creator — so do everything just as it should be done. This is why Micmac

13

people don't mark the days of the week. They go by the moon."

I asked, "But there is the time of harvest, and of gathering things."

He answered, "Yes, of course. We gather different plants throughout the year. For example, we have a certain kind of tea they gather now [summer] and put away for the winter, and they brew that tea all winter long. It's traditional tea, and it comes from the mother earth, no grinding or machinery. We mix it strong, and it's good for your system. It gets you through the winter."

WHAT TIME IS IT?

14

Grandfather Turtle walked in front of me out the door and down the long hill that led to the banks of the Miramichi River that flowed by his land. On the property was the naked frame of a teepee, which he said he used when large gatherings were held here for teaching.

At the bottom of the hill, against a wall of trees, we found a little cabin where I was to stay. He opened the door and entered. I followed him inside. There was the hovering smell of smudging: sweetgrass, sage, and *tchee-choss*. There was a simple bed, and a number of ritual objects were placed here and there on shelves and tables and around the room. An eagle staff stood in one corner, a medicine stick in the other. A painted drum stood against the wall. I didn't know the significance of any of these objects, but took everything in. I watched every move he made, every detail, not knowing what was significant and what wasn't.

The cabin was unfinished, with pieces of insulation tacked up here and there. He picked up a jacket patch off the shelf that said "Micmac Indians" on it, and handed it to me as a gift. I accepted, wondering what jacket I would sew it on.

"You're a Micmac? Wear this patch with pride."

"Here's some feathers."

"Are these your only ones? I don't want to take your last feathers, or your last patch, for that matter."

"More always comes to replace what we give away," he answered.

I accepted it, recalling all the gifts I never gave away.

He sat me down on a chair at the table against the back wall, and placed a clam shell in front of me. He handed me a strand of sweetgrass and a piece of fungus, and asked if I knew what to do with them. I didn't.

I glanced up and shouted in surprise to see a large hawk hovering over my head, his brown, grasping eyes staring down.

"What's that?"

"That's a red-tailed hawk. He's the protector. Nothin' to be afraid of. We call him *bee-boo-gwess*, because he makes that sound, *bee-boo*. That's not a real live bird. He's mounted. He'll protect you when you travel in the spirit world."

I had no luck burning the sweetgrass whatsoever, and I got up from my chair. He sat down and began to show me the finer points. He was very patient. He showed me how you have to get the sweetgrass braid rather hot before it will burn by itself. He showed me how the corners of the cut fungus burned best, and how to fan them before you put the single strand of sweetgrass on top of it.

I asked him what the words for things were, absorbing them

like a dessicated sponge in a summer rain. We walked outside again and sat on the grass.

I asked, "What is the word for the river, like the one over there?"

He answered, "That's called *see-poo*."

Eventually it got to be about two in the morning. The sun had been replaced by stars and the river was no longer visible, yet we were still talking.

I looked up at the stars and asked to know the word for them.

"*Gu-lo-o-witchk*." I tried it on my mouth. I liked it.

Up until that moment I had been looking around and asking the names of visible and familiar objects that I could point to, colors I could point to. It was now too dark to see anything but stars and I was running out of words to ask. My mind was going blank in a pleasing way, filling up with stars, perhaps. The timelessness of that perfect summer night had placed me in a trance. I shook it off and asked, "What time is it?"

He shrugged his shoulders, "Two, three, four o'clock?" Neither of us were even yawning.

It was then that it dawned on me to ask the obvious question, "What is the word for time?"

I had begun to notice that native people often sleep irregular hours, up all night at gatherings, then sleeping it off all day when the opportunity comes. I myself had lived this way, especially when working on creative projects, but not to the extent the elders do. Being here with the elder, I almost forgot about time altogether. But it seemed like a great question. An easy one.

"There's no word for time," he responded, enjoying a puff on his pipe.

I couldn't speak. My mind was knotted. This was a major revelation to me. Until that moment, I had held to the unconscious assumption that all languages were roughly interchangable, that there was one word in each language that could be roughly matched to each English word, and that all people agree on what they are looking at, but call it something different. How wrong I was. I began to see that going back to my traditional roots was going to take a long time. "My whole life," he said!

THAT'S HOW LONG IT TAKES

Grandfather Turtle continued, "There is no word for time in Micmac. Indian people never use time. There's no time in anything you do. When you're doing something you do it till you finish it. That's how long it takes. '*Bo-ech-nuk-qo-choy dan del lippi djadun*' means, 'There are no time limits. When it's finished, it's finished!'"

At first I thought he might be pulling my leg, but I didn't laugh. Elders are tricky sometimes. I later asked a variety of Micmac people about this curious non-word, and they all responded the same way. Their answers seemed to imply, "Oh we don't believe in that!"

Since then I've seen the remarkable beauty and incredible power of a people free of the constrictions of time. I've seen groups of Micmac people gather at a non-time and non-place and begin to work together spontaneously without a word passing between them. All that's required is a trust in what so many profess to believe: that there really is an intelligence in the universe that is working things out through us. I've seen this intel-

ligence at work as an organizing — and sometimes healing —
force among native people. It doesn't run on a schedule, at least
not one known to us. It is an exact sense of time shared by
flocks of birds and herds of deer and elk as they turn together
and stop together in synchronicity. It is this same synchronicity
that science is struggling to understand.

In the talking feather circle (or talking stick ceremony) the
one who is passed the feather is permitted to speak as long as he
or she wishes without being interrupted. That can be a long
time or not at all. You never know how long that circle will last,
and once you enter it, you are not supposed to leave until it's
finished. I have heard stories from people whose entire village
or town entered into a talking feather circle to get to the heart
of a community problem. Such circles can go on for days (taking the nights off to rest); and there is always a grandstander
somewhere who's been saving it all up for weeks. It's part of living in a world where there is no word for time.

The longest talking circle I entered into must have been
fourteen hours, but I wasn't watching the clock. And yes, there
was a race for the bathroom afterwards, if you must know.
That's biological time.

You can't see or do time, and most Micmac concepts are
expressed in terms of events, in terms of doing or seeing,
regardless of whether they are mental, emotional, or physical
events. If you can't do it or see it, you are not really living, at
least not in the fullness of Algonquin life. You can't do time
unless you are in prison. You can't see time except while watching the clock — something most native people try to avoid. So
time is not real unless you are in prison.

Emotional events are often described as something you do or

see: "My heart is not in place." "I am in darkness today." "You light a fire in my heart." "My heart goes into a million pieces." These are events, not abstract halfhearted constructs. Native people live wholeheartedly and go through each stage of life viscerally and fully so that it is a healing transformation. You can't become transformed this way in a weekend seminar.

Biological, rhythmical time is very real, but in Algonquin it is described in terms of what it does, and what you can see. A phrase such as "Leaf Turn Moon" (the moon when the leaves are becoming red) would be much more meaningful and useful to a traditional elder than "September" or "vernal equinox." He or she would know what you meant. It describes one phenomenon of biological time in that region, but makes no pronouncements about absolute order in the universe. You might ask that elder how old he was by asking, "How many such moons have you seen with your own eyes, grandfather? And how many winter snows have you walked upon?" This is honoring the rhythm of the seasons, and the importance of the elder's experience of them. "Time" in itself has no meaning, but every experience we encounter has meaning which becomes a story we share with others.

I have been told that before Europeans came, there were no fixed "months" in native speech like "starvation moon," or "fish nesting moon," or "cranberry moon," as traditional people use today. Some elders say long ago, people knew these days by many names, whatever was appropriate. When the Europeans came and asked "What do you call February?" these labels came about. It is said that the old ways of speaking were much more creative, more subtle, more artistic, than anything we can experience today. They made you think.

19

CLOCKS

Our life is a medicine story that has no beginning or end. We don't begin a story with "Once upon a time, at 8:05 P.M. on a Wednesday..." we just say, "*Nauqte negwew... One day....*" Algonquins recognized the power of connecting with this moment now. Clocks and watches often dilute that power and make us believe there is something going on which is not part of now. Clocks make us worry and split us into pieces. They conflict with biological time. Algonquin people used to call this device "Captain Clock" because it seemed to rule the white missionaries with an iron hand, or perhaps brass. To this day, many choose not to understand, and not to be ruled.

A drumming song often has a regular beat, but like the human heart, it has its subtle lags and bursts which betray deep-seated feelings, or perhaps the tiredness of the person who is beating. It doesn't just beat time, it creates sacred space. Clocks have a beat that is heartless. They have no feelings, they are never tired, they don't respect we who do have such limitations. Many native people learn various mental tricks to fit in with clock time, often learned later in life, but need to get away from clocks in order to be themselves.

Living in the mainstream, I find myself trying to abide by the clock as if it were some heartless conqueror striking me with a whip, making me anxious and fearful. I fret over what I imagine other people's sense of time to be, and feel bad when I make someone wait, whether they care or not. I measure my own productivity by how many minutes every task must take.

When I find myself doing this, I try to notice that I am losing track not only of the quality of my life but also of the quality of what I'm working on, and I slow down. I know many readers will secretly identify with me, and probably never admit it. It takes a lot to keep us from the here and now, but measuring our very beingness with judgmental little minutes and seconds can do just that. Somewhere within each of us is a five-year-old still resisting the words, "Hurry, hurry! We have to be on time!"

DRESS FOR LONG-TERM SUCCESS

Most dress-for-success books tell you a winning attitude includes being on time. I can't argue with that. Many native people strive for success in the marketplace and are punctual. Nobody likes to wait. But native people also know we can do better than that. It's better to remain calm and unhurried; it's better to be well prepared both physically and mentally; it's better to understand why a certain meeting time has been chosen than to accept it without asking; it's better to remain in a spiritually awakened state than to go into the unconscious anxiety-driven state which can lead to ulcers, stomach cancer, heart attacks and also a hardness of heart. It's good to remember that real productivity is measured by the long-term effect of what we are doing and how well we are doing it, not by the quantity of activity.

21

THERE'S NO HURRY

No time, no rush. Like innings in baseball, things are best done in their natural order, first things first, but they "take as long as they take," and no short-cuts are needed or asked for. If Algonquin people sometimes seem like "Sunday drivers" to harried, clock-driven city folk (and I know, because when I first returned to this way, I had become one of those city folk), maybe it is because every day is the Sabbath according to the teaching of the elders.

Wabanaki elders have told me that most of the household crafts as they were practiced by their ancestors a few hundred years ago required immense patience. There was nothing you could flick a switch and create. An expert could make a birch-bark basket in a few minutes, but that was the exception. The whole quillworking process takes 80 to 100 hours, to soak, pluck the quills, to prepare the dye and then dye the quills, to dry them and weave them together. It took days and days then, and it still does now, even with Rit and other modern conveniences.

Fishing, hunting, and gathering plants takes tremendous patience, but since it is all part of the sacred way of life, it is like a Zen meditation rather than work. (Early Zen monks didn't think much of time either.)

ANOTHER TIME

Among those who follow the spirit there are some who have pierced the veil of appearances through fasting, sweat lodges, pipe ceremonies, prayers and offerings, and through dreams. "Sitting in your chair and going somewhere" is yet another way that some native people have pierced the veil. Those who have encountered the spirit world sometimes tell of visions of the past or future which prove true, or of prayers which affect future events, or perhaps even past ones! Clock time can seem to skip backwards or forwards, and some say even physical time travel is possible. If even one person can experience this, doesn't our conventional view of time blind us from seeing and experiencing such events? Where there's no word for time, nothing is surprising.

23

FAST ONE

It was my first *sooneywen*, or fasting ceremony, and I was eager to get started.

"When can we begin?" I said.

"Well, if you really want to begin the teaching, you need to do a four-day vision quest."

I stumbled for words for a moment before responding, "That would be great."

Grandfather said, "The vision quest means you go four days without food or water, and there are many tasks you have to perform. You start with a sweat lodge, and that water you take in there is the last water you're gonna get for four days. And then you have another sweat, and you drink water again, and that's the end of the fast. You're gonna see a lot of things in there, and that will be part of your teaching."

"I understand. What's a sweat lodge?"

He paused, and sighed again. "Maybe you do only two days. Nobody's trying to hurt you with this."

"I've done fasting before. Four days shouldn't be hard. Let's start right away."

"I think we'll do two days. If you do well, you can come back and do four next year."

I was disappointed. I wanted to prove myself. I was in a big hurry to "get it done" whatever it was; start at the end and go back and fill in the foundation later.

We stayed up late talking, and I told him that I had already started the fast. "I'm going to do four days anyway," I said.

He just answered, "Hmmm."

"You're going to need some sleep. Tomorrow we have to go to town and buy you tobacco and some ribbons. There are still a lot of things you need to know before you start your vision quest. Friday morning, we'll prepare the sweat lodge for you."

I complained, "Why can't we start the fast now?"

"Do you have the ribbons? The tobacco? Then show them to me!"

I couldn't understand his lack of appreciation for my enthusiasm.

He seemed at a loss for words — he went to his shelf and picked up two heron feathers. He gave them to me to take into my fast. "Here's two crane feathers to use in your smudging. It's not as strong as an eagle feather, but it's pretty good."

He said, "Look at the cranes by the river. They will teach you patience. We call them *dtumgwaleegunidjk*. That means,

24

'His neck is broken' — that's the way he looks. But he's very patient. He stands there, sometimes on one foot, and waits without moving for hours. Then, when he sees his breakfast swim by — whoosh! — he snatches it in one motion. That's his power. He is showing you how to live *sah-be-u-wen*, the spiritual way of life. Wait as long as it takes for things to be ready, then act fast.

"Sometimes you will see a crane flying around, and he's telling you to be patient in everything you're doing."

I nodded my head, but still wouldn't eat. I went to bed without taking in any more food.

The next day he put a glass of water on the table and left the room. Eventually I sipped it. He returned unexpectedly and said, "Fast is over. Can't drink water while on a fast! Your next fast will start in the sweat lodge, the right way, just like I said."

Needless to say, it was a great traditional fast.

25

THE POETRY OF CONTEXT

I came to know Ben Payson as Geezeegool Meektcheektch, "Grandfather Turtle." He once gifted me with a fox fur hat. I wore it as I danced in the circle to honor it and then the elder said, while gazing with proud eyes, "You look good in that hat."

Some might see this episode as only an environmentally foolish waste of a fox's life. To an outsider, it might simply be a generous gift. The elder's words might indicate only a preference for the fashion, or that my coloring went well with the rust red of the fox fur. But to me it was poetry.

I dread cheapening any poem by explaining it to death, but since not everyone will immediately understand the Wabanaki poetry in his haiku-like one-syllable words, I'll do so anyway, just this once.

The fox energy has much significance to Micmac and other Wabanaki people. For one thing, it embodies a strong, attractive male energy (whereas the otter embodies the attractive female energy). His words said, "It's okay to be masculine." "The male animal is nothing to be ashamed of." It "looks good." Just that acknowledgement tapped an inner strength I was searching for. It encouraged me to be myself, to overcome shame and guilt. It also empowered me to take the leadership role in my personal life as well.

The fox is also a very clever animal. He is smart in a way that the Wabanaki people understand and respect. When I first entered the Native American world, I tended to rely on cleverness as a defense. At first the native people distrusted it and gently corrected my urban ways. Clever words do not come from the heart.

At that moment I had just utilized my cleverness to pull together a difficult gathering, which had gone well. The words said, "You have a native cleverness the people can respect. You are trusted. You are resourceful, not manipulative or deceitful."

The words he spoke reminded me of *weleeakamkook,* "everything is looking good for you today," which is a joyful blessing.

The fox hat is the kind of ceremonial garment an elder might wear while speaking in the circle. From that day forward, I sat with Geezeegool Meektcheektch and the other elders in each of his talking circles and spoke as a teacher. I was not told to do this — it was understood. It was an initiation, my entrance into a deeper level of "the teaching."

The power of those words was not in the words themselves. They were like common stones arranged as a burial marker in the forest, powerful because of their user's intent.

THE WHOLENESS THAT IS HOLY

What is sacred is not just transcendence; what is sacred is not just the world of things, it is the relationship between the two. Sacredness makes every step of the journey both into and out of the world meaningful. Transcendence — withdrawing from the body and returning to the source — that is one direction of the wheel. What is sacred is the whole wheel, creating, maintaining, and withdrawing from the world. All the directions are sacred, but only because of each other. Place one over another, leave out one direction, and the sacredness is lost. It's the *messkeeg*, the wholeness that's holy, the *opsetgo*way and the relatedness of all things that is "everything."

But how can completeness be expressed poetically? What words can express the wholeness of any thing, no less everything? No words alone do service to the "great mysterious" as some native people call it,[3] but actions offered in expression of the Creator can. Through living the four directions — to walk, talk, think, and pray everything you do and believe — you can live the sacred manner and your speech will match the poetry of the *nogomaugh sa'aq*, "the old ones."

The Algonquin speech that the European can recognize as "poetry" is really part of something much greater. Plain,

27

unadorned speech that arises out of a sacred space, a momentous time, and an illuminated state of mind, is sacred poetry. Such words are *eltaeegen gamalamun*, they fly true like a strong "arrow to the heart" of the moment. [4]

During that first visit, Grandfather told me someday I might have to choose between the Micmac way and other ways I'd learned about.

I answered, "All roads are good."

He said, "If you try to walk on all roads at once you might get confused."

"What do you mean?" I said, understanding but not liking what I heard.

"Keep it simple or you will lose your heart."

Those words had a lasting effect on my life, and partly inspired my first book of epigrams, *The Secrets of Wholehearted Thinking*. [5] I'm still working on both the understanding and the liking part.

These moments of poetry are around us even in urban society, usually during critical turning points when a loved one passes over, during an emergency, or when a child grasps the essence of a new experience and puts it in a "nutshell." These moments open our eyes.

Reading is not living and we have a difficult time putting these sacred moments into writing, into story. Flowery poetry and literary devices are a poor substitute. It's easy to forget that every ounce of truly memorable writing is distilled from gallons of hard-earned experience. The same is true of the high speech of the elders.

LYING IS WORSE THAN DYING

I knew a Muskegan woman (the Muskeg are another hoop of nations from the South) who always used to say, "Lying is worse than dying."

I won't forget the first time it came up. I heard her knocking, and opened the door, expecting to be greeted by her usual cheerful hello. She gave me a hard look and said, "You've been eating sweets, haven't you?"

I said "No, not that I remember."

"You've been eating sugar lately, and red meat too. I can tell. It's been in the last three days! It affects your spirit, you know."

"No...well, I don't remember!" I knew that she was a vegetarian and considered wasteful eating a huge moral issue. She was right. It had been nearly three days since I'd indulged, and we Northern people evolved needing more meat than our Southern cousins, but I didn't have the nerve to face her wrath on any of these points. I thought I was taking the easy way out, but I was wrong.

"You know lying is worse than dying!" she said fiercely and with conviction. She really scared the heck out of me. "The only thing worse than killing cows and chickens for one's meal is lying about it afterwards!" I felt smaller and smaller. There was no way out.

Then she took me to her house and made me a beautiful salad full of avocados and sprouts. She said, "Vegetables are your friends. They love you, and want you to eat them. They are medicine." I felt like looking down at those little loving vegetables and saying "I'm sorry I lied. Do you forgive me?"

29

They were very forgiving, and so was my Muskegan woman who was trying to guide me back to the native way.

Honesty is what knits Algonquin society together. Lying pulls the people apart. "You have to speak from your heart" is heard constantly as the secret to everything from relationships to spiritual power. Imbedded in these words is an understanding that is perhaps similar to the Vedanta belief that the man who always speaks the truth will be powerful in his actions and that his words will become manifest.

In America, truth has become a marketable product of self-hypnosis and linguistic programming. As time passes, the world, even India, seems to become more oriented towards truth as an artifact of culture, but the traditional Algonquin man or woman still holds to a truth that cannot be co-opted. Some call it "our connection to the earth." It takes a combination of humility and fearlessness to be that honest in modern society, and only a handful maintain that truthfulness every day, but it is the only way that works. We need to keep trying.

Urban society is filled with "spin doctors" who use words as a means to acquire power and control and, since the Industrial Revolution, worldly Western and Eastern people alike have given up seeking inner mastery and control in favor of controlling others, and the use of speech is at the heart of this reversal. According to typical Algonquin teaching, we are the truth, the truth of what the Creator made us, but when we pretend to be something we aren't — even the person we'd like to be — we split the self into two parts. Then we become "lost," an odious fate for people of a hunting culture.

The sage strives not to impersonate a *sagamaugh*, a wise and well-respected elder, but to actually become the person he wants other people to see, a whole person without projections, fantasies, or delusions, uninsulated by false pretenses and prejudices. Even a trader hopes to trade on his good name and become prosperous in balance with his integrity. For if his economic survival ever comes to be based on wearing a false face, how will he ever remove it?

In the Micmac view, cleverness of speech is opposite to sincerity; clever words close the heart. Unless entertainment is the objective, and the Micmac can be very entertaining, it is best to be direct. We are all here to help one another, not control or deceive. If you are lost in the woods and you ask directions of someone, you don't want to hear riddles, any more than you want an over-boastful wild guess. Woodland people know this instinctively. I've sometimes seen a Micmac turn his back and walk away from a person speaking too boastfully or making light of someone else's pain for the sake of a joke. Footsteps speak louder than words, and in the Micmac language, they thunder.

Even among hikers and climbers from big cities, you sense a change in consciousness; once they get out on the slopes, they start taking each other seriously. Sincerity becomes sacred once again. Put them in a storm together and they become regular Algonquins, using speech to strengthen one another's spirit, praying in humility to the forces of nature, thinking with care about their actions and each other, and walking with purpose.

Grandfather talked to me about the connection between healing and honesty that first day. He said, "The person has to help themselves, you can't do it for them. They have to be honest with you and tell you the problem. You have to help that person conduct their life the right way. 'Be honest with me.

Then I can help you.'

"You see, our Creator doesn't lie, he doesn't cheat anybody. When you work with spirit you have to be honest, no matter what you've done wrong. For me to help this person the spirit of God has to work through me to them, and if they are not telling me the truth, how am I going to solve this problem?"

I asked, "Do you mean we must always be honest with everyone? If you were captured by your enemies and they asked you, 'Where is this person?' Would you lie to them?"

He answered, "No, no you don't lie to these people. You only have to tell them, 'Yep, he was around here a while ago. He could be over there, I don't know, but he was here.'"

"I deal with a lot of anger in people. They come into the sweat lodge and I know what they are thinking. I know what their problem is, but they have to work it out for themselves. That's why some of them get healing and others don't. You can hear them crying in the sweat lodge. The spirit comes and does the healing.

"If you start to speak from your heart, spirit will come."

It was one of those simple phrases again, the ones that echo in my mind like poetry.

32

EMBODIMENT

The essential poetics of the Algonquin might be called "poetry in motion," or becoming one's own medium of expression. Certain customs, objects, and gestures are recognized as embodying certain feelings, thoughts, and energies, and can be varied to express almost anything in physical form without words. I call it "embodiment." Everything that really matters is enacted. Even the flow of events we call time are embodied by the river. That is why storytelling far outweighs every other poetic process — it uses action to show, rather than tell or presume. Stories are three-dimensional. Everyone will have a perspective on what it means according to where he or she is standing, just like life.

Few things are abstract, everything wants to become grounded in reality, to complete the circuit between heaven and earth, which is so important if Creation is to continue. Life wants to manifest fully, and the traditional person offers himself or herself as the vehicle.

A dominant theme in Sacred Christian European tradition is to separate and prepare to leave Creation with all its problems.[6] The Sacred Tradition of the East is to accept and merge with life as it is.[7] The Sacred Tradition of the Algonquin is to work with the Creator to keep Creation, with all its beauty, going in a constant process of change and exchange.

For a traditional elder, smoke, or *bigsod,*[8] is an embodiment of prayer and takes the prayers and songs of the Algonquin with it on the way to heaven. The combination of smoke and sung prayers rising to heaven are found in creation stories in both North and South America and are central to the ancient rites.

The six ribbons used in prayer are an embodiment of the directions: the six visible of the seven sacred directions, and all that they represent. The South, the West, the North, the East, the Sky, the Earth (white, yellow, black, red, blue and green, respectively) and the Within. They are sewn onto the calico prayer shirt, also called the "*mayomee*" or "ribbon" shirt so you can carry them with you wherever you go and hold them while

33

you pray. The seventh direction has no color. The Abenaki say it is hidden in the heart where it is hardest to look.

Like the colored prayer flags of Tibetans, Sherpas, and other Mongolian traditions, these ribbons or the more traditional strips of dyed cotton, are tied to living trees and bushes, and left out for some time, to blow in the wind. The wind blows them and frees the prayers to fly upwards to heaven.

The feather embodies the spirit of air and is a mover of energy. I have seen Algonquin people use it to fan the *bigsod*, or "smudge smoke," or to move away bad spirits. The eagle embodies the elder energy in any form. Therefore the eagle feather embodies not only air energy, but that of the elders, which comes down from the highest elder to this world. The energy in it is one of power and authority, which should be respected. The power of the eagle is also the power of the communicator, the messenger. "Bring me the message!" we call out, and the eagle hears us. I can recall many times that eagles have appeared at gatherings or during travels with my elders regardless of the surroundings. They circle us and remind us of the power of the Great Spirit and how it can make us strong in wisdom if we stay in balance.

The elements embody energies beyond themselves. The sun embodies the grandfather's creative energy, while the moon embodies the grandmother's creative energy. The sky embodies the father energy, always distant, always invisible, while the earth embodies the mother. Even a clump of soil embodies the whole of the earth mother's spirit, in the hands of a *bpoo-ohin*, or "spiritually gifted elder" (medicine man).[9] Even a puff of air embodies the whole of the sky's spirit and can work magic from the lips of an elder. *Ooch-dju-zen* means "it (the wind) comes from that direction," and is the word for wind, or any moving air.

The sweetgrass and cedar are not only medicine, they each embody the four elements. The earth womb they grew from, the water that nourished them, the sun-fire that enlivened them, and the air that they breathe — all four elements. To burn them while smudging is to change them from a sleeping to an active state.

PURIFICATION AND SMUDGING

◆

I n Algonquin life, as in many cultures around the world, smudging is used to purify oneself, as if bathing in the smoke. Its calm energy washes away confusion and self-hate. Purification is the first step in any ceremony or healing process. It slows you down and helps you enter the timeless world of spirit.

Religious purification through ablutions, sweat lodges and saunas, and fasting are cleansing practices that we can all understand and that rid the body of toxins that can cause disease. But purification through smoke is just as universal, and is harder to understand. [10] Perhaps there is a chemical change in the body through inhalation of the burning herbs, such as the relaxation one feels when smelling sweetgrass. Perhaps the energy released in the smoke has an effect on the aura. But one thing is clear: the burning of the plant is a ritual offering in itself and the smoke embodies the prayers of the people as it rises to heaven. To stand in the midst of such prayers must be purifying to the open heart.

In Micmac tradition, you smudge or "purify" the air (or

"vibrations" as the people today might say) by lighting a braid of *kji-m-tsee-goo*, "the Great Grass" (sweetgrass), a smudgestick, or a large shell containing *ka-cho-see* or "cedar branches" mixed with other healing plants. Sometimes it takes a steady application of fire before the smudge can stay lit by itself. Once lit, one shouldn't blow on the fire or the smoking end of the smudge stick, as this can only disturb the spirit of the fire. A flaming braid of sweetgrass can be put out simply by shaking the braid slowly, and the same slow shaking motion will keep the glowing ends kindled. Fanning the ember with a feather or feather fan is preferable.

Before smudging, the eyeglasses and watch are always removed. Jewelry is also removed, even if it is traditional. Everyone who will be smudged is asked to do the same. Even though it is a regular public and social activity, smudging is a solemn occasion, not to be laughed at or done in jest. Intent is important.

When the smudge is held before someone, they use at least one hand to brush the smoke towards them and into their hair. Hair is powerful to the Algonquin. It collects the vibrations of the energies around you, and is important to purify carefully. Hair also holds the smell of the smoke a long time. This is part of why native people don't cut their hair.

Traditionally, the smudge wand or triple braid of sweetgrass makes a circle around the person four times clockwise, one turn for each of the cardinal directions, creating a shield around them that wards off harmful energies. The experienced Algonquin can create a spiral of smoke around someone from head to toe that makes four complete circles and then comes back up. It is healing on many levels at once.

The Micmac and other Wabanaki people smudge themselves every day, often stopping for a quick *bigsod* many times during the day. They smudge gifts before they're given, they smudge gifts when they're received, they smudge their houses, their yards, their tools, and their pipes. They smudge their cars, animals, their clothes, and each other.

The first time I met my Miramichi Indian Aunt Helen, she gave me the gift of sweetgrass to take home. "You burn it and it smells nice," she said, but there was a lot more to the story. Over time I have come to associate it with prayer and "speaking as one with the Creator." If I have a dream of a plant or object and *bigsod* or smudge smoke is rising from it, I know it is going to be medicine for me; that it "prays for me."

There is something very comforting about the smell of smudge. I quickly came to expect it and sometimes in an urban setting where the smell of sweetgrass or sage is absent, I feel something missing, something empty about the air. The Algonquin people are woven together not only by custom and speech, but by the very air they breathe.

OFFERINGS AS EMBODIMENT OF CHANGE

The sacred tobacco, called *dtemaway*, (or *speebaq'n*, a mixture of red willow, natural "Indian" tobacco, and other herbs such as sweetgrass) plays many roles. It is medicine, it is from the earth, but once you have prepared it, it is an embodiment of your own energy. Through your thoughts, words, and deeds, you can transfer almost any energy into the tobacco, so that it becomes a medium. It is also a medium of exchange which spirit recognizes. The Algonquin don't make animal sacrifices,[11] but they make the sacrifice of their own tobacco into the fire. Exchange, trade, sacrifice, offering, change, are all the same word in Micmac, *sa-syeh-wyn*. It is understood that any offering of tobacco is sure to bring a fair exchange, an equal return from spirit, so the idea of self-sacrifice in the conventional sense is foreign.

Originally, sacrifice meant simply "to make sacred" (*sacre facere*), which is very close to *sa-syeh-wyn* (sacrifice) in meaning, but which convention has twisted into something regrettable. When you give up everything for your people in the *soo-ney-wen* (fasting ordeal) you do it for the sake of others and for the earth's sake, but you also do it to strengthen your own spirit, your own vision, and your own gifts. *Soo-ney-wen* (fasting) is the basic "technique" in the Algonquin path of knowledge. You give up everything as if preparing for death and, before you are reborn from the sacred sweat lodge, spirit honors you with gifts many times over, and all is new and refreshed. *Sa-syeh-wyn*, sacrifice is the embodiment of Creation, but you have to do it yourself. No one can do it for you.

EXCHANGE IS THE AXIS

A lgonquin people are not stuck in some clockwork universe that has already been wound up and left behind, as the Deists once believed. The *ulnuq* "We the People" wind it up every morning with ceremony and keep it going every moment with mindfulness toward the many life forces. And exchange is the axis on which the world spins — it keeps Creation going.

Every living thing must give and take in order to participate in Creation. Even the earth and sky exchange gifts with one another. All is change, all is exchange. In order to receive, you must give of yourself. This belief is shared by many other peoples, and the Vedas refer to sacrifice as "the knitting together of the worlds," which connects humans with the substance of nature.

Why the Wabanaki (and other Algonquin people) use tobacco as a medium of exchange with spirit is a mystery. Elders will tell you, "That is what the Creator told our people." In the Creation story, Glooskap, the first man, walks all over Turtle Island and asks each plant what it is used for. Each plant answers, and Glooskap names each plant accordingly. As the story goes, tobacco was the only plant to tell him to use it as a medium of exchange with spirit.

The Hopi use cornmeal; the early Jews used salt, a valuable commodity in the desert, as a similar medium of exchange; the Greeks used libations [12] in the same way. Recently, I observed an urban Italian-American as he threw salt over his shoulder after finishing his pizza. Presumably for "good luck," these and other customs around the world may have their origin in ancient rituals, practices whose purpose was to insure — through some form of self-sacrifice — the continuation of the world, which is certainly much more than lucky.

In Algonquin culture, the offering of something of the self, such as tobacco, in ritual, not only keeps Creation going, it is a re-enactment of Creation. The Vedic word *Rta* (with a vocalic R)[13]

39

can mean "sacrifice," "the way," "the flow," but implies the beginning of things, or Creation. The Vedas say, "Nothing came before *Rta*," and, "The Gods are all first-born of *Rta*." In Native American Creation stories from South America, the gods fling their own hearts into the volcano, or the earth, and up come food and water and all the good things in return. This "self-sacrifice" seems to encourage personal surrender to the Creator, in exchange for a role in Creation. (However, the well-known Aztec abuses of this image are as horrifying to most native people as to Europeans.)

We surrender our heart to God figuratively, a self-destructive act only in the Zen sense. As Shunryu Suzuki said, "When you do something, you should burn yourself completely, like a good bonfire, leaving no trace of yourself." In Western psychology it is called "letting go of ego." When you let go of the tobacco and let it fall into the fire in devotional offering, with it should go part of your self. The Buddha interpreted "sacrifice" figuratively, saying the real sacrifice was the giving up of selfishness.

Once while fasting, and praying to Geezeegooisk Oetgasenook, Grandmother of the West, I learned how to cleanse my heart of fear and anger by pressing the tobacco to my heart, letting it absorb the "bad medicine" and then flinging it into the fire. At the end of the day I felt my heart was clear and empty and all selfishness had been burned away. For me, the sacrifice was both real and figurative at the same time.

NO DEAL

My mother (along with other relatives) taught me about the native teachings in bits and pieces, but didn't want me to smoke, so she never mentioned the tobacco. When I finally found an elder who agreed to teach me the secrets of the spiritual path, he kept asking, "Where is your tobacco?"

I'd answer, "I don't have any."

The next morning he said, as he pulled a truck driver's baseball cap over his head, "Get dressed. Let's go to town to get tobacco and ribbons for your fast."

"That's a long drive," I said. "Maybe we'll talk some more and then go later."

He just looked quietly at me. I walked away. He wandered over to my car and planted himself beside my passenger door. I found him standing there some minutes later, just smoking his pipe, staring at the sky like a statue, not saying anything.

I got in the car and opened the door for him. He got in, still smoking his pipe. "Where do you want to go?" I asked.

There was no answer.

"Oh, the tobacco. Okay."

I started up the car. We made the long journey to town and at a milliner's, he helped me pick out six long ribbons: red, white, yellow, black, green, blue. I said, "Let's get purple too."

He gave me a patient look. "There's no purple direction."

When we reached the tobacconists, I found several brands of pipe tobacco. I touched a can of Prince Albert and looked at him with eyebrows raised.

He said, "It doesn't matter what brand. It's for spirit."

I touched a pouch of Walter Raleigh and looked at him.

He said, "It doesn't matter what brand. Spirit doesn't care."

Then I picked up a pouch of Sail tobacco and looked at him. He gave me a big smile and nodded his head enthusiastically. "Now that's a real nice blend of tobacco."

I commented on the exorbitant price and he answered, "The more it costs, the more of yourself you put into it, the better for your prayers. Give more of yourself for spirit. It's a good trade."

I carried the tobacco out to the car feeling I had done my part for tradition.

On the way we met an attractive Micmac woman in fine store-bought clothes sitting on a bench. She seemed to know Ben and looked on us both with disdain. Her glance seemed to say, "Losers!" Ben pulled me along. I guess not all natives believe in tradition. That's free will in action, free to become a slave to passions and possessions.

Standing near the car passenger door again in the parking lot, Grandfather silently held out his hand. After a long embarrassing moment, I figured out that he wanted the tobacco. Startled, I pulled it from the shopping bag and handed it to him, wondering what the deal was.

He held it up in the air in his fist and stated triumphantly, "Now we can begin the teaching!" He proceeded to teach me about the spiritual life day and night for three or four days after that, some of which has become part of this book. Those teachings have never stopped.

But it isn't only the elders we need to offer tobacco to, we need to offer it to *Geezoolgh*, to the fire, to the grandfathers and grandmothers, to our ancestors, and to the earth and its plants and animals. For the Wabanaki, no other plant does what tobacco can do. This is a point which sticks in the throat of many Westerners and those who took college courses in science. However, the scientific method does not say, "If you don't understand it, it's false." The scientific method says, "Try it and see if it works."

STORY TELLING

◆

I f there is an art form of poetry among the Algonquin (outside of the many songs they sing), it is storytelling. Perhaps the most powerful form of storytelling is that which the Micmac call *ahdooga'chn*. The verb form is *ahdoogwit*. This is a form of storytelling that serves a purpose. The elder will tell an old story, perhaps a legend or teaching tale, but will change it around so that the arrows land pretty close to home. It is rare for an elder to criticize someone directly, but it is not necessary when one has mastered the art of *ahdooga'chn*, which can reduce a grown man to tears. It can be used gently, but also can be devastatingly brutal, as there is no way to retaliate. It is like a poison dart — you can't quite put your finger on where it is lodged, but it hurts. The *adoogwit* story circles around you and then catches you by surprise, a high form of big game hunting.

When I first asked Grandfather Turtle to teach me the native ways, he needed to test me to see if I was really serious, so as we drove to get the tobacco and ribbons, he told me the story of the boy, Weesuckerjack (in some areas, his name is Sacajaweah)

43

who wanted to fly with the geese (in some areas it is eagles).

It was a hot day and I was veering in and out of some rough traffic while listening to him. We passed a very attractive girl who was walking alone on the side of the road, going our way, and I glanced at her for just a moment. I thought she was likely to cause a traffic accident on this bad road we were on, and was only concerned for the public good. I don't think Ben saw it quite that way. As the elder told the story of Weesuckerjack, I realized he was talking about me.

DON'T LOOK DOWN

"Weesuckerjack was a man who saw Canadian geese flying overhead and wanted to become one of them. He collected Canadian goose feathers for a long time, and then one day he made wings out of them and fixed them to his arms, and called to his geese brothers in the sky to help him fly. They swooped down and carried him up and set him into flight, which was what he had always wanted. He flew along with them, and was able to turn when they turned and dive when they dove, but it was very tiring.

"'Don't lose your concentration!' they told him. 'And whatever you do, don't look down!'

"The boy just laughed, and said, 'Don't worry. I won't look down.'

"They flew for many miles, and the boy was happy, and remembered to keep looking up.

"At some point, they flew over an Indian village on a river

bank, and some young girls were paddling a canoe. They looked up and saw that he was a man flying like a goose, and they started laughing and calling to him, telling him to come down. They waved and called and giggled, and eventually he just had to look down.

"He had not seen a woman in a while and was struck by their beauty and forgot where he was for a moment. His wings faltered, and he fell like a stone, right through the boat. Luckily, he didn't kill anyone, but he hit his head hard and had to be pulled to shore by the Indian girls, who just made fun of him for not flying straight, and left him there to recover on his own.

"He was left with nothing, and as his wings washed down the river, he was very sad.

"He was foolish to want to be like the geese, a real 'sucker'...and even more foolish to look down...that's why they call him...."

"I get it. I'm Wee-sucker-jack, and you're one of the geese," I muttered. He had me practically in tears. I pulled the car over to the side of the road and turned the key to the off position.

"You can fly and I can't. Is that it? Why don't we just forget it? If that's the way it is, why don't I just quit now, let you off, and go home to New York? Why are you wasting your time with me if that's what you think?"

Ben was quiet for a minute. "I'm not telling you to give up. I'm not saying this will happen. It is just a teaching story, and it's a warning, too."

I'm simplifying the story, but it was told very pointedly, emphasizing the ignorance and eventual humiliation of the boy. I felt the arrow in the story and was very upset. I said, "Are you

45

saying you won't teach me?"

He responded, "I'm tellin' you not to look down!"

THE BOY WHO WANTED TO FLY WITH THE EAGLES

A year later, a non-native friend of mine who loved Indian lore and surrounded himself with Native American books and artifacts, invited this same Micmac elder to come stay with him in the suburbs. He promised to take care of him in exchange for teachings, yet the man did not take care of his own family and financial responsibilities.

Grandfather Turtle and his helper came and were treated well. By and by, the *ahdooga'chn* time came, the teaching tales, and the man was devastated by the invisible lightning bolts that seemed to hit all his secret targets. I dropped by to see how the elders were doing, and the man's eyes were still red, still sobbing uncontrollably from the stories he'd heard earlier in the day. I never saw a man cry so much.

I asked Grandfather Turtle what happened. "I told him a story," he said quietly, with a loving look, "'bout a boy who wanted to fly with the eagles."

The man's wife didn't understand that her husband's crying was a part of his healing and refused to provide any more food for the Micmac elders, who had no car.

Grandfather Turtle took me aside and said, "We're starving; we haven't eaten since breakfast. The same with my helper here." He gestured towards his helper.

"You got a car?" he asked, as I nodded. "Maybe you'll give us a lift to the store?"

I gathered what was going on and drove them to a house where food was available, and everything was fine. Incidentally, after they'd had time to simmer down, the man and his wife became frequent visitors of Maine and the Maritimes, becoming good friends with Grandfather Turtle and his family.

GIVE-AWAY

Gift giving is a great Algonquin tradition which puts unselfishness and gratitude to the test. Ben had already given me many feathers, a patch, food, and Polaroids of his family as gifts (not to mention teachings) before I gave him anything in return.

Long ago in India, there was the practice of *dana*, where things were given away freely, as part of a spiritual meeting, and something was always given back, in the form of service, teachings, or a gift. I have found this true among Algonquin people and, when a gift is given sincerely among friends, the compliment is always returned generously. The Sac, Algonquin people from the Midwest, say "Sharing and giving are the ways of God."

Today, many Algonquin people still engage enthusiastically in a "give-away" ceremony, often at the end of a gathering or for some special occasion. Then the one who accepts the gift will either wear the gift or hold it up in the right hand as they dance in the powwow dance.

47

The gift is seldom store-bought, although there is no taboo against store-bought items; they should simply express some aspect of the relationship between the two people. Often, a gift is worn or used for about a year before it is "gifted" to someone else. It is a special honor to wear a shirt worn by one's elder or friend. It is a badge of intimacy. The Micmacs don't say of the shirt, "It was second hand." They say, with appreciation, "It was danced."

At times the nature of the gift speaks volumes, or communicates some hidden message. The gift can be given casually, as between hunting buddies, or with humility, as from a young person to an elder. Sometimes the giving is quite dramatic, as the following story illustrates:

A few years ago I attended a kind of New-Age spiritual gathering in Minnesota, and a number of other Native Americans attended. I ended up arranging for a strong and proud young Ojibway man named Steve to stay in my hotel room. (The Anishinabe, or Ojibway, are close relatives of the Micmac, though they live and work around the Great Lakes.) Throughout the weekend, he walked around the hotel with only a leather vest and jeans on, a gigantic bear-claw necklace around his neck. The giant sharp claws of the brown bear seemed to dig into his brown skin as he walked. Most of the attendees were non-native and those who asked him questions found themselves and their beliefs challenged by a barrage of penetrating bear energy. As he swiftly challenged or corrected their misconceptions as he saw them, that imposing necklace became a symbol of his fierceness. Most of them "crawled back into their holes."

As the gathering ended, a group of non-natives said goodbye, standing in a circle with him. I'm sure many of them were convinced he didn't like them, but I knew he did; he was just giving out some strong medicine. He expressed interest in keeping in touch with them, though they were doubtful if he meant it. They were all timidly looking at his necklace.

Without a word, he tore the precious bear necklace from his neck with a yank from his strong hands. He pulled a pair of wire clippers from his pocket and to everyone's horror, slashed the necklace to bits and separated the claws. He then presented each person with one of the huge bear claws so that they too could be more fierce in their convictions. He then gave a long bear hug to each participant. There were tears as the people began to speak of their love and respect for each other. I couldn't help shedding a few tears myself.

All life is a cycle of exchange. The earth holds the water, the water replenishes the earth, the fire of the sun draws the water into the air, and the clouds give the water back to the earth in the form of rain. These are all sacrifices which keep the world new. The root word of *sa-syeh-wyn*, which means to exchange, trade, barter, etc., is nothing more than "change," which is the root of all offering.

When the Wabanaki eat, they take some food out of the bowl and give it back to the earth, as an offering. Animals sometimes leave part of their meal to be enjoyed by the next fellow, or perhaps it is an offering to the Creator. The Tibetans offer food to the *dakinis*. When you cut a tree down, you first offer tobacco to its spirit, and ask permission. When you pick a plant, you make a bit of tobacco offering as a trade for the plants you need and you leave the rest. When you gather stones for the lodge, you offer tobacco to the largest rock. The *bpoo-*

ohin (one with extraordinary spiritual powers) lives his life as an offering to spirit, in exchange for the blessings of heaven. There are no selfish or unselfish acts, only foolish and wise acts.

VISUALIZATION

"E mbodiment" of life forces through dancing, gifting, and ceremony is important to Algonquin people, but so is visualization. The reader may conclude that an Algonquin without his sweetgrass would be vulnerable, a person who loses his tobacco would be grief stricken, but not so.

All of these embodiments help balance and connect heaven and earth, but are only teaching tools, amplifiers of the inherent power of visualization. I have seen Algonquin people, stuck in a situation without a braid of the great grass *kji-m-tseegoo*, or "sweetgrass," smudge themselves with gestures alone, and I have been instructed to do the same. If you've smudged a lot before, going through the motions is just as powerful, but you have to see and feel the purification happening. There are some situations where you might simply close your eyes and visualize being smudged, and receive help from the spirit of the great grass. You might even smell its smoke around you! The inner action is powerful too; however, we need to keep the inner and the outer life in balance.

I've seen native people, stuck in an urban situation without American Spirit (an organic tobacco popular among native people) or other traditional tobacco, gather a few cigarette butts together, tap the contents into the hand and make a very powerful offering. After all, the quantity of tobacco doesn't change the message, just as the size of the lettering doesn't change the meaning of a word.

The sacred objects allow us to "walk our talk" and renew life by bringing the sacred powers into this visible world. This earth plane is the testing ground where we find out what is real. The Lakota talk about enfolded and unfolded dimensions and beings. The Micmac know this aspect of life too, but don't use those words. They know that Creation is a movement from the invisible to the visible, and that "We the People" have been using visible objects to catch, and connect with, the invisible for thousands of years, bringing it into this world of the created.

Even in dreams, we see the spirit forces embodied in dream objects. We dream of a moose instead of the old ones, we dream of a colored ribbon instead of a direction or entity, we dream of a medicine stick instead of power. Throughout the in-between worlds of dreams there are embodiments of all kinds, and using those same objects in this world strengthens the connection between all the worlds, especially if we choose them ourselves out of our own affinities.

Once a person becomes skillful traveling within dreams as a conscious entity, reading and using the "embodiments" as tools and signs, he begins to see waking life in a similar light. This is what I have always called "Dream Walking" — something understood by most Wabanaki people long ago — that this life is little different from a dream — a dream we can walk around in.

Perhaps he also learns to "sit in your chair and go somewhere," a popular Algonquin update of an old expression which means that, when you think deeply, sometimes you find yourself somewhere else altogether. All these are part of the infinite

51

variety of means available to the person who seeks to be a stronger embodiment of the Creator, as well as its tool: *El-loo-goq Neesgam*.

As we travel the easterly direction in spirit, back to the source of life, we sooner or later pass beyond all embodiment, see the invisible world directly with the eyes of the soul, and glimpse the Great Mysterious *Geezoolgh*, which is known through the heart. The Great Invisible, as it is also called, has no form or substance other than *gesalk*, love. This great love can be sensed directly by the purified heart, but it has no form of itself. Since the Great Mysterious has no embodiment in particular, any object in creation can be an expression of *Geezoolgh*. In fact, all Creation is its embodiment — not the objects themselves, but the eternal dance of those objects in motion through the generations. Put away time pieces for a moment, and the world around you can become whole again, a world that flows and changes according to the music of that sacred dance.

DANCE AS GESTURE

There is an old strain of Indic teaching that holds to the belief that all language and form arise from the dance of Siva, his forty-nine steps becoming the forty-nine Sanskrit letters. Siva's dance is the Mahamudra, "the great gesture," but today, mudras are more often than not referred to as tokens, or "stamps." Today, the "godly language" of the Vedas is speech and the sacred symbol OM, as opposed to gesture and rite.[14]

However, gesture is still the "godly language" of the Algonquin, epitomized perhaps by the Eagle Dance, a dance that is never photographed because it is so sacred. There are many types of eagle dances for many purposes, and each one embodies a vision or prayer and makes it an event, a motion, so that its power is felt on earth and then amplified. It is also called an "Honor Dance," and accompanied with song is used to honor people and things. There are other honor dances, and people honor gifts such as hats, belts, moccasins, through wearing them in an honor dance. Such a gift is not fully owned or honored until it has been "danced." The gift is held aloft with the right arm four times during the dance, as if to say, "How joyful I am at receiving this beautiful gift." The word "dance" itself is used to refer to everything, every life process.

I've always been a wallflower myself.

53

While sitting on the sidelines watching an inter-tribal pow-wow dance at Big Hole Reserve a few years ago with my elder, Geezeegool Meektcheektch, "Grandfather Turtle," I ventured to ask, "What is the word for dance?"

He answered, "The word for dance is *eenoodahain*."

"Is there a different word for sacred dance?"

He answered, "No, same word," and added, "all dances are sacred in the powwow, even social dances."

I looked at him doubtfully. "There must be a linguistic distinction," I thought to myself.

"There's some good dancing right now," he said, waving his pipe to the direction of the dancers. "Why don't you join in?"

I knew the last word had been spoken on the subject. Swimming lecture over; time to be thrown in the river!

I overcame my shyness and became part of the dance, and

lost myself for two sacred days as the dances continued to the stunning thunder of drums and the mezmerizing sounds of chanting. He was right — nothing could have been more sacred than that experience!

Two-step or "powwow" dancing (any native dance with a double hop on each footstep) is the perfect folk art because it is so easy to begin that everyone can do it together, from age four to a-hundred-and-four. A whole village could dance in step with one another and dance out their differences, walking away at sunset with a feeling of love and closeness with each other. While nontraditionals might be just learning the step, others might be whirling, ducking, and flashing feathers and beads in a way that would earn them prize money in the big cities. It all harmonizes together, and after a couple of hours all hearts are beating as one with the beat of the drum, the *batchkeegadaaygoway*. Today, there are reservation-wide powwows somewhere in Micmac country every weekend of the summer and everyone dances the social dances together.

There is no line of demarcation between high and low culture in powwow dancing, but everyone knows and appreciates the really great dancers. Their names are legend. Reserves pay or trade for "head dancers" to come from far away to lead and inspire and instruct the people by example. I've heard the same said of Tai Chi in China — the best and the least can work out together and learn from each other.

Physical gestures or deeds accompany most messages because actions speak louder than words. Give-aways and exchanges of gifts are almost as profuse among the people as compliments are in some cultures, and serve the same reassuring purpose. They too can be a sort of dance.

In India, Siva is both the dancer and the observer of the dance of the cosmos. One could easily parallel Siva with *Neesgam*, the sun, who watches everything on the earth, as it dances in a sacred circle around her, continually nurturing its Terran daughter.

The eagle spirit that is within all of us has a wind dancer aspect and a keen-eyed observer aspect as well. It is important for each person to be aware that they are already a part of such a dance, both as observer and partner.

My elders say, "The eagle is the messenger because he flies so high and sees so far." Part of walking in balance on the earth is balancing the observer self with the one who dances with Creation. Krishnamurti said, "To understand truth, one must have a very sharp, precise, clear mind; not a cunning mind, but a mind that is capable of looking without any distortion, a mind innocent and vulnerable."

55

Wittgenstein said the same thing in much fewer words, "Don't think, look!"

Among Western metaphors, dancing is perhaps the closest we can come to describing the essence of the Algonquin way. Dancing is sacred poetry in action; it expresses balance, exchange, relationship, beauty, animal-like grace, and tradition. But you can't do it and analyze it at the same time. You have to let go of yourself as a fixed object in position, and flow with the music into the long, shining river of life. [15]

GESTURE AS DANCE

Gestures are an integral part of the Algonquin art of speaking. These subtle but important gestures can change, complete, or underscore what is spoken. The high language is even richer with gesture and is even more filled with ambiguities. Many words drop out and become shadows. The expressions make you think long and deep about their meaning. Sign language is still used between tribes, although usually combined with speech.

The sideways, flattened hand, moving up and down in the air (like a slow gentle karate chop) is a famous native gesture of noble discourse. We see it in the occasional statue of a native orator who may have lived in Colonial times, and we also see it in the movements of our native orators today. One hand moving in a beseeching gesture could mean "I don't want to have to say this again."

Some objects are pointed to but not named. I've seen Wabanaki speakers point to themselves in place of the word "I" or "me." In the old days, it was considered childish and self-centered and I've heard a ninety-year-old *geezegodwit* quoted as saying, "*Neen* ['I'] is a babytalk word." It is replaced by a gesture, a humbler stance.

To an adult, a Micmac elder might make a gesture which I call "*Neen ach geeol*" The me-and-you gesture, and then perhaps would say "like to stay."

Arms folded across the chest doesn't mean "I'm not listening," but means "I'm standing my ground, but my ears are open." However, if people turn their backs to you for no reason it may mean they are not listening. The stance of the *geenap*, or "strong elder," is a congruent stance, the stance of someone walking in balance on the earth. It is hard to describe in words because there is nothing to it, it just is, like an uncarved block of wood. [16] The problem with body language is that it can be misinterpreted. It is important to trust the intuitive reaction created by words and gestures in context. Listen with your heart.

The "Micmac hug" is with right hands clasped (some Algonquins say left) in handshake, embracing the other person with the left arm, head to the left. This hug is often stoic, brisk and hearty. Traditional people don't shake hands often, but there is a handshake that is reminiscent of the "Indian arm wrestling" grip which is very jovial and friendly, generally between men. [17] These gestures are part of the poetics of the Micmac and they are practiced by the people every day.

Animals are very highly revered in the Algonquin world and gestures are parts of language we share with animals. It helps us feel close to them in spirit. Native American dances often imitate animal motions, as do many Asian martial arts movements. [18]

The motions of the hands when we speak, or in the pipe ceremony, help to bring together body, mind, and spirit. In older forms of Tibetan Buddhism, physical gestures are also important in spiritual practice. [19]

Words often become dispensible altogether. Many native chants and songs do not have words, but "vocables," syllables with no objective meaning. In Tibet and India, chanting often consists of mantric sound, such as *OM* (or *Aum*), *Hum*, or *Re Re Re*. They speak the language of Creation and, years ago, they may have been sung. In Wabanaki culture, the syllables "*Hey-ya-hey*" seem to focus or stir up quite a lot of feeling and power, whether sung or chanted.

Chuang Tzu, the Taoist elder of China circa 500 B.C. said it well: "The wise man gives instructions without the use of speech." The Wabanaki elders seem to share this sentiment deeply.

FREE TO SURRENDER

One of the biggest disputes in time-oriented Western philosophy is free will versus predetermination. Europe has seen numerous proponents from each camp, with no victor in sight. However, in Algonquin culture, one has the choice to exercise personal power, or to strive to become purely the tool of the Creator (though to do so may require strength and will power). This sentiment is echoed throughout the world among earth-based peoples.

A pipe man told me, "You don't carry the pipe, the pipe carries you." This is basic medicine teaching. For this reason, I am pleased when I read that the ancient Chinese sage, Chuang Tzu, said "To hold on to Tao, just hope that Tao will keep hold of you!" I have also read of an expression in the ancient Kashmiri Shaivite tradition which goes, "In the beginning, we practice speaking and breathing the mantra. In the end, the breath of the mantra practices us." [20]

Will power is not discipline, control is not mastery. The eagle does not fight the wind or tell it where to blow, he takes it as it comes and works with it. The medicine men and women tend to do the same, and avoid "telling the Great Spirit what to do," which often makes havoc out of plans and schedules, but which makes living a fresh and powerful experience. I jokingly call it "karma surfing."

We can have our free will if we want it, but according to ancient teachings, there is a better way. When we come to know our own power, only then do we have something of value which we can truly offer up to the Creator in exchange for becoming Its tool.

CO-CREATING

icmac traditionals say *Eloogoq Neesgam*, "(I am) the tool of the Creator." The moment of Creation, as set down in Creation stories and myths, may have happened a thousand generations ago, but it is still happening now. The story continues and you are a character in that story. Miracles are not uncommon in Algonquin daily life because the world is still under construction, and we are often the tools used to build it.

59

To find oneself a character in the ongoing Creation Myth is a heavy responsibility at times, and when such a man's tools of Creation are taken away, when his culture is taken away, the weight of that responsibility to the Creator crushes him. He may turn to the tools of self-oppression instead, the drink, the drugs, and he tries to forget. The modern person is accustomed to having blinders on, which allow the fast mind to operate, to survive in an impersonal and inanimate technological environment, and not go crazy. These blocks have been there so long, no one knows that they have them or what they are.

The more options you have, the broader your temptations, the more blinders you need to keep focused on your own priorities and issues, and the more you develop. The way I see it, the Algonquin people did not have or need as many blocks to the unconscious, irrational mind, for which the Newtonian world is an anathema, and often are reluctant to join technological society for this reason. The Newtonian world not only separates living beings from inanimate ones, but seems to favor the inanimate ones, in an effort to control and explain reality according to an agenda of rationality, ignoring the fact that we ourselves are not rational, inanimate objects. In fact we are magical beings as well as wise and cautious ones. We can't have one part of a person without the other. In the native world, both are accepted, but when a native thinking person enters into high-tech society where predictability is worshipped, there's no telling what will happen!

People of an oral tradition have long indelible memories, and that can make twentieth-century living very painful, as the mind of the Algonquin becomes crowded to bursting with useless information and slogans and lies. Sometimes alcohol seems to promise some sort of refuge, but it doesn't heal anything. It embodies the break between the people and their tradition. Drink is not traditional to Algonquin people. Drugs are not traditional to Algonquin people. The view that drinking and drug-taking are harmless is not traditional. And yet many lose their way to this trickster.

When the *geenap*, or "strong elder," gets back his belief, he is once again with Creation, and begins to heal himself and others. Once they have healed, individuals start to act as part of Creation and walk close with the Creator. To begin the journey, the *geenap* says to spirit, "*Geh-doo nemeedoo nadgo'o-eh!*" "Let me see something!" and he is given a vision of what he is to do. There is no book to tell the Algonquin what is right or wrong, or what to do next; the way is revealed each moment from within. The most important language to learn to read is the language of the heart. You have to find your own answers, perhaps by slowing down and letting spirit catch up to you. Correct inner guidance from the Creator speaking through the heart is a treasure worth any sacrifice, and many do make the ultimate sacrifice rather than live without it, but usually it just takes a little extra courage to uphold one's right to follow that guidance.

Where you are standing is sacred ground and every day is the sabbath. Outsiders sometimes have trouble understanding traditional native behavior, why they are so serious about looking for signs, why they are so sensitive to insensitive people, why they are so mindful of small matters, how they can be so patient, why they approach others so gently and quietly, and why sincerity is so essential. If traditional people are reluctant to change the people and places around them, it is because where they walk is sacred ground. They are helpers of the grandmothers and grandfathers, and are themselves tools of the Creator, but so are others.

Everything you see, in the sweat lodge, in the vision quest, in your dreams, in your walk on the mother earth, becomes a part of Creation and a part of the teaching to share with others. Share when spirit moves you to tell the story that pours through your heart and you shall move others. Those tears shed are the Creator touching and healing others through you, and you are touched as well. The Algonquin art of speaking is sec-

61

ond to this touching, for poetry is the result of the way, not the cause of it.

FEASTING

Food exchanged is a very important dance of fellowship and family. "All my relations," *nogomaq*, is said just as much through exchange of food as through words. The traditional Wabanaki wigwam (*wee-goo-ohm* or "where I dwell") had soup simmering over the fire for relatives and friends to share at all times, and this practice is still held by many traditionals.

Feasts are very important and no expense is spared to provide just the right foods whatever the time of year. Even the feast has a poetry of its own and each food has spiritual significance. The salmon on your plate represents Nedawansum, the first *geenap* or "strong elder." The nuts in your bowl or in your meal represent Neeganaganimq(oo)zeesq(oo), the first young woman who was born from the leaf of a tree.

Nothing could better express caring for one another than the sharing of food, which comes from the earth and gives life to people, and that is what a feast is about. The people feed each other all the time, out of mutual respect, but especially at feast time. Feasting is mentioned in the Creation stories and is used to honor individual successes, the completion of a fast, or to bring the nations and band councils together. There is a feast for marriages and the birth of children. There is a feast for baby's first step, first tooth, and also a "walking out" ceremony as soon as the young boy (*ulbadoodjeedj*) or girl (*ebeedess*) can wear cermonial regalia and walk around on his/her own two feet. This too is honored with a feast. I once was privileged to serve the food at such a meal, serving the circle of feasters in clockwise fashion. In the old times, a boy was feasted when he killed his first moose, thereby entering into adulthood and becoming eligible to marry and to vote. We can safely assume he helped in eating the moose as well.

Micmac people are incessantly thankful for the gift of life and give thanks constantly in their prayers, "*Wellalioq!*" [21] ("Thank you all!") to the four directions. There was always a feast at harvest time, in thankfulness for a good crop, and also to fatten up for the winter while the food was still fresh (and full of vitamins, as we would say now). When the Algonquin Squanto showed the Pilgrims how to farm, I'm sure he told them that part of getting a good crop was being deeply grateful in advance. I can imagine those hungry Pilgrims sending out the Thanksgiving dinner invitations in May. Gratitude is Lesson One of any Algonquin course in philosophy.

There is a feast held for someone who has died, usually one year after their dying. This helps honor the one who has gone on, and it ends the grieving year. At this time, the men and women stop cutting their hair in mourning and try to return to life as usual.

Traditional feasting food includes venison, nuts, salmon, bannok bread, or *looskinigun* bread, and eel meat. Meat was prepared with a wide assortment of herbs. There are four types of food eaten at the traditional feast, and they are served by (usually) four men, and eaten at the same time. These are 1. *looskinagin*, or fry bread; 2. vegetables, nuts and berries; 3. herb teas and liquids; and 4. meats and fish. These honor the four directions— East, South, West and North.

When I completed my first *sooneywen* ceremony, a fast of two days preceded and followed by sweat lodge ceremonies with Micmac neighbors of all ages joining in the sweat, I was honored with a traditional feast.

The day before the fast, I'd finally agreed to eat again, and Grandfather Turtle took me and his helper Grandfather Eagle to a little shack by the Miramichi River where some guys were selling live eels and lobsters. We had a traditional pre-fasting feast of lobster right there beside the river. Lobster (which they call in Micmac *Injun Djugedj* or "Indian Crab") fattens you up for a long journey. It was also a delicious apology for tricking me with the water glass.

The elders opened the shells with their bare hands and ate heartily. Bees gathered around them, attracted by the aroma, but the elders never swatted at them even when they landed on bare legs and arms. I tried to copy them, only succeeding in cutting up my fingers until they were bleeding. I was too busy swatting at the bees to worry about the blood. I knew I had a lot to learn and was doing the best I could.

They slid the eels into plastic bags to save them for my post-vision quest feast. That was my incentive, I suppose, to finish the fast, although fried chicken would have been more effective. The elders put those lively bags on the floor of the car. As I drove back to the house, they wiggled their way under the car seat and we had to find them. I was worried they had escaped from the bags and were hiding somewhere in the car waiting to strike.

After the fast was over, the elders cooked the eels in pans with butter. Micmac neighbors came and joined in the feast with great joy that I was rejoining the tribe. They heartily enjoyed all the other dishes, but only took small portions of the eel meat, because it was my distinguished honor to finish the eel. Not a scrap could be left behind. They wouldn't leave until I'd forced the last bite down my throat. To look at the live creature was not so promising, but once cooked and skinned, it really did taste like chicken. We shared one guitar and sang songs and had a good time, a better time than the poor eel.

The traditional feast song starts with the call for the eagle, "*geetpoo!*" followed by non-literal vocables.

Geetpoo, eegunday, kwey yo hey
Kwan a lee a kwan do dey
Kwan a lee a kwan do don a hey a hey yo!
Dey ya kah! Dey ya kah!
Kwan a lee a kwan do dey
Kwan a lee a kwan do don a hey a hey yo!
(as sung by Mr. George Paul and others)

Most ancient earth-based peoples celebrate with a feast ceremony, but each in a different way.

FASTING

The essential technique to higher consciousness, at least in the Algonquin tradition, is fasting. Everything spiritual has a way in which it can be enacted, embodied, and completed, and the way to undergo the process of spiritual transformation with your whole body, your whole self, is through fasting and prayer. Fasting, or *soo-ney-wen*, is purification on all levels, including the physical. It is the act of giving up what is precious to you so that others can have it. It teaches you to appreciate the basic nourishment in life so that you don't abuse it. Fasting also sensitizes the body to nonphysical vibrations, and to one's own inner workings.

My experiences fasting with elders have led me to believe that the body and other aspects of the self are essentially good, but absorb confused and unhelpful energies and substances from the environment (toxins), and need a little help in passing them off, hence the importance of purification. Once purified of these confusions, the body and mind become strong and healthy and work as better tools of the Creator.

In the Wabanaki way, less is more. The less you bring with you on the fast, the better. The Japanese word *mu* means "no," or "not," and in Zen implies "not two," comparable to the Hindu *neti neti*, "not this not that." It is said that "once you grasp *mu*, you grasp Zen."

Interestingly, the everyday word used for "not" in Micmac is also *mu* ("moo," but cut short). If you feel "not-good" (perhaps sad or sick to your stomach), you might say *"moo-wel-oh-day-gn!"* If you were fasting and the elder saw you about to drink water or read a book, he might say *"mo-chwah"* ("no"), or *"Mook!"* which means "Don't!"

Many Asian cultures share the Micmac emphasis on fasting. In *The Woodcarver*, Chuang Tzu writes, "I fasted in order to set my heart at rest. After three days of fasting, I had forgotten gain and success. After five days, I had forgotten praise or criticism. After seven days, I had forgotten my body with all its limbs." This describes the way a *sooneywen* feels. One's confusion lifts a little bit at a time, until one is free from doubt and confusion.

Most people who experience the *sooneywen* agree that the first day "up on the hill" seems to last a very, very long time. It seems there is no one to talk to and nothing to do. The thoughts are still agitated and restless. During the second day, the mind slows down, becomes less aware of the passing of time. By the third day, we have already entered the spirit world and are too busy talking to spirit to notice the passing of time at all. The fourth day we spend almost in eternity, and when the elder comes to take us back, we are reluctant to leave our new home — at least this has been my experience.

As there are seven directions, all told, in Wabanaki traditions, one could speculate that in ancient times, fasts were seven days long, and indeed, I have heard this stated by an elder. According to histologists, those who work with allergies, it takes seven days to clear the body of a foreign substance, such as an allergin, so a purification fast would have to be seven days long to be complete.

The *sooneywen* is done without food or water and this abstinence is usually for two or four or perhaps eight days. During this time, the fasting person contemplates a single question or spiritual goal and seeks visions which will bring the answers to that question. It is a waste of energy to ask a million questions, for you'll get back what you put out, a confusing jumble of information. Ask but one question, and you will get a singular answer. There is an old Algonquin saying that you are more likely to hit water by digging one deep hole than by digging a thousand little holes. The same is true with the fast. Each well-considered question can lead to a whole universe of wisdom, because one insight leads to another as the answers come. Every good question is the key to the universe, so choose one and dig!

I have always been used to fasting and was not fearful as the day of my first *sooneywen* approached. The day arrived. I awoke at dawn and Grandfather Turtle came in ready for business. He said that my ordeal was to keep a fire going for the entire forty-eight hours.

He showed me the logs that would be used in the ceremonial fire and handed me an axe and said, "These need to be split up!" Then he left.

I tried swinging the axe in their general direction, but didn't make much of a dent. It was hopeless. Grandfather Eagle sauntered down from the house and saw what was going on. He grabbed the axe and without a word, split several hard logs in two, *whack! whack! whack!* and piled them up, ready for the next two days.

Then he brought the twelve "grandfather" stones together in a pile, stacked more wood around them, then lit a good blaze with expert mastery and efficiency. I stood around the fire, wearing only swim trunks and a wool blanket, which was draped around my shoulders. The air had a cool bite to it, and the grass was still dripping with dew. I shivered slightly. My mind was blank.

After the sweat lodge was over, Grandfather Turtle took my six ribbons and tied a knot at the top. He handed them to me and said, "Hang these in the trees to hold your prayers. You'll need them."

I did as he instructed. We walked back to the cabin together. He said, "It's important to keep the fire going no matter what. When you keep the fire going, you don't blow on it, or you

68

might blow away the spirit of that fire. Use a feather instead, like the one I gave you. And don't use paper. Only use wood.

"Keep an eye on that fire and don't let it go out. If you need help, offer tobacco to the *buch-tyiew*, the fire spirit. Place a little tobacco on the fire and you'll get help."

He started to leave and I panicked. I said, "Hey aren't you going to help me? I was never a boy scout! I've never kept a fire going before. I don't know what to do!"

He turned his back on me and walked away, saying, "Yer gonna learn!"

PRAYING

The word for prayer is *ahl-soo-tu-my,* which means "speaking as one with." You don't have to go to church at a certain time to do it. You can spend your whole life speaking as one with, and if you do, your life becomes prayer.

Wabanaki don't invoke the gods through repeating a long poem or chant verbatim. They speak as one with Geezoolgh (the Supreme Being) or Neesgam, (the Creator/sun) or with Noogamee, the grandmother. The words come from heaven, along with the wind of the Great Spirit, like birth water along with the newborn child. Out of this continual process will come chants that gradually become "set" and are repeated. When you pray for help, the words should come freely from your heart to heaven like the prayers of a mother for her children; however, you must address the spirits by name, and the animal powers by name, and you must tell them your name as well, if you want them to enter your life. It is good to speak in the old native language, for it is a powerful language, but it is much more important to speak from your heart, for that is you and you, too, are sacred.

Praying is a communion with the Creator and with Geezoolgh. It is best to ask for things of the soul, such as visions, wisdom, or understanding. These bring the best harvest, and help us as co-workers, making the Creator happy. You can say, "Let me be the tool of the Creator. I am in your hands here and now." In the Micmac language, this same expression would be, *"Eloogoq Neesgam! Neegeh geel ekpidinq aym!"*

Some people pray for healing, love, and harmony, which is all right too. You can say "I pray for my people today!" which might be said *"Geezkook ahlsootumokeek nogomaq!"*

Yet others pray for more money and more cars and more jobs and more houses, not to mention fame and fortune, without thought to the chaos and damage in human ecology it might cause. All things are related to spiritual life, but there are no traditional words in Micmac for these things. Petitioning God to give you more than the other guy is not "speaking as one with," but separating yourself from the Creator.

Kabir says, "All know that the drop merges into the ocean, but few know that the ocean merges into the drop." He was speaking as one with.

Seng Ts'an said, "The one is none other than the All, the All none other than the one." And Huang Po wrote, "Every single thing is just One Mind. When you have perceived this, you will have mounted the Chariot of the Buddhas." He was speaking as one with the Creator Mind.

The Taoist *"Wu-wei,"* which implies non-doing, or nonaction, is really perfect action — acting in harmony with the whole (*kriya* in Sanskrit). Things done rightly are done effortlessly, in accord with nature and with our place in the scheme of things. This too, seems to be an expression of the Micmac at one with.

Lao Tzu said to the anxious student, Keng Sang Chu, "If you can only know when to stop, be content to wait, listen, and give up your own useless strivings, this 'melts the ice'" (the ice of inner confusion). Native prayer is not meant to be yet another vehicle for worldly striving, but to be a time to heal confusion and to be thankful for the way things are.

Once we see the real truth (the Micmac word *dellia'o-weh* means real truth) then we can do what's best. What more could we want?

FIRST LIGHT

t was dawn by the banks of the Miramichi. I was standing alone beside the fire, about to enter my first sweat lodge. I had received sketchy instructions the day before in what was involved in Micmac prayer, but I'd never actually tried it. I felt very strongly connected to my ancestors in that place where they had once lived, and I felt I knew what to do, as if I'd done it a long time ago.

I faced the fire, faced the direction of the east, faced the red of the morning sun, and holding a bit of tobacco in my fist, I raised it up in offering. I closed my eyes and said, *"Ellabadu Niskam, Wedjibeck, Nogomaq,"* blessings of the Grandfather, the

Creator, the Sun in the east. All my relations!" I opened my eyes and threw the tobacco into the fire. (*Wedjibeck* means "where the tide comes in," but it was the only word for east I knew then, and from where I stood, it was somewhat accurate.)

Then I walked to the north of the fire, careful not to step on the spirit trail that led from the fire into the lodge itself, and turned to the south, where the Miramichi lapped against the sweetgrass just beyond a thicket of trees. I took another bit of tobacco in my right hand, and holding it aloft in my fist, I faced the southern sky and said, "*Geezeegool Geetpo Up-kweh-tess-nook, may-da-lain! Nogomaq!* Grandfather Eagle of the South, greetings to you! All my relations!" I added, "Bring me the message for how I should live my life." Then I tossed the tobacco into the fire, and stood there for a while looking into the flames.

Then I walked to the eastern side of the fire, and facing the dark of the night receding in the western sky, I lifted up another pinch of tobacco and said "*Kis-koo-wisk Oet-gkas-en-nuk, a-bochun-moo-ee geez-kuk. Nogomaq!* Grandmothers of the West, help me today, heal me today! All my relations!" I threw the tobacco into the fire, and stood there for a while to soak in the energy from the fire, and to pray inside myself to the grandmothers.

Then I walked around the fire, and facing the north, facing the sweat lodge where Ben was already preparing the ritual space for us, I said, "*Wel-al-in, Geezeegool Mo-in Oh-aht-nook! Wel-al-in geez-kuk! Nogomaq!* Thank you, Grandfather Bear of the North. Thank you today. All my relations!"

I had asked Ben to teach me one whole sentence in Micmac, and I had never gotten a chance to use it till now and it seemed to fit. I threw it in.

"*Welalin don del meetugut au naq'n-aa mah-gooum!*"

I think I said, "Thank you for coming today to the sweat lodge." At least the Bear of the North understood me. I always wondered why he had taught me that phrase. It was something for a leader to say. When would I ever use it?

In one short prayer round I had used every Micmac word I knew, and probably incorrectly, but it was my initiation into the tribe. I was surprised how quickly I had learned the various words, although I had to spend a lot of time before each prayer remembering what to say. It was worth it. I didn't want to be a tourist, I didn't want to introduce any change into this ceremony, now thousands of years old. I wanted it to change me, and threw myself totally into becoming what must have been me in a past life. It was the deep tap root I was seeking. I knew I was finding a part of myself that would make the superficial parts function better.

Everyone prays differently, and prayers are different every day. This was my first try. I think the grandfathers understood me.

MY FIRST SWEAT LODGE

A number of Micmacs showed up for that first sweat lodge, including a young teenager named Buck, with whom I felt a rapport. We watched studiously as Grandfather Eagle untied his hair and prepared the Y-shaped stick with his hatchet. Probing into the fire with the forked stick, he knocked the burning logs away and herded the first of the twelve glowing rocks into the lodge, perched gingerly in the fork of the stick. Then came the other eleven grandfathers. They looked like miniature suns traveling along the ghost trail into the darkness of the lodge. He placed them in a hole dug into the ground at the center of the lodge. Ben was already sitting silently in the north of the lodge, working with the spiritual energies.

We entered our sweat lodge, the women on the west side, the men on the east side. We knelt to enter the small opening at the south of the domed, blanket-covered structure, and as our heads passed under the door, we said *"No-o-go-mach!"* which means "all my relations," a most ancient blessing. The oldest members of the group sat in the back next to the water pourer, Ben, who could be dimly seen in the back. We were seated by age, and being next to youngest, I was positioned toward the door, legs crossed "Indian" style. For my convenience, Ben had placed a few small rugs around the sides of the lodge, but there was also cool, dark mud, and damp grass as well. Buck was handling the door, and Grandfather Eagle was the doorman, the *ga-a-na-djit,* and stayed outside, passing in the *samgwan* in water jugs for us to drink, and taking care of those of us inside.

Most of the ceremony was in Micmac, and yet I felt at ease. There was a mixture of smells to be enjoyed as the flaps went down: the subtle dry smell of burning rocks, the residue of smoke in the blankets, the smell of clean sweat, tobacco, cedar, and wet earth. Sitting in that dark lodge around those rocks, surrounded only by native people, chanting and praying in a language I was not yet familiar with, I got the impression that nothing had changed for 10,000 years, and that, in fact, I could have just now slipped back to prehistoric times at this very spot, experienced the same thing, and still felt like I had been there before. If what Ben had said about coming back until you learned your culture was true, I could have been in sweat lodges with Ben since the beginning of Algonquin time, over 10,000 years ago. It was a most healing experience, a brush with eternity. Most emphatically, I felt I was finally home.

Ben took his sacred cedar bough, dipped it in the bucket of water sitting next to him, and splashed the water onto the blistering rocks with a wild *tch tch tch* rhythm as each of the needles let go their drops of water differently. It was an intense sizzling, frying sound that reminded me of a jazz drummer in freefall. Our faces were met with a blast of riveting heat. I could feel the heat seeping into my pores and healing me. At times I had to breathe through my towel to adjust to the air. Tears of sweat rolled into my eyes and stung, and I used the towel often to clear them.

"Pray hard, everybody! Pray hard to the Creator! Heal!" It was easy to pray hard under these conditions.

As the rattle came snaking around in the utter darkness, I could feel the confusion being rattled out of my head. A grand looking medicine pipe, called *te-maq'n,* made of a tee-shaped piece of red pipestone and a carved stem of wood was passed around during each of the four rounds. I had never learned to smoke it, but I did the best I could to keep the glowing bowl of *spee-bach'n* — a special mixture of red willow bark, tobacco, sweetgrass, and other herbs — from dying out. I learned it was best to pass it along quickly if you don't know what you're doing.

After opening up with a prayer to the East, we did a round for the Eagle of the South, asking for the message. I hoped to see the eagle light in the sweat lodge during the eagle round, but I was too self-conscious, perhaps anxious, and didn't see it.

There was a break, and we opened the doors for a moment, but were not to leave. Water was passed in. The next round was for the Grandmothers of the West. We sang songs to the grandmothers, and I saw what Ben called the grandmother-light at the top of the lodge. We went clockwise around the circle within, offering our thanks and prayers. When it came time to ask the grandmothers for help, I said, "Grandmother, let the wall fall down. Heal my heart and let the wall that surrounds it fall down!" The others responded in a chorus of *"Daho!" "Hey!"* and *"No-o-go-mach!"*

Until that time, I couldn't have put my finger on what was bothering me. When the spirit moved through me, my mouth knew what to say, even though my head did not. Too many complications in my life had caused a wall to build up, cutting me off from my feelings, and it was time to bring it down, through the help of the ancestors, spirit guides, and our Creator.

Between the rounds, the flap to the door was opened: Ben said, "Bless yourselves!" and we all slapped ourselves on the arms and legs. The flap went up, and the light came in. It was during those moments I could see Ben and the others sitting around me. Ben was totally transformed, his face illuminated by Geezoolgh, the Great Mysterious One, his long white hair flowing down over his chest as I had first seen him, the light playing on his face in strange ways, his eyes closed, his face one of concentration without thought.

To me, he embodied the spirit of both the Neanderthal shaman, shaking his rattles, yelling strong syllables to the nature spirits, and also of the concert artist, Mstislav Rostropovich, the Russian cellist and conductor whom I had seen at work during my days in the music conservatory, deftly working the magic of his art form, riding and yet controlling a wave of emotional and intrinsic experience, in balanced relationship with the creative forces, precise yet with abandon. Watching him in the lodge spanned all of my lifetimes and connected them. I was in a land before time, but also here and now, gaining understanding about my own life.

I saw nothing of the Grandfather Bear as we did the round for the North, but was fascinated with the song Ben sang about the boy and the bear, and tried to sing along.

The door flap was closed again and we went into the fourth round, the round of the East. I saw the brilliant blue light of Glooskap in the lodge, our ancestor and teacher, as we spoke our prayers. It made me happy to see something of my own in the lodge, and the light was uplifting, joyful, and healing. As I gazed gently at it, I worked on opening my heart, as if with a large pair of soft pliers, and let my body twitch to get the kinks out.

Ben had taken my six prayer ribbons into the lodge, and had looped them and hung them from the sapling framework that was visible from the inside. Ben's lodge was a small one and he let it get very, very hot, which seemed to please the other Micmacs there.

As the sweat lodge was winding down, I became very relaxed, and had a vision of a crane, or heron, *tdumgwaligunidj*, in front of me. Perhaps it was the same bird who had donated the feathers Ben had given me. He was coming to remind me to be calm and patient in my pursuit of Micmac wisdom. Ben

77

had said the night before that whatever you see in the lodge becomes part of your teaching, and you can share it with others.

At the end, Grandfather Eagle handed in through the door a welcome surprise, at least for me: a bowl of blueberries and a big spoon. We passed the bowl clockwise to the back of the lodge, to the north, where Ben sat. He said some hushed words in Micmac and offered the bowl to the four cardinal directions, and to the sky and to the ground. He thanked the rocks for doing all the work to heal us, and suffering for us, and giving us their energy.

There was a gentle, fatherly, singing quality in his voice as he spoke to them that made me feel love for the rocks also, love and compassion, and I believed that he or whatever was speaking through him truly cared for the rock spirits represented there, and intended to heal their pain. Ben spooned out some blueberries and placed them on the hot rocks.

The door was open, and light from the south lit up the inside of the lodge so I could see the blueberries frying on the rocks. They were gratefully eating them up!

When it came time to leave the lodge, I was relieved to get out of the hot, steaming lodge, and into the daylight, but I was also beginning my vision quest ordeal, and was not to touch water again, nor speak to anyone save Ben. The other Micmac guys were being quiet around me, and I realized this was serious business.

LISTENING

The fast or *sooneywen*, is a time for listening. Listen to the wind in the trees, to the fire and the cracking logs, to the bees and the sound of the river. Listen to the voices in your head and let them rattle their way out like the pebbles in the turtleshell rattle.

If you fast long enough, you go on a journey and reach a place where there are no words.

When you return, your words, like water, will be fresh and new. Trying to hold it in your hand, where does the water go? Life is like the wind and blows where it will; trying to hold it in your hand, where does the wind go?

Words are like flowers and flowers are beautiful if they're allowed to grow wild. Pick them, separate them from the earth and hold them for a while, they wither just as people's hearts wither holding onto empty words. Flowers are miracles, but trying to hold them in your hand, where do the colors go?

The grandfather doesn't listen to your words. He listens to your heart and knows your feelings. Talk leads to more talk, but silence leads to wisdom. Incessant talkers babble on and on and on like water, but water is never repeating.

In the Micmac Creation story, Glooskap, the first man, was created by lightning bolts. In the Abenaki version, the seven openings in his head were also created by lightning bolts. Glooskabee, as he is called by the Abenaki, was lying on the ground without senses until *Too-see-noo-ahsk*, the Creator, gave him two nostrils to breathe in the sweet smells of the earth, two eyes to see everything in depth, and two ears to hear two sides to every story, each opening made in a flash of lightning. Then the seventh bolt of lightning came and gave him only one mouth, so that he would only speak half as much as he listened.

Likewise today, native people are encouraged to inhale the sweet smells of the earth, see things in perspective, listen to both sides of every story, and to speak only half as much as they listen, a Wabanaki formula for success and happiness in daily life.

Chuang Tzu said that the Tao communicates itself in its own way, in the right moment. Otherwise, it cannot be communicated. He also said, "The purpose of words is to convey ideas. When the ideas are grasped the words are forgotten. Where can I find a man who has forgotten words? He is the one I would like to talk to."

80

IT BURNS TO ASHES

Humility is the altar stone of Algonquin prayer and way of life. Inner peace and humility are so integrated into daily life they are not usually spoken of. *Sooneywen*, "fasting," can also mean "you humble yourself." The elders must constantly humble themselves before their Creator in order to work with the medicine. They do an excellent job of keeping their youngers humble as well, through the most subtle humor and *ahdoog(w)aq'nn* or teaching stories.

The *bpoo-ohinn* or gifted elders smudge themselves with the smoke from the *tdjee-choss*, a tree fungus that grows on elm trees. The word means "it burns to ashes," and it does. This trait is always pointed out to young people who are new to the medicine path as something to be noticed and perhaps imitated on their journey through life. It is the way of total humility in service to the Creator — you burn with the fire of the Creator's energy until you are reduced to nothing. In the end we become *geezeegodwit*, "elders who are like an old dry pine tree, ready to fall over," or like the *goomoodj*, "the tree that is good only for firewood." This is the humble goal of the true *bpoo-ohin*.

In Taoism, one admires the "cosmic humility of the man who fully realizes his own nothingness and becomes totally forgetful of himself, like a dry tree stump or like dead ashes." [22] This statement is remarkably Micmac in nature. In Buddhism, the term *nirvana* is derived from the word "blown out" or "burned out." The tree fungus *tdjee-choss*, like the devoted elder, gives of itself totally. It doesn't go out, its fire stays lit until it is ashes, all burnt out.

81

Grandfather Turtle often says that when he conducts the sweat lodge he is taken up by the spirit and heals the people, but outside the lodge, he is "just like everyone else." This is such a refreshing statement in comparison to many of today's gurus — "avatars" whose power comes from being different from others.

In a similar vein, Chuang Tzu wrote, "The sage recognizes himself to be as other men are. He does not set himself apart and above others. He is different in his heart when he centers on the Tao and not on himself."

Chuang Tzu is also known for his "turtle" story, where he states that it is better to live as a plain turtle dragging his tail in the mud then to be made an offering for a prince and venerated for years. Grandfather Turtle often weaves stories about an old turtle into his teachings. "He goes slow (dragging his tail in the mud) but he never makes a mistake. He takes a step, then looks around, then waits and takes another step. He always has at least one foot on the mother earth."

In Western culture we equate "being well grounded" with getting there on time, mastering the way of the clock. But watching Wabanaki elders has taught me that there is another way. They are grounded in the earth and in their bodies, and in the Creator, and get there at the right time spiritually. They tune into the flow of events which emerge from the source of Creation. When you are one with Creation you can do that.

Once, when I was walking in the Himalayas, I met a yogic master on the path wearing a white robe. He grasped my arm, looked into my eyes, and said these words to me: "A man's energy and strength come from the earth. His heart must be rooted in the soil like a great oak tree if his branches are to reach to the sky." He then walked on. I was speechless. It wasn't until I was shown this teaching by Wabanaki elders that I understood his words. This is what it means to be "grounded" in Native American traditions.

PEACE

New York has many peace fesitivals, including the renowned festival held in Amenia each year, where peace is proclaimed in every major language. While Grandfather Turtle was visiting New York, a message was given to me to ask him on behalf of the Amenia Festival what the word for peace was in Micmac. I agreed to ask.

When I found Grandfather, he was sitting against a rock in

the shade, puffing slowly on his pipe and looking out at the beauty of *oositgamoo*, "the surface of our mother," and at the blue sky above him, his head leaning back with pleasure. He and the rock were as one, rooted in the great earth, strong, enduring, unchanging. He seemed timeless, as if he had always been there.

I explained the situation to him — the person who passed the message to me needed an answer by three o'clock. It was urgent.

He didn't look at me but continued slowly smoking his pipe, just as he had been, his eyes unwavering.

"What's peace?" he answered. "I'm not sure of this word. What does it mean?"

I didn't know what to say; my mind went blank. I didn't know myself.

83

"Does it mean there is no war going on? There will always be war — somewhere. You can't stop that. We don't have a word for that kind of peace. When someone gets angry at you, you try to talk to them, you try to understand each other. Just like husband and wife; they're not always peaceful.

"The way I'm sitting here? There's no word for that. You just do it. It's that simple.

"You ask these people what they mean by peace, and I'll tell you in Micmac."

Some time later he taught me a few phrases for an inner peace, each including the root syllable *wunt* — one of which was *wunt-taktek* or "peaceful." But he made a memorable point that peaceful afternoon.

HEAVENLY LIGHT

The word for heaven, or "in heaven," is *hwa-so'q*. The word for light — the whole big light we might see in a vision — is *hwa-so-hwy*, "I am lit up." These two are nearly the same. So heaven, in a sense, is light.

The little blue light of heaven that we see in the sweat lodge is called *wasoweck*, "the bright little flower," or literally "it is turning bright," or "it is lit." It may also visit us in prayer. Entities may appear as lights and colors, but heaven is a whole big light. Purple light is considered the color of truth, and when the truth comes to you in this form, you are well blessed, even if you don't understand.

The Ancestor, Glooskap, the first man, the million-year-old man, is seen as a beautiful blue light in the spirit world. He is a powerful guide and a teacher for Micmac people today. The Abenaki ("Dawn Land People") call him Gloo-ska-bee. The Naskapi of Labrador ("the People From the Place Where Things Disappear") call him *Mis-ta-pe-o*. He takes people on inner journeys through the spirit world and protects them when danger arises. Some Micmac believe he is still alive "somewheres," others believe he will be reborn in another form, perhaps as a "white" or "black" person — to test the vision of native people. Glooskap once said, "When the Indian people need me again, I will come back," to unite the tribes of the Algonquin people. The Miskwaqi call him Nadabozo. The Cree call him Weesuckerjack. Each Algonquin nation seems to have a different name, but they all look for the return of this great-grandfather.

Some elders speak of a little spirit light behind the right

shoulder which they name *Biboogwess*, the Hawk. You can't see it with your normal vision, but it is there sometimes, and looks out for you as your protector.

The Taoist Liu Hua-Yang said, "Human nature and life are contained in the light of heaven (between the eyes), and the light of heaven is the Tao. These are the most important secrets of the Tao." It would not be surprising to a Taoist, then, that the Micmac words for "light" and "heaven" are so alike.

This heavenly connotation of light is worldwide. It is found in the Kabbala and in Jesus' sermons as well. Although the experience of inner light is universal, each culture and tradition has a different understanding of it. That "whole big light" the Wabanaki elders speak of is part of a very deep teaching. As they say, "It'll take you your whole life."

85

A CLOSE WALK WITH CREATOR

My second day into the fast, I was already far away from what people call ordinary reality. I was experiencing what might be called an NDE — or near-death experience — a journey with one foot in heaven. I was walking close with the Creator — I don't know when it started, but suddenly wherever I went, I could just whisper to It, chat with It, and It would answer casually, without hesitation.

It was so easy. I could always do this, I just seldom remembered to try. Whenever I asked a question, the answer was there.

This was going to be interesting! I placed the log on the fire, and when I made another prayer to the spirit of fire, *unk-tchi-*

buch-tyiew, the fire lit right up. I sat in the beautiful warmth of the sun, and watched the fire with satisfaction.

I crawled back into the lodge to do a meditation, and maybe come up with some good questions. I closed the flap and it was night all over again. I found the ribbons in the dark, hanging from the frame of saplings overhead, and held onto one of them, running it through my fingers. When life is simple, and you're alone to face your thoughts, little things can seem gigantic, a single word can seem like a billboard sign. A ribbon can seem like a lifeline from heaven. I said my prayers.

I asked, "Who is the true teacher here in this place, in this lodge?"

I didn't hear an answer, but I had the urge to open the flap, to see what ribbon I was holding. It was the black one, the ribbon Ben had said was the color for his teacher, the ninety-six year-old elder, Abe Buffalo Calf. His spirit was with me, he was the teacher here and Ben was his helper.

I asked, "Who is the true teacher in this place, this earth?"

This same simple voice in my heart told me a story. "Many years ago, in the beginning days, there were these four men. They were all friends, four equal partners. They met often and decided what they would do together. Eventually, one of them became more powerful and wise than the others, and had acquired more experience than the others, and when he spoke, the others knew to listen. There was no reason to call him 'leader,' or even 'teacher.' His teachings were good, so he began to lead.

"A good teacher is one who has good teaching. If Ben's teaching helps you, he is a good teacher. Some day you too will be a good teacher. But start small. You have much to do yet."

I was cautious to take the word of someone I couldn't see. I asked out loud, "What kind of spirit are you?" just as Ben had taught me. I asked, "Who is speaking!"

The silent, booming voice spoke like a crashing cymbal, in perfect clarity that could never be doubted by anyone who heard it. "Geezoolgh!"

I was truly shocked. Geezoolgh is the Great Mysterious One, the Invisible Oldest Spirit of the Universe...God the Absolute, Uncreated, Unmanifested. Ben had told me we could chat with the Creator as a friend, that It was right here in our hearts, and everywhere, and I thought It wise teaching, but here It was becoming a solid, audible reality, and It was more real than anything else in life.

"I answer to Geesoolgh, or God, or many other names. It's the same thing."

I collected my wits for a moment, then asked, "Who am I?"

I heard Ben's voice again as if on tape. "Yep. You're an Indian!" When he'd first said it, it was meant as a joke. He was looking at the utter mess in the back of my car at the time and shaking his head, but now those words had a different meaning.

The Great Spirit Voice said, "Your mother is of the Micmac and that makes you welcome in this tribe, but you are also strong in Micmac spirit. You were here in a past life."

"There are many vehicles for the teachings, all over the world. The Micmac is one of the oldest, and one of the few still intact, still on the same land. But there are many teachings, each with an integrity all its own. There is a reason for the existence of each one, otherwise they would never survive."

I asked, "What do you look like?"

"I cannot be seen. No one sees me. Open your heart and you

can feel me. Open your ears and you can hear me. Open your mind and I give you wisdom. But you cannot see me for I am invisible!"

I had many, many questions, ones I'd forgotten to ask of life all along. The Great Spirit answered into my right ear.

I felt the tingle in my hands again. I asked for healing for the numbness that had been bothering me for five years. There was no answer.

In my vision I saw a burial mound on a hill of sand near the ocean, a hill covered with grass. I saw a fence around it. Where was I? I felt I was near Indian Island, Canada, a place I'd heard of once, but had never been to or learned anything about.

I later asked an elder, and he said there was such a place, and it wasn't that far away. It could have been an ancient burial ground. My ancestors from long ago could be buried there.

I asked again about my spiritual life. Geezoolgh said I was a teacher in my church and a teacher of teachers. I should continue teaching with full sincerity, and try to be honest and candid about my position on church politics.

"You will gain strength from the path of your ancestors, and freedom too. No one can trap you. When your home is the broad earth, you always have room to walk around a trap. You can always come here to Micmac country, and to this lodge. With that strength you will speak to your people back at home with a new honesty. It's up to you to heal your people. They need words of healing and truth."

I asked this being to open my heart more. It replied, "Tomorrow, I will open it a hundred times wider. Be patient."

I'd sung the first of three spirit songs many times this morning, but after returning from this journey with Geezoolgh, I received the second. It was a joyful song, and I sang it happily.

I closed the lodge again to contemplate and rest. The Great Spirit had left me alone to think about what it had said, some of which I have yet to understand.

I looked at the light coming through a worn spot in the old blanket that served as a door. I saw the White Buffalo Child's face in that light spot, and gazed at it for a while. I finally pulled it open, and walked outside. It was getting dark again. I spoke to the wood and fire with tobacco, and the fire billowed right up again.

I went back into the cabin, feeling more at home. I placed the *tchee-choss*, the tree medicine, on the clam shell that sat on the old table, and lit it, and with my cupped hands, wafted the smoke into my hair and again took the sacred smoke in my hands and crossed my chest. I placed the sweetgrass against the glowing fungus and lit it, and smudged myself from head to toe in a spiral with four loops, one for each of the cardinal directions. This was all as Ben had shown me to do. Then I picked up Ben's drum, the one with the buckskin head painted with a sunrise, and played it for a long time, as I tried out the two songs I had been given by the Grandmothers and Grandfathers. I sang a new set of lyrics, just for fun, "Beauty is reality, beauty is love, love is all, Oh Geesoolgh." I felt the love of the Creator filling me up like rain in a hollow tree stump.

89

SINGING

Algonquin people often receive their messages from the grandmothers in the form of songs. The words to these songs sometimes have meaning and some-times no meaning, with vocables such as *hey-hey-ya ho*. Sometimes the two are mixed. The grandmothers will know what it's all about when they hear it. Some sacred songs are sung in the lodge to invite the grandmothers and grandfathers in, and to thank them. Like many group songs, they are sung more or less the same each time.

Singing is very basic to prayer in most earth-based cultures. The *Wallum Olum*, the "bible" of the Lenape people, was sung. The Tibetan *Bardo* chants were probably sung over the deceased. Each of the hymns of the early Vedas were sung, with specific rhythms and pitches, much as they are today. Early Christian hymns were chanted in plainsong, which evolved into modern choral music. Algonquin prayers are no different. Some songs come down to us from the distant past, with words we no longer clearly understand, and other songs come to us while we are fasting and give us a personal link with the ancestor or helper who gave it to us.

There are many types of Micmac traditional songs. Some powwow songs are invigorating, involving high-pitched scream-ing which gets into the high overtones of the voice. They revi-talize the body and keep people doing the two-step for hours. Some songs are plaintive love songs, others are lullabies. In many traditions it is felt that if the love song works and brings you a wife, why not use it as a lullaby when the children follow?

Most solo songs are accompanied by a lone drum, and group songs are done with group drumming, and the rhythms might be very complex or very simple. Some are "heartbeat" rhythms, while others tick off sixteenth notes with a pit-a-pat-a rhythm. Most Wabanaki drummers I've seen use a stick or a leather-wrapped drum beater with a rawhide frame drum, rather than hand drumming on a tomtom like in the movies. If a drum is not available, one beats the ground with a sturdy stick.

Once, when singing for elders, I sat beating on my ankles with my bare hands and was insistently handed a stick to correct my mistake. As the Micmac drumming tradition evolved out of a hollow log (often made of a burnt and scraped-out birch log) beat with a stick, hand drumming seems a bit alien even today. I beat on the ground with the stick as I continued singing, with the elders smiling and nodding at last with approval.

91

In many traditions, the drumming pattern and melody might go on without a repeat for ten minutes or more. This takes years to memorize. Songs like this develop out of the collective thoughts and experiences of the whole tribe and are fixed by tradition in a set pattern.

In *Metis* (the people of mixed blood) fiddling music, the Scottish sound of the violin strikes us as "mountain music" but if you listen carefully, you'll notice the rhythms are like nothing from Europe. They don't repeat, they don't fall into four-four time, and yet they get you moving.

The sound of the Eagle Bone Flute is a sacred sound from the wingbone of a sacred bird. We follow it and it lifts us high into the *mussehgeesk*, blue sky, with its high piercing whistle sound. This is a very ancient Micmac instrument which is used only for ceremonial purposes and is heard in the black dream-time darkness of the sacred sweat lodge. One might wonder, "Is it the *bpoo-ohin* playing, or is it the spirit of the eagle calling those who fast to the spirit world?"

You may hear the sound of the Eagle Bone Flute in your dreams and in your fasting, or whenever a great spirit is near you. Always stop and listen and let your spirit soar when it does.

Confucius (China, 500 B.C.) taught the importance of "friendship, ritual, and music." Later, reformers tried to elimi-nate each of these pleasures, demanding "purity and universal love," while outlawing any physical expression of them. But friendship, ritual, and music are essential to communion, com-munication, and community, and no theory can erase that.

Each person in the Algonquin family is a poet, singer, friend, ceremonialist, teacher, student, storyteller. At the same time, each person also has a speciality, and certain things require years of exacting training. As with anything native, always begin at the beginning.

WHERE SONGS COME FROM

The second night of my vision quest, I was feeling a little dizzy. I was used to fasting, but the energy com-ing into that lodge was intense. I went into the cabin to rest. As I closed my eyes a stream of images reeled past them — people, places, things, that I couldn't quite recognize, although they seemed familiar somehow. In the lower right cor-ner of my vision screen there was the image of a campfire. I was puzzled at first, and looked at it carefully. It was moving with the wind, growing bright and flickering down again. I realized it was the fire outside. Spirit was allowing me to keep watch over my fire and have my rest too. I went outside and walked to the clearing. The fire was just as I'd seen it, and I understood. I returned to the cabin and set myself on pursuing the answers I had come here to seek.

I began to hear songs in my head, "ceremonial" songs, that repeated over and over. Ben had mentioned something about how the medicine man hears melodies, complete with words, in his inner journeys during his vision quests, and these become part of his medicine kit, he uses them in the sweat lodge, and in healing. I was just beginning, but already the songs were coming. I knew how to write down music, so I made notes in my notebook, drawing the five staff lines freehand, and preserved the songs for such a future occasion. Grandfather had forbidden me to write English during the fast, but he had never said anything about musical notes. Over the next twenty-four hours, I heard about a half a dozen songs in this way, some with the kind of "nonsense" syllables one often hears in medicine songs, *hey, hey, hey.* Later on during the vision quest, a song was to come through me that was so strong and powerful, it made me forget the others. I used it over and over to pull me through the second day of the quest, and I found that it helped awaken the fire spirit in the campfire.

In the minor scale the pitches would be as follows:
8 8 — 7 8 — 5 7 8 — 10 9 8 — 5 — 7 7 — 5 7 — 5 7 8 —

Nis-gam Nis-gam, o-oh way o-oh way, oh Nis-gam Nis-gam o-oh way.

Each person receives his or her own song in the lodge and it has power for that person.

To tell you the truth, my elders like country-western music outside of ceremony, a popular music form which may have native roots. After my vision quest was completed, Grandfather asked me to sing some of my songs. When he heard the "country" songs, he invited his wife and some of her friends down to hear them. They hardly moved until I'd run out of material!

TRICKSTERS ABOUND

Most native traditions have stories of a "trickster," or deceiver, and the Algonquin are no different. The best-known native American trickster is the Heyoka, a Lakota word for clown, or literally, an unnatural or anti-natural spirit. In winter he goes naked, while in summer he wraps himself in a buffalo robe. Micmac lore is filled with stories about a trickster, Lahks, and also Malsum, whose name means "wolf" in Maliseet, [21] although some Micmac people believe it is derived from the word for blood; i.e. "he is related to you." The message is that you have that same ability to lie and cheat and to throw people off balance, but you don't have to use it. The world has enough in the way of confusion already. The medicine people are supposed to help others see all the tricks and tricksters, and not to add to the confusion but to dispel it. Some don't see it that way.

Writing is a great vehicle for modern-day tricksters, at least according to several Micmac elders I've known. They firmly espouse an oral tradition — you always have the person's face to look at, and that's where the depth and inflection come from.

The face is a part of speech in an oral culture. In literate cultures, you have books, and although the words may be clever there is no face. No face, no eyes; no eyes, no tears. You can't look in a newspaper's eyes and see if it is lying.

THE WAY OF JOURNALISM

I t is interesting that there is a parallel between the way of the Wabanaki and the way of the Columbia School of Journalism, a path I came across briefly as a cub reporter for a local newspaper. Perhaps because newspapers knit literate society together the way speech knits oral societies together, the editorial principles handed down to me by my elder editors are close to the ethics of Wabanaki speech and thought handed down to me by my Wabanaki elders.

95

(Journalism) No sparkling generalities. Substantiate your facts.

(Wabanaki) The whole is incomprehensible. Go step by step. Make no generalizations. We are all unique and each moment is new. One tree is not like another, one rock is not like another.

By presuming to know the whole, you limit your experience of it.

(Journalism) Always distinguish opinion from fact.

(Wabanaki) Speak from experience. What's important is what you see with your own eyes. What you don't see, you don't know. God is in the details. The truth to you is that you saw it, or that you heard someone say it. If they are wrong, it's still true that you heard them say it.

(Journalism) Always identify your sources. Don't plagiarize.

(Wabanaki) Don't be a magpie storyteller. If you tell someone's story, be sure to say whose it is, or you will lose the trust of the people.

(Journalism) Don't commit libel.

(Wabanaki) Don't say anything bad about anyone. Better to be silent and let them live their life, unless they get in your space. Everyone has a place on the wheel, but it doesn't have to be in your house.

(Journalism) Don't pass judgment. News is news.

(Wabanaki) Don't pass judgment. You can despise someone's behavior, but you don't despise them. We are all greater than the sum of our acts. The Creator knows if what they do is right or wrong but doesn't withhold love either way.

(Journalism) Don't say anything bad about the sponsors. Without them, we wouldn't be here.

96

(Wabanaki) Respect the elders and spirits. Pray and give thanks to *nau-ql*, the four directions, and to all the grandmothers and grandfathers, to the ancestors, and to the sky and earth. Without them, we wouldn't be here.

MOCKINGBIRDS AND OTHER TRICKSTERS

As I lay there that first evening of my *sooneywen*, my head was rushing with images. The spirit world was fully populated. The question was, which were helpful spirits, and which were not helpful?

I saw a spirit of a man before me. He disappeared. I asked

Ben inwardly what or who that was. His words came back to me: "When you meet a spirit, it is very important always to ask, 'What kind of spirit are you?' Some animals have a certain message for the Micmacs, but you should always ask what that message is, rather than make guesses which might be wrong."

I lay down to rest again. There were the spirits again, and there in the corner was the flame, as always. I saw Ben. He vanished, and then I saw the Micmac woman I'd met earlier in the tobacco store with Ben — I called her "Mockingbird." She was very powerful in my vision, luminescent eyes, long black braids, and a hard, mocking mouth that repelled me. We were standing face to face in the other world. She looked at me up and down, from head to toe and back again, laughing a raucous laugh. She blew her breath at me and disappeared. I spun inwardly, wondering what was happening to me. Somehow I hadn't expected such a pretty woman to be so cruel — not a logical presumption at all, given my life experience, but one which I had then, all the same. Perhaps Ben was using her to point out a weakness. I remembered the story of Weesuckerjack. Hadn't I met her in the shopping center right after hearing that story?

I was aware of lying on my bed again, and when I looked at the picture in the lower right corner of my vision, the fire had nearly gone out! She had blown it out! It was late at night and I was tired, but I could no longer say, "It's just a dream." I knew better.

I pulled myself out of bed, threw the small plaid blanket over my naked shoulders and went outside to the clearing. The fire was just as I'd seen it in my split screen vision. It was nearly out, with only a single ember remaining alive, and that just barely.

My first impulse was to blow on it, but then I remembered Ben's words. I chopped at it, used pieces of dry bark, pieces of sweetgrass. I even tore off a little piece of that newsprint I'd found at the edge of the clearing and tried to get it to light. I got a flame going two times, but the bigger logs just wouldn't catch, and I had run out of ready tinder.

I was frantic! My only job was to keep the fire going for two days, and that woman had made a fool out of me. I worked harder at the embers, but to no avail. I used more newsprint, which Grandfather had told me not to use. Soon, I was covered with ashes and dirt from head to toe. I was being humbled, *sooneywen* in Micmac, *humbleche* in Lakota.

I'm not one to give up easily, but there is something about surrendering to a higher power that's very effective. I call it "the surrender strategy," and it's definitely for winners. It may seem to the ego like giving up, but actually it is stepping aside as a bull-headed slave-driver of the self, and becoming a willing tool for the Creator. Men seem to especially need to act out their humiliation, covering themselves with ashes, letting go of pride, outer appearances, position, posturing. It means letting the light go out, giving up wishful thinking, and it means fasting, weeping, and wailing. Out of this death of the self comes a new birth. It sounds like a vision quest.

I was resigned to the fact that the fire had gone out, and that I would have to tell Ben sooner or later, but I surrendered to the Great Spirit in all sincerity, and asked if there was anything I could do to make up for this. The answer was loud and clear. "Make the sacred tobacco offerings!"

I was surprised. I had forgotten all about the offerings. They would be a helpful ritual to help me focus my thoughts, and ask for forgiveness. I pulled out my pouch of tobacco. I didn't have much left, so I had been meting it out in small pinches. This was time for extra strength tobacco. I took a double pinch and walked to the fire and faced the east, the dark black sky where the sun would most likely come up in a few hours, in spite of my sacrilegious blunder.

I made a long prayer in Micmac and English, holding the sacred plant in my outstretched fist, asking for help and forgiveness. I spoke to the Grandfather of the East, and he told me to talk to the *Buchtyeow* spirit, the fire spirit, so I prayed to the fire spirit to help me. Then I tossed the double pinch towards the cold ashes. Some of it fell on the ground, and some on the logs.

To my amazement, a few flakes of tobacco landed on the embers and burst into flame, catching the other kindling on fire. With a little bit of help, it had soon caught the logs on fire as well. I was, to put it mildly, overjoyed. I returned my hand to the tobacco pouch, and performed the rites for the three other directions, and as I did, the fire glowed heartier and warmer, and its warmth was comforting. I had learned an important lesson: Talk to the fire spirit if you want fire, and don't talk to strangers (inner or outer ones) unless you want strange experiences.

99

A HEALING JOURNEY

The next morning, I was feeling lightheaded, and a headache which had started earlier became stronger. I sat up in the cot, breathing deeply to relax. I saw Ben's face before me as a grandfather clock. The image was humorous and innocent, like something I'd seen as a kid on Captain Kangaroo. (When my sister met Ben, she commented that he looked like Captain Kangaroo). His mustache formed the two hands of time, as if it were 8:20 A.M. Perhaps it was. I got the message. It was time.

I thought it meant it was time to fix the fire, so I went out and did my pyrotechnic duties. Nothing seemed out of the ordinary, so I returned to the cabin. After a while, Ben opened the door and sat down next to me to talk with me. He said it was time for me to journey to the other worlds.

He said he knew I was feeling sick. He moved the chair to the middle of the room and had me sit in it. The pain in my head and eyes got worse. He smudged me extensively and rubbed my arms and back and neck. His hands felt strange. He pushed my hair up and smudged under my hair.

He touched my chest and said, "This is the doorway to the heart. Niskam can enter here to heal you. Pray to Niskam."

Then he took me on a learning journey. He stood behind me and placed both his hands on the back of my head. First, I saw the blue light, mixed with white. When I described it, he exclaimed happily, "*EY heh-yah! EY heh-ya!*"

Then we went to the grandmother together. I saw an old, old, native woman with a wrinkly, wrinkly face and shining dark eyes. She had a feather in her hair, and a look of waiting, listening, absorbing, withholding until asked. Her face was poised in balance between question and answer.

Ben said, "Ask her for the medicine for your sickness."
I asked.

She answered, "There's no medicine but love. Love is the healer." She said the word as hEEl-eRR, and it soothed me and drew me closer to her the way she spoke.

Then she vanished.

He said, "We should be seeing the yellow light in the west now." I looked, but could only see it faintly. The headache seemed to sqeeze my visions away rather than help them. I was in discomfort, but this was all part of the healing.

We journeyed to the north. I clearly saw a fire. I knew that wasn't usually found in the north, but in the east. Yet I saw it and it didn't go away.

Ben said, "Ask the fire for medicine."

I spoke to it. "You are the fire in my body, and so you also know the medicine for the fire in my body, don't you? Tell me what it is."

"WATER!" came the crystal clear answer. "Water is the medicine for fire."

101

I felt stupid. Everyone knows that. Why didn't I think of it? The cure for the fire in my arms and legs was water. Water was what I was always reminding myself to drink, but was too busy to go get. I knew the answer all along, but was shocked in surprise when I heard it.

We journeyed to the east, and he asked me to look for Niskam. I saw a clouded new moon in an inner sky. Then I journeyed farther and saw a small, red flame in the distance. I described it.

"That is the grandfather, the old one, Niskam. You can journey to that flame, but beyond that, no one knows what's there. Ask that grandfather there for healing. Ask for medicine."

I asked and waited, but got nothing verbal. No sound or visual symbol to give me a clue. I told Ben and he didn't seem to react like there was anything unusual about it. He waited, then brought me back into this world.

My nerves flared up like a brush fire. The flame within me spread from my right side, up my body, and swept across me to the left, and then up into my head. My face was buzzing, and then the fire went to the top of my head with a tremendous surge of flame.

He exclaimed, "You will be healed in four days!"

My body continued to burn for a long time, and I couldn't stand up for awhile. He left to let me sit there and absorb all that happened. My headache was gone.

Later, as I was fixing the fire, a song returned that I had heard in the lodge, the prayer to Niskam. It was very powerful again.

I fell asleep in the cabin, not long after the journey with Ben, and had a medicine dream. Ben had said that it's good to get to sleep after a sweat lodge or healing journey, because many of the answers will come in dreams.

I dreamed I was back at 2016 Peabody Street again, my childhood home. I was in the pale yellow kitchen where I used to stand and talk to my mother while we were cleaning up after dinner. In the dream, there were sprouts growing everywhere, in large planters, something which had never actually been there. They looked good and ripe and I wanted to eat them. Scattered around the kitchen were various healthy morsels of food. There was a health cake of some kind, a sandwich, a glass full of some kind of juice.

On the table was a portable black and white TV. I stood in front of it to watch. A baseball game was on, but it was raining and raining. The tarp was over the diamond, and the outfield grass was soaking in torrents of raindrops as they fell from the sky. The crowd had been driven from the stands long ago. The announcers were silent, as if it had been raining for so long they ran out of anything to say, and no alternate programming had been arranged. It was very peaceful to watch.

An Italian friend of mine, Valeria, appeared in this kitchen from my past.

As I looked closer, I noticed grey smoke rising up from the sprouts. This puzzled me. I stared for a while. Then I looked and noticed that each of the plates of healthy food had a small trail of smoke rising from its heart up to heaven. But the room was not smoky. What was this dream telling me?

I woke up, and found the dream still strongly with me. I realized that the smoke was sacred to the Micmacs, that when something burns, it carries the essence of that something toward us. When we burn sweetgrass, it purifies our spirits and carries our prayers to heaven. The sprouts were my purification, my medicine. They were ready to give up their life energy for me.

The other foods were medicine too. I needed to eat healthier.

Why was Valeria there? I had been taking Valerian herb for a while to calm my nerves, but when life got even more hectic, I stopped taking them, which was not sensible. I needed more — not less. Seeing her reminded me to take the Valerian.

But what about the baseball game? It was a rain-out. What does that mean? I thought about it a long time. It could only mean rest, and lots of it. It meant surrendering to nature the ambitions and battles of modern society. It also meant water from heaven. The fire spirit had said its medicine was water, and here it was again in another form.

As an avid baseball fan, I had become conditioned to think of rain as the enemy, but rain delays are as much a part of the game as pennant prayer flags, bases in the four directions, and sacrifice flies.

I walked out to the fire again and then Ben came. I told him my healing dream. He mentioned that I could also make some sweetgrass juice by pulling a single strand of dried sweetgrass from a braid and soaking it in a glass of water for a day. If I then drank the charged water, it would help heal me. It sounded like the "roo-bub" juice my Aunt Helen prepared for me, so I tried it. It was milder than the rhubarb, but it worked.

He sat down, lit his pipe, and told me more about the medicine wheel teachings. He removed the beautiful, hand-crafted medicine wheel made of willow from the wall and held it in his hands. He tried to explain the meaning, but it was over my head. I had to ask him to go over it again and again. It was such a deep teaching and I was trying to be so literal, but Grandfather had endless patience.

I still contemplate what he said about being born in the east and traveling clockwise around until we reach the east again, perish and ascend into a greater loop. He told me how the elder was like a snow plow, making a trail for the younger ones walking behind (see "He Dreams," p. 158). Just after that, a bulldozer pulled up unexpectedly and started plowing the new driveway up the hill from where I sat contemplating the meaning of it all. Ben wasn't any ordinary snow plow, he was an earth mover!

WRITING

When I finished my *sooneywen*, I entered my second lodge, happy to drink the water that was passed around. During that ceremony I was given a new name, Abachbahamedtch, or chipmunk. It means "little brother of the squirrel people." The chipmunk is also the musician of the forest, making funny little noises. The word also includes information that he has a little fluff of white on his back, which I take as a possible reference to my mixed blood.

Being part Micmac and part Celtic, I'm like a chipmunk between two rows of trees, scampering back and forth between two worlds, delivering messages from one to the other. Sometimes that job involves a bit of writing.

The native teachings are never learned from books. It is ironic to be writing this down, for all that I have learned about Algonquin wisdom and the art of speaking over the years has been learned by experience and by listening to my elders. This means that you the reader are getting it from a book, which is not part of the traditional way of life at all. You should be out doing instead!

For better or worse, I am a "born writer." It's in my medicine bag. Yet according to at least a few elders, the traditional way of the Micmac includes only the writing of "hieroglyphs," or pictographs on birchbark, writing which the Micmac developed to a high art and still maintain today. I was invited to study this art from a *geezeegooisk*, a woman in her nineties, but she passed away before we could meet. Grandfather Turtle constantly reminds me that writing in the English way is an unnatural thing to do and causes confusion, yet Micmac hieroglyphs also are confusing — to all but a very few elders.

Most of the traditional Wabanaki people I have worked with do not own books, do not read, and do not intend to. They are not interested, pro or con, in this writing project and do not care if I use their words or not and do not want to be mentioned by name. If you were wondering why there are so few direct quotes here — books are not part of an oral heritage. When they speak, they speak to me, not to anyone else, not to a book, an inanimate object. My teachers did not "write" these teachings. These expressions are shared by many people, and they have been passed down through time. No one can take credit for Micmac wisdom, least of all me. Like the low rolling hills of the Miramichi Valley and the river that runs through it, this way of life has always been.

PROBLEM SOLVING

Many Algonquin elders, so I've observed, have an innate genius for problem-solving and managerial skills, especially where people are concerned. They think around things with holistic minds. They see the world in three dimensions. They look to the future and to the next seven generations. They never built suspension bridges and superhighways, but then they never had to levy taxes and tolls to pay for fixing them each year, either.

Once we did a sweat lodge and a woman was upset because the door to the lodge kept falling closed. She felt it was the presence of "bad medicine" and began to talk to others about it. At the next lodge, the elder asked her to be the *ga'an-nadjit*, or door keeper, a great honor, and stayed outside with her, helping her keep that door from falling closed. She too became part of Creation.

When things are going badly, it is difficult to know when to separate those involved and when to bring them into relationship. It is the wisdom of the Wabanaki to know when.

STEPPING STONES

That first stumbling attempt at ceremony was a long time ago, but I still have a lot to learn about native tradition and working with nature. Recently, I was helping Grandfather conduct a gathering in Maryland, near where my family lives. We were to go several days and needed lots of lodge stones for the sweats.

I was emerging from the woods and an elder asked me, "We're running low on grandfathers. Maybe you could help find more good sweat lodge rocks around here somewhere."

I answered, "Sure," but I knew that choosing lodge stones was a tricky process. Many stones are not suitable and will explode in the fire, or not give enough heat. Others will be too large for the Y-stick. I know because I had chosen all of those stones at some point in the past.

I noticed Grandfather Turtle walking up a hill in the woods some distance beyond, obviously looking for stones, and I thought, "I'll join him. Maybe I'll learn some pointers."

I had a strong desire to help with the lodge, and I also wanted the knowledge I knew was necessary to be really helpful.

I walked quickly down the hill before me, and suddenly found myself at the edge of a creek I had forgotten about. It was November, and the creek was cold and spangled with orange-red leaves. I wondered how he had gotten across. I thought, "I didn't know I'd have to walk on water to keep up with this elder!"

I was in sneakers, but I survived the crossing as best I could. I ran to catch up with the elder. He showed me what kind of rocks he was looking for. I asked if he could give me tobacco for the rocks, and he said he'd already taken care of it.

I asked him about the word for "things falling together" and he showed me how the Micmac terms for "a gathering" (*maweeyomee*), "gathering stones" (*mahweegundow),* and "things fall together" (*mahweedahdjik)* are all related.

108

I chose good stones, and we had a good gathering. Things fell together.

I gathered several rocks, and made my way back down to the river. From this direction, I could see that there were stepping stones spanning the creek, but that each stone was covered neatly by a large orange-red leaf. A trained woodsman would spot those leaves that were unmoved by the current and know that rocks must be underneath, suitable for holding one's weight.

I crossed the current with ease, appearing to walk on water to those standing on the other side who were unfamiliar with the terrain. Not only was I walking on water, dancing on floating maple leaves, but was carrying two heavy stones, just to show off.

What I realized is that it takes more than love and strong

desire to serve God in order to solve the problems of the people. It takes understanding as well. That's why we need good teachers, and lots of experience.

When the elders heal people, it looks to the outsider as if it's all magic. It looks like "walking on water." The same could be said of a great poem or piece of music. At first listening, Mozart seems to "walk on water" too, only with notes. When we ask questions and take the time to learn the secrets of the craft, we sometimes find there are stepping stones in between those leaps of faith, but they're covered with maple leaves.

TRAVELING

" "Everything put together sooner or later falls apart" is a line from a Paul Simon song, and it's true. All the water systems of New York City, the bridges, the railroads, the cars, are falling apart all the time, and will have to be repaired and maintained for the rest of time. People will have to spend more and more time repairing things until there is no time for anything else. A river, on the other hand, should never need fixing.

Roads have to be repaired, too. People criticize the Indians, saying "they couldn't even invent the wheel." But the invention of the wheel elsewhere has brought its share of problems. The wheel harms the soft earth and the hard rock earth damages the wheel; they don't get along. Dragging sharp "travois" poles was a good solution in its time, and is still used by the Sami of Lapland, those trans-Atlantic close cousins of the Wabanaki. [23] A poorly designed highway cuts off the flow of water and creates two stagnant marshes on either side of the road. Those marshes are full of dead trees, plants, and even animals. Modern roads cut the mother's veins.

The ancient Algonquin world of a thousand years ago was a Garden of Eden in many ways, one where transportation was slow but free. Today, driving on the Garden State Parkway, you need a coin bucket on your lap to get anywhere. In the old days, the Miramichi River was a highway, creeks and streams were roadways and streets. Lots of people lived on Turtle Island long ago and, until the European settlers came, each group of people lived near the water. You could visit anyone by water travel, because everyone lived on or near the riverbanks.

Seepoo is the word that means river. It was the same or similar word in Algonquin villages from coast to coast;[24] you could travel from the Atlantic to the Pacific or anywhere in between. The Illinois River was once a great waterway of the Midwest, but its great majestic flowing way was built over with the concrete, pipes, and brick walls of Chicago, a city called "the Venice of America" for this reason. Now those walls are falling apart, with billions of dollars in damage claims. (Venice also has its problems!) The earth and its rivers are stronger than anything man can create. That is why everything unnatural falls apart.

There were always trails along a river, and trails branching away from the river and climbing into the mountains. Native people all over North America developed transportation systems based on long-distance running. The Mohawk Trail, approximately 250 miles, was used by messengers who could run the entire distance in a twenty-four-hour period, linking the six nations of the Long House people together, carrying messages from one place to another. [25] According to Trudy Lamb Richmond, a Scatacook from Connecticut, these runners kept in shape by playing lacrosse games where the goals were several miles apart.

A few years ago, I started running a lot of 10K races, and found it came very naturally to me, partly because I used to backpack twenty-five miles a day in my youth. I believe that most young people today could run forty miles in one day under ideal non-polluted conditions. But they'd have to get in shape!

Seven miles per hour is a comfortable run for most people, but native runners used to sustain ten per hour over long periods. Imagine leaving New York City after breakfast and arriving in Philadelphia in time for dinner — by foot! This was once possible. Travelling by foot gives you a sense of personal accomplishment no other mode of transportation grants you. It also gives you a sense of how big our Turtle Island really is. (You would also grow very strong!)

111

"THINGS FALL TOGETHER"

There is an expression in the Micmac tongue which says it all as far as the Algonquin worldview is concerned, and that is *Mah-wee-da-djik*, "Things fall together." Even now, when the high of addictive substances and high-tech pollution and high-pressure economics are pulling manmade things apart, the people of the traditional ways still have faith that natural things fall into place for those who can find the Red Road.

Creation is ever-unfolding and all-pervasive and so the wisdom of the Creator is in all things at all times, not like a hand forcing things where they don't want to go, but a natural gravity of the spirit, where things fall together as if by magic. That gravity could also be called universal love, but that's a very European way of saying it. The *bpoo-ohinn* speak of "sharing the love of our Creator," and when you do that, you help things fall together.

Gravity, as understood in modern Newtonian physics, means "things fall together." But when the Wabanaki began speaking of this thousands of years ago, they weren't just talking about how planets form, how atoms form, how molecules form, break up and then reform according to ionic principle. They weren't just talking about how galaxies congealed, or how gasses become crystals, or how water becomes ice, or how the ecosystem balances itself out in ways too complex for the human mind to grasp. They were talking about each of us in our hearts and in our interactions with one another.

No need to worry. Things will fall together at the right time. Creation is still happening and we are a part of it. Let things fall together. When you are making something, you don't have to plan it all out in advance on paper each time. Bring out the best materials that you have at the moment, and see where and how they want to join forces.

HOW THINGS FELL TOGETHER

When I was in my mid-thirties I had wandered far from the native way and wanted to find my way back for myself and my family, but there seemed to be no quick fix. I went to a Native American "program" near my home in New York. There I was chided for wanting to "be Indian." I asked the presenters if there was a Micmac medicine man or someone else who could teach me about the Micmac way of life. They were discouraging to say the least. Finally a brusque woman gave me a phone number in Canada for a self-styled Micmac medicine man she had met. She jotted it down on a napkin but got the numbers crossed. When I dialed the number a voice said, "Department of Fisheries and Wildlife."

I was certainly surprised, but the man seemed friendly, and I ended up chatting with the fellow, a non-native, as I remember. He told me the person I was looking for was a charlatan and not even Micmac. He just happened to know him. He also happened to know the phone number of the Red Bank Band Office and gave me the name of the chief's wife. I called right away. The chief's wife picked up and talked my ear off for a half hour. She gave me the number of a man named Stephen, and even mailed me her own original copy of an article about him from the local newspaper.

In the months to follow, I called that Band Office a dozen times and later went there in person, but that woman never appeared again.

I called Stephen and he gave me a list of names of those who could teach me the way of his people. The only problem was none of them owned telephones and he had no addresses. I would have to come up in person.

One thing led to another and I did come up, but the day I arrived, every single person on the list was in Maine on a Penobscot-owned blueberry farm, stooping over, picking blueberries out in the bush. When I got to the bottom of the list, I almost gave up. With fading hopes, I tracked down that last man and eventually found his house.

The last person on the list, Grandfather Turtle, happened to be home that day. His daughter was sick and so he was not in Maine with the others. After testing my resolve a little at the kitchen door, he gave me the answers I was looking for. Since my Micmac grandfather had died before I was born, I asked him to adopt me as his grandson and he agreed. He sat me down and gave me "the turtle teachings," about how important it was to go slow, step by step, so you don't make mistakes. I have called him "Grandfather Turtle" ever since.

That is how everything that led to this book fell together.

NO NEED TO CONTROL

There's no need to control everything in a world where things work together without your controlling them. There's no need to be anxious when the more you fight, the less the "magic" which makes things turn out beautifully can work. If you believe in the ongoing falling together of things, you can relax within yourself, you can stop hurrying, stop pushing, stop rushing, and simply let things be. That doesn't mean you get lazy, because a lot of things may want to fall together at any moment, and the plan definitely involves you, the tool of the Creator, to help make it happen.

When a joke or story makes us laugh, it is because something surprises us when two statements or things fall together. When the light suddenly dawns and we see how two parts of our lives fit together in ways we didn't before, that is the same thing.

Creation happens by itself, but it includes you as part of it. Don't tell spirit what to do, let Geezoolgh tell you what you can do and, if you listen and follow the wind from spirit, you will see yourself as one of those pieces falling together. It's a beautiful feeling to be like a red leaf in autumn, swaying, floating gently on the wind and then landing in just the right spot.

The natural world falls together; the poison plant grows near its antidote in most cases. All things are inter related in such a profound way, there's no end to it. But when the people stop fighting nature and start flowing along with its way, they too can find their lives falling into place in many ways at once. The far-flung parts can fit together because they came from the same source in the beginning of Creation and still fit even today.

The medicine people say the love is what heals us, it is love that fills the Creator. Love is not something you can define, but we say young people "fall" into it; maybe there's meaning behind this expression, for love brings people together by their affinities. In a village full of young people, girls and boys, it's likely that over time the ones that are wrong for each other will drift apart and the ones that are right for each other will fall together and maybe fall in love. It is a wonderful thing, it is a joyous magic. Let's not forget how beautiful this is.

115

SPEAKING

In Algonquin life, conversation is nothing less than an art, one which some may develop more than others, but whose standards are high, even in comparison with European art forms.

The Micmac language (the Wabanaki tongue I am most familiar with) not only lends itself to witty conversation, it possesses a degree of poetic sensibility equal to any I have personally encountered. The antiquity of its origins makes me wonder if, as technology advances, men's hearts decline. Even though certain individuals become more aware through the advancement of science, does it really liberate and enlighten the average person? I suspect that poetry in everyday language declines as utilitarian communication increases. Language as it "evolves" becomes simpler, it becomes more practical, more universal, but it loses its heart along the way, and it loses in depth what it gains in breadth.

Martin Ling, quoted in *Parabola* magazine, wrote, "The further we go back in time, the more powerfully impressive language becomes. It also becomes more complex, so that the oldest known languages, those which are far older than history itself, are the most subtle and elaborate in their structure... (while) grammar and syntax become more and more simplfied." In the *Incompleat Folk Singer* Pete Seeger wrote, "... English, with its great generalized and unspecific meanings, leaves lots of room for poetry. (At the same time I didn't find a single person around the world who thought English a beautiful language.)"

A lot of Micmac terms are borrowed from European languages to accommodate new European realities, and other imported concepts are described in new Micmac terms, but there is an underlying core of pre-contact spiritual and traditional words which is fascinating to me.

We have been led to believe that without the benefits of modern socialization and education and the comforts of technology, we would become narrow, plodding, superstitious, and insensitive brutes; "prehistoric hunter and gatherer" does not paint a flattering picture in most people's minds. I could be mistaken, but the botanical knowledge, wit, poetry, and spiritual understanding I glimpse in those ancient phrases give me a totally different picture of our venerable ancestors, and a different picture of ourselves today as well. Do we really know more? Do we really live longer? Are we happier? Do we understand our own hearts more profoundly? Are we really more creative? More imaginative? More spiritual?

To me, the free association, the depth and insight, the layers of meaning in Micmac phrases would indicate genius if it were written by an individual. It is a well of fresh metaphors and ways of seeing that are just now being explored, even as they are being lost.

It could, for example, inspire a new generation of writers looking for a voice with which to speak of the sacred.

There is the Micmac "babytalk" spoken by children, there is adolescent banter, and then there is the mature speech of the council. Beyond this, however, are many levels of speech which equal our best poetry. There is "High Micmac" and several levels even higher. It's said that "when a *geezeegooldjeedj*, an old elder, gets into the bottom of his language, very few can understand what he means any more." The way is being lost, and much of it probably will be unretrievable within the next twenty years.

Oral cultures communicate very differently from literate ones. Literate cultures speak along straight lines, avoiding repeated words and phrases. Messages and ideas are listed from a. to b. to c., like the phonetic alphabet from which they are made. Oral speech is almost ceremonial in that it goes in cycles and winds back on itself. A prayer might start with naming and describing the self, "I am Black Crow, and I am standing here on this hill this morning..." address the spirit by name, make a statement, and come around again, repeating the beginning in another way. It loops and loops, each time going into the subject a little more. There is much repetition of key words, which is part of the rhythm of native poetry. We can see traces of this in European storytelling, but this cyclical pattern doesn't generally happen in writing, and such writing would meet with resistance among many readers.

In India, the *Baul* singers are inheritors of an oral culture and encourage contrary opinions and non-conformism, much as in the old Algonquin oral tradition. "Nobody tells a Micmac what to do," is an old saying, and so it stands to reason that there is no one specific body of Algonquin wisdom. Inconsistencies abound... consistently. Some elders show a *Baul*-like desire to play with speech, and not answer questions directly, but to weave the words into the moment with a touch of humor and mysticism. In India it is called *Sandhya* or *Sandha Bhasa*, "twilight language." It is in this realm of twilight that some elders are able to create shimmering orbs of meaning with words alone.

118

Most oral traditions abhor a direct question for they are too linear. P.L. Travers wrote, "The Irish, as a race, have the oral tradition in their blood. A direct question to them is an anathema, but in other cases, a mere syllable of a hero's name will elicit whole chapters of stories." [26] Oral lore isn't that which has not been written down, it's that which *cannot* be written down.

Another thing about oral languages: the individual becomes very important. Since nothing is written down, each person becomes responsible for preserving the language. When the people were free and safe, and living their own way, this was not so hard. Everyone had a good knowledge of the language. Today it is a crisis. Today, an old fisherman could have a stroke, and the meanings of fifty key words relating to fishing would be lost. The individual becomes a treasury of stories or words or knowledge, so the sense of responsibility is greater.

Since nothing is written down, there are also more changes made. Dialects change from place to place. Usually, there is an old dialect and a newer dialect, with variations. The old people speak the older dialect, the younger speak the newer; the newer reserves *speak the modern, while older reserves speak the more traditional way. Often the newer dialect simply drops *g* sounds at the beginnings of words and replaces *q*'s (as in Iraq) and *ch*'s (pronounced as in the Scottish "*loch*") with glottal stops. But often, whole words change. Since there is no dictionary, words mean what people think they mean, and that can change from person to person. Families, cliques, or groups develop their own humorous idioms and slang, and sometimes it catches on. Much of oral language is colorful slang, so each phrase has to be learned individually; sometimes there is no guessing what an idiom might mean. In some areas, people will greet you with

*Reservations in Canada are called "reserves."

"*May dalain!*" ("How are you feeling?") or "*Maydaleeoolain?*" ("How are you feeling?" plus "How's the world treating you?"). You might be greeted elsewhere with, "*Nikmaq!*" ("hello kin-friend") or "*Needap!*" (Friend) according to local custom.

Micmac is difficult to learn, but like most languages, was never meant to be studied by outsiders. It was "meant" (whatever that means) to be grown up with, lived with, studied your whole life, and passed on when you die. It is more difficult for a foreigner to jump into high Micmac speech than for an "Indian" to jump into playing in an orchestra.

Chuang Tzu said that the sage is like an artist or craftsman. He utilizes but never submits to fixed rules or external standards. He incorporates but doesn't imitate. This creative, artistic approach is the best way to describe the way the Algonquin live, work, and even speak.

In oral society, a long and accurate memory is taken for granted. No one writes anything down. It's all incorporated into the *ochtdup*, "the body-mind complex," and comes out from the heart.

This expectation and ability to remember is one of the first things that one is struck with when entering traditional oral culture. It is startling at first. Once, as we were walking through a marshlands area, a mile away from the nearest pen and paper, my Micmac friend chose to give me lengthy directions to his house in the mountains in another part of the United States. I took it as a compliment that he thought I'd remember. I did find his house months later, but it wasn't easy.

Unfortunately, too many people have a powerful word for those who try to uphold the responsibilities of an oral tradition: "illiterates." It's interesting to note that the Kabbalist and

Ayurvedic medicine traditions are oral traditions which have only been written down in the last century by outsiders. Plus, there has always been an "oral Torah" (*she-be'al peh*) handed down from Mt. Sinai in addition to (and different from) the written. Negro spirituals were not written down until recently. These were obviously oral by choice, so why is it so far-fetched to suppose that much of Native American culture is also oral by choice?

On the subject of "the world's greatest books," Coomaraswami wrote, "Of these books many existed long before they were written down, many have never been written down, and others have been or will be lost." This is a good response to the question, "Where is the Native American's great contribution to world culture?" One only need listen.

121

WORDS AND PHRASES

There is a great ocean of difference between the Indo-European world and that of the Algonquin, those two great language groups. The distance in perception between English and Micmac is especially pronounced, but not unique. Not only is there no word specifically for time in Micmac, consider the following: There are very few "nouns" in Micmac; before the world was crowded with material objects, most things were alive and therefore "verbing." Imagine English without nouns.

Colors are verbs; most colors in nature are part of an action.

There is no gender, unless you have to point it out specifically. The prefix *otch* could mean his, hers, its, and could refer to animal or human. Once I tasted a language not burdened by cumbersome "he and she" I never wanted to go back, but I seem to have no choice.

Words are relational, and the grammar of the language reflects the interdependent state of the world in the Micmac view. A phrase I've heard from Tibetans, "Things arise simultaneously," happens to express the Micmac view exactly. This means that although there is a root syllable for "eye" or "leg," it's always "his eye" or "its leg" in actual use.

Micmac often does not compare with English because where the English will see only "woman," the Micmac will see a young girl, an adolescent, an adult woman, a grandmother with grandchildren, a spiritual grandmother, or an old woman, all of which are described by specific terms. There are a similar array of words for man, depending on if it's a young man or old. The term *geezeegooldjeedj* denotes a little old man. In connotation, some would add: "He is about ninety years old."

Colors are verbs, as are many adjectives in Micmac; in nature, things change color, and always for a reason. When green grass becomes yellow, it might mean it has become dry. If a leaf has become red, that action is part of its getting ready to fall. When the sky is becoming gray, it may be preparing for snow. Color changes in nature are part of a vast pattern of action and reaction, subject to daily or monthly change. Colors are full of meaning. A blue sky is a dry one, green grass is healthy and full of life. In English, when we say "red" we usually mean the pigment, or red paint, rather than ripe, burned, flushed, as the case may be. Most of the time, we don't know the difference.

Blue is *moos-seh-geesq-chamough*, which means "it is being

the color of the sky." Green is *neebuchtamough*, which means "it is being the color of the forest in spring." The word for yellow, *wadtuptek* means "bright as a flower." *Neeskanamough* is the color of a bruise, or purple. My favorite is orange, *wolquasamough*, which is "the color of the setting sun in the west." Sheer poetry — and these are everyday words.

The Wabanaki culture of the Northeast is not only quite ancient, it has retained much the same form throughout history. Referring to the Clovis people, the first known Native Americans, David Hurst Thomas wrote in "The World As It Was," (a section of the excellent book *The Native Americans*), "Clovis ritual vanished long ago, but perhaps vestiges lingered on among the Naskapi Indians of Labrador. Maybe, like the Naskapi, Clovis medicine men addressed the animal spirit [by name] by entranced drumming and singing."

123

Although native and non-native scholars alike debate the authenticity of shamanic practices among the Micmac, nevertheless they are quite widespread and, if you ask me, very effective! In the Micmac shamanic ritual as I've seen it, you always address an animal spirit by name, and speak your own name as well. The Micmac have been living, working, and hunting alongside the Naskapi for centuries; it should hardly be surprising that they would have so much in common spiritually.

Most "nouns" in Micmac are sentence-like descriptions of the unique qualities of the object, a snowball of parts of other words rolled together in various ways to create a picture so that even if you hadn't seen one before, you'd know something, or quite a bit, about it.

Native languages (like Japanese, so I'm told) are relational and contain words which refer to other words, which refer to still other words. The Micmac word *maulgh-dyew* or "blood" means "it comes from meat." *Buch-dyew*, or "fire" means "it comes from the wood." There are a number of "dyew" words.

There is a basic syllabic level where sounds are used by convention, but upon this is built a body of knowledge which some would call "scientific." The language itself stores knowledge the way we store knowledge in big computers, by branching and menuing. This knowledge largely concerns plants and animals — how this is like that, how this differs from all other things — but it also conveys a great deal of insight into human psychology.

In my talks to English-speaking audiences about Micmac language, I often use the word for "groundhog" as an example, *moo-lumpb-gwetch. Mool* means "dig," derived from *moal-ayhe*, "to dig." *Lump* is short for *lumayg*, or "under the ground." *Gwey* is short for *gwetch*, which means "someone," usually an animal with four legs. So this one word tells you it is "someone (with four legs) digging under the ground." The word for "mole" is even more interesting: *moo-lump-gwe-djeedj. Djeedj* means "it is small," so *moo-lump-gwe-djeedj* is "someone-small-with-four-legs-digging-under-the-ground."

In a similar way, the Micmac/Cree word *peepeesisikwe(oo)* or "*Pipsissiwa*" refers to a little plant that grows in the forest, but literally means "it breaks up" which is short for an older word which means "it-breaks-up-kidney-stones-in-the-bladder," which is even more helpful if you have kidney stones. Plant and animal names as well as the "Indian names" given to certain people by their elders, often have two parts, one that places it in a group or category, and one which sets it apart from the others in that category. Take *goo-goo-gwess*, for example. *Gwess* is

a meat-eating bird of prey, and it refers to the one who calls
goooo-goooo late at night: An owl!

If the high Micmac language is lost in the next few years, it
would be to them as it would be to Americans if our computer-
stored knowledge were lost forever due to some tremendous
short-circuit. The language reflects the philosophy that all
things arise interdependently, and are interrelated. If anyone
understood all Micmac speech, they would know exactly how
all life related and what was unique about each thing. They
would also be very old by the time they were finished. The language holds this much knowledge.

SPONTANEITY AND INNOCENCE
IN ALGONQUIN LANGUAGES

At the heart of spontaneous action is sincerity. The
Algonquin uphold personal freedom, especially in
any artistic expression, and it allows for spontaneity
within the framework of tradition. The Sahajiyas, or
"Spontaneous Ones," in India are examples of a similar spirit in
Asia. [27] The ancient Wabanaki of the Northeast always preferred
wigwam-style dwellings (in hut-like and cone-like shapes as
needed), and briefly, tee-pees, as opposed to French-style houses, because one could spontaneously pick up stakes and go elsewhere, like Moses and his moveable first Tabernacle.

Micmac solutions are fresh, insightful, and immediate, like
those of a child. These perceptions often become stored in the
formal language of the people. A five-year-old who doesn't have

a word for yesterday, will say "the day we already slept from." Tomorrow becomes "the day we haven't awakened to yet." I have been told that the Micmac word for today, *geezkook*, has derived from "the day you have already awakened to." The word for night, *depkik*, derives from, "you have already arrived at the end of the day."

Spiritual elders cultivate a childlike quality on purpose. Children are admired for their spontaneity and openness to spirit, and elders admonish adults to be "the mother earth's little children." Zen master Takuan said, "Zen is to have the heart of a little child." When a little Micmac child gives advice to an adult, it is taken very seriously.

I believe that the linguistic capacities of "tribal" people are expanded, just as children's are, and tend to share a nothing-for-granted freshness that linear languages have lost. Words in written languages have become codified.

When I told my five-year-old son I was taking him to the hardware store, he exclaimed, "Is that a place where they don't sell anything that's soft? Why do you have to go there?"

I answered, "I need plumbing supplies."

That only added to the confusion. "What's plumbing?" he asked.

"That's pipes and faucets and things that bring water."

"I thought a plum is a fruit!" he exclaimed.

"Why do they call it a hardware store where you buy things to bring water, and water isn't hard?"

I was at a loss for words. I said, "Well, pipes are hard I guess. I don't know."

Children listen hard to words and expect them to mean what they say, but sometimes English doesn't measure up. On the other hand, Algonquin words and phrases fill the mind with pictures.

I believe that in old English many more words "meant" something, in and of themselves. Words from the German such as wildebeest, doppleganger, and meistersinger are more fresh and direct. Many French-based words are the same way such as portmanteau. Latin, in its day, was very self-descriptive and poetic, and some linguists make extensive comparisons between Micmac and Latin. Even today our slang is fresh and direct: "eighteen-wheeler" and "whatchamacallit" are words that children are naturally attracted to. Tribal language is closer to this kind of poetry than codified English.

The words for objects and creatures in Micmac seem filled with a childlike magic to me. They pick the unique quality out that makes the animal different from all others, capturing for me the wonder I felt at first seeing these things as a child. *Goh-beet*, the word for beaver, literally means "someone with teeth." *Gw-* is short for *gwetch*, "someone" (usually an animal with four legs) and *beet* is the root syllable of tooth (*nee-beet* is "my tooth.")

The word for moon is *dep-kun-o-set*, "the one who shines/walks during the night," and the word for sun, *na-goo-set,* is "the one that shines/walks during the day." The word for hurricane is *weh-ga-lam-sin*, which means "the wind is very angry." The word for one's lover is *zeezee-bem* or "my bird" (not necessarily tame!). All of these are parallels to a poetry of innocence that is becoming lost in the English language.

Some Micmac words that relate to European inventions (and animals) actually do capture recent historical "first beholding with wonder" moments. The word for window, *du-oh-bu-dee*,

127

seems to mean "it is outside and inside at the same time" or contains elements of all those words. The word for horse, *de-zee-boh* (like "beau"), is from the French language of the people who introduced them to the horse. It seems to say, "Is it not beautiful?"

The word for a wooden frame house, *gwen-djee-goo-um*, means literally "where the French dwell," (or more superficially "French-house") even if a Micmac is living in it. The word for cow is *gwendjoodeeyam*, which seems to say "a Frenchman's idea of a moose" ("French-moose").

The word for my car is *noo-tabag'n*, which I've heard Micmac people translate as "my toboggan, my vehicle, my dogsled, my rig." The word for apple, *wendjoo-so-oon*, means "a big French cranberry." You can still get a feeling of what confusion the first introduction these things might have created, the Frenchman trying to describe it in his language, and the Micmac trying to be diplomatically correct.

Some well-used Micmac phrases have a poetic sensibility to them:

> *"My heart is not in place."*
>
> *"I am an arrow to the sun."*
>
> *"Keep the circle strong."*
>
> *"I am in darkness today."*
>
> *"My spirit goes someplace."*
>
> *"Light a fire in my heart."*
>
> *"My heart goes into a million pieces."*
>
> *"It was beautiful the way I slept."*
>
> *"Things fall together."*

128

"Walk straight behind the plow."
"The truth is happening now."

These sound almost like titles to poems, but they are part of the everyday art of speaking, the poetics of an ordinary people.

EVERYTHING IS ALIVE

The natural wisdom of the Algonquin is not opposite to European attitudes or any other kind of way, it is just different. This path of action I am speaking of, a path I have glimpsed in the actions of Wabanaki elders, is not short-term thinking. It is immediate thinking, it is here-and-now concrete thinking, but it is long-term in application. It is based on the experience of this very moment, and we often say *geezkook,* "today," or *neegeh,* "now," to refer to this moment, and *ga'cha-mee,* "here and now," to refer to this place we stand. But it is also based on the experience of the people as a whole and the teachings of elders who have talked with seven generations of people. That is long-term thinking, which is prized very highly, for it is an inheritance of much value.

All of the things in our life have power, and how we use them and take care of them strengthens or limits their power for us. In the traditional way, everything has life spirit in and around it and should be treated with caution and respect, and perhaps awe. Everything is sacred, yet to say that Wabanaki are animists and everything is "animate" is not quite true.

In all Algonquin languages nouns (thought-clusters) are either animate or inanimate (strong or weak, respectively). In

129

Micmac, although all humans and animal creatures are linguistically animate, the other "nouns" such as those for geographical features and plants and man-made artifacts, are hard to predict. Trees are animate, flowers are not. A spoon is animate, but a knife is not. A mountain is animate, but a river is not. Cheese is animate, but meat is not. A cup is animate, but a fork is not. A star is animate, but earth is not. The moon is animate, but the clouds are not.

Ent gamulamun, "my heart," is a Micmac word very close to *gamalamin,* "to breathe" (and *gamalami,* "breath"). When the heart beats, it is said, "Your heart is breathing." The Micmac recognize a close relationship between life, breath, and the heartbeat, and yet the word for heart is inanimate. At the same time, fingernail and knee are animate. It is hard to fathom many aspects of Wabanaki speech and this is perhaps the hardest. There are stories in which inanimate rocks become animate when used by one of the characters. The Passamaquoddy word for candy, *zugol,* is animate in Canada, but inanimate in the United States. Chalk is animate, but pencil is not. The list is endless and baffling.

This does not mean that some are alive and have a spirit and some are dead objects. No one today knows why there are these differences, but the use of the pronoun for "it" would change in each case, depending on whether there was an animate or inanimate noun. The word that means "it-he-she" applies only to animate nouns.

Robert Leavitt, Director of the Micmac-Maliseet Institute in New Brunswick, conducted an experiment which intrigued me greatly. As he did his field work with Maliseet speakers, he presented each individual with his hand-held tape recorder and

130

asked how they would refer to it in their language. Each person without exception referred to the tape recorder as an inanimate noun, but when asked about the tape inside it, each person referred to it as an animate noun. Why? No one seemed able to explain.

As the language, with its complex grammar, contains the knowledge of the Wabanaki people, so the distinction of animate and inanimate words must tell us something. I don't know what it is. Perhaps if we studied the Wabanaki languages well we would have our answers and be surprised.

PARTS OF THE WHOLE

Each thing we encounter on our journey is either the embodiment of one spirit or soul, *otchitchahau-mitch(oh)*, such as a person or moose or beaver, or it is imbued with a greater spirit or soul which can also be embodied elsewhere. A single blade of the great grass sweetgrass, *umptseegooabee*, puts you in touch with the spirit of sweetgrass everywhere, just as much as a whole armful would. It is all one spirit.

Even a large mountain can be seen in one glance, but a river has no clear beginning or end to the viewer. In Algonquin tongues, a river is usually named in sections, according to its characteristics in that region — as far as the eye can see but no farther. Their names told what activities happened there. Skowhegan Falls is from *enskow-hegan* which includes a kind of ceremonial greeting as well as a reference to spearing fish. Perhaps it was a place where two tribes met to fish for salmon.[28]

131

Everything is relative, a part of the whole. Everything we experience personally is personal. The Algonquin people I've encountered have taught me that you can't have it all, you can't know it all, you can't explain it all, and it's a good thing. It's bigger than we are. Life is much more enjoyable when you take it as it comes. "Keep looking, you'll find your answers," is a phrase one hears a lot. But the answers you find are not final ones. They are your answers, in the present moment, and there is much more to the story. Keep looking. Creation is not only a mystery, it is still happening, and it's happening around and within us. Step by step, this point of view has become a part of me.

RESPECT FOR HUMAN NATURE

Respect for nature and its infinite variety is admired by Native Americans wherever it is found — which includes, logically, a respect for human nature and its infinite variety as well. It is this second respect that newcomers to ancient ways find so astonishing. They are accustomed to perceiving man as something opposed to nature. How could a people respect both?

In the Algonquin way of life, as in good literature, a person's own spirit and own nature work through them, hand in hand with the Great Spirit and with all of nature, to heal them of confusion, sorrow, and smallness. Healing and purification ceremonies provide constructive outlets for this transformation, a safe space where screaming, spitting, vomiting, and moaning are expected. Our "human weaknesses" are natural, even if they seem to go against nature. Deprived of these outlets, they fester and become poison, a pollution of the heart.

WHAT DO YOU MEAN "WE"?

There's an old joke where the Lone Ranger and Tonto are surrounded by disenfranchised native peoples, i.e. "hostile Indians." The Lone Ranger says, "We can handle this!" whereupon Tonto, a First American himself, says, "What do you mean 'we,' white man?"

This tale points out an interesting separation between "*wabeys*" or white people, and native people, beyond the obvious inconvenience the Lone Ranger is experiencing. There are actually two words for "we," in native language, and there should be. If you and Tonto are talking to me and you say in English, "We are leaving now," you need to make it clear who will be leaving. If you mean you and Tonto, that's fine with me, but if you're including me, then you are telling me what to do and where to go, and I may get annoyed with you and walk away.

In Micmac there's no confusion; you would say *nee-nen* if you meant "me and my friend over here are leaving" and would say *gee-noo* if you were including me in your plan.[29] There is a big difference between one "we" and another, and one is always careful about *gee-noo*. As the Lone Ranger learned, you never really know what another person wants or needs, until you ask.

One reason I avoid the word "we" elsewhere in this book is because it causes misunderstanding. I don't wish to either automatically include or exclude the reader from "We the People."

By now you probably know if it feels like home to be hearing about the Algonquin way of life. If it does, you are included in the word "we."

NO WORD FOR TREE

I once asked my Micmac language teacher, "What is the word for tree?"

I was surprised when he answered, "There's no word for tree. There are pine trees, maple trees, elm trees, and so forth; there are young trees, shade trees, and old trees that are only good for firewood. All these deserve specific terms. But there is no word for just tree."

I countered, "But you have only one word for human being — *ulnu.*"

"Yes," he answered. "People are all alike, they have two eyes, a nose, a mouth. They have to eat and sleep, they need love, and to find their purpose in life, but trees? They're all different!"

I wondered about this, but remembered a conversation with a "tree doctor" who works in the Brazilian rainforest, Dr. Margaret Harritt. If you have a hundred trees and remove four of them, if you don't know what you're doing, you may be removing three out of four species present, leaving a monoculture. The problem with a monoculture is that it might not last two generations. If they are clones, they will be prone to the same diseases, bugs, and blights. The new science of genetic diversity is in its infancy in the United States, but the Algonquin art of speaking insured diversity centuries ago.

134

A few months later I was walking in the forest with my Micmac language teacher and came across an old tree that was already half dead. As I looked at it, the word *goomoodj* came into my head, almost as if someone spoke it in my ear. I turned to my teacher and said, "What does *goomoodj* mean?" I couldn't remember.

He answered, "This word refers to a tree that is so old and so nearly dead that it is good to cut it down for firewood. This tree here is *goomoodj*. Cutting it down will make more space for other things to grow. You are learning!"

Actually, I'd forgotten, but some part of me remembered. It was another step in my education on how the human interacts with nature. We have been a valued part of the forest for thousands of years — we clear out the dead wood.

Categorized diversity is at the heart of what Algonquin language teaches us, and it is an important lesson. It has taken the Creator millions of years to develop genetic diversity on this earth. We cannot create any meaningful diversity ourselves, yet in the past fifty years, we have removed much of the earth's genetic diversity (an eight-year-old told me that forty-seven species a day are becoming extinct), not to mention linguistic, cultural, and religious diversity. What are we doing? We don't know because our language doesn't force us to look.

By carefully recording biological diversity, the Algonquin language has taught the people who speak it to look more closely at the wonder of nature. The people know not to hunt all the animals at once, but to weed out the runts and old ones from the herds. They know to leave a portion of herbs ungathered, especially those whose roots are to be pulled and used in medicine. They know to gather the deadfall first and cut down only

135

goomoodj for burning. When saplings must be cut for the lodge, they offer tobacco to the mother of the saplings, and do not cut them all at once.

FOREST FOR THE TREES

I took my Micmac language teacher, Stephen, to Vassar College where I introduced him to the head of the Anthropology Department, and they talked a long time. I took him to see many of the various sights in the Hudson Valley. I would drive and occasionally say, "Look at that!" He took it all in very casually. It was no big deal. He and his wife and children took me to Kentucky Fried Chicken in thanks for my efforts.

Later that day we were driving along through the woods, chatting, and suddenly he pointed and exclaimed, "*Look at that!*" I thought he had seen a bear, but it was too close to the suburbs for bears.

I said, "I don't see anything."

I slowed the car to a crawl, looked high and low between the trees, but couldn't for the life of me figure out what he was pointing at.

"There. See that?"

I looked again, but saw nothing.

Finally, he said in admiration, "If my grandmother could see all those white ash trees standing together like that, it would make her the happiest grandmother of all the Micmacs! She could make thousands of baskets out of those trees!"

Stephen went on to explain how they cut the large trees of

ash and split them down the side in long bands, perfect for baskets.

I looked, and suddenly my vision reversed. Instead of looking around the trees as if they were some obstacle in the way of beauty, I began to see their beauty, their usefulness; I began to see them through the eyes of his grandmother.

"There are tons of white ash around here," I said. "Tons! They are sort of nice, aren't they?"

"Sort of nice? Our white ash are disappearing due to acid rain, and taking our basketry industry along with it. Do you think we could log some of those out of here?"

I didn't know, but I thought that with permission, it sounded possible.

I learned a lot that day, and offered to help him sell the baskets in the New York area.

137

WE ALL HAVE A PLACE ON THE WHEEL

The human race started out with our ancestor Glooskap, the first man (like Adam, or like Manu in the Indic creation tale) who was formed when a lightning bolt hit the clay. The next stage of "evolution" began when he was hit again with lightning and rose up and walked around. The third stage of evolution began with fire, which was ignited by a third bolt of lightning. From that grandfather fire, seven sparks flew out.

In one of the earliest Vedic hymns, the grandfather fire of

Creation gives birth to seven sons from which (or whom) Creation proceeds. Most Vedic scholars won't venture a guess as to what it means, but the parallel to the Creation story of the Micmacs is remarkable. Elsewhere, in an Indic story of Creation, Indra throws the lightning bolt which splits the clouds and starts the rain. This is the event that creates the oceans that give rise to life on earth. This is reminiscent of Glooskap in the Creation story.

From the seven sparks which came out of Glooskap's first great council fire, came seven tribes. From each of those fires, seven more sprung forth, and then there were fifty fires, and then fifty Algonquin tribes. Each tribe is necessary and unique. Without any one of them, the hoop would not be complete. (See Appendix for a partial list of modern Algonquin peoples.)

138

My personal elaboration on the theme of seven sparks from seven sparks would be as follows: There are seven inner planets (this is one), and on this planet, seven types of creatures (mammals being one), and of mammals, the human is one. Of humans there have been seven races — the Native Americans being one, and of seven great families of nations of Native Americans, the Algonquin people are one. Of the seven great families of Algonquians, the Wabanaki are one. Of the seven Wabanaki tribes, the Micmac are one. The Micmac therefore have seven council districts, and seven geographical areas in which they have always lived. Take away any of these groups and the hoop of life is broken. They are all here for a reason and all are different in some way.

A DIFFERENT DRUM

We ourselves were created as individuals for some unique purpose we don't exactly understand. We are each different from all others. Our form and function are linked. We each look different from anyone else, we each have different mannerisms, thoughts, and ways of doing things, different talents from anyone else. We have different metabolisms and a different pace of life. This is how we were created because we each also have a different path to follow from anyone else.

When Henry David Thoreau wrote, "If a man does not keep pace with his companions, perhaps it is because he hears a different drummer. Let him step to the music which he hears, however measured or far away," he echoed a viewpoint that underlies much of Wabanaki culture.

139

Each person is a part of Creation both as an individual and as part of a group and, although the needs of the many outweigh the needs of the one, the needs of Creation outweigh the needs of the many, so there is a balance between the individual and the tribe. The tribe has the right to include or exclude whom it wishes, but cannot tell anyone how to think or what to do.

The Algonquin person is therefore free to follow his or her own heart as long as it doesn't endanger others within the group. It is not that the people don't work together in cooperation, they do. But the harmony among a community of elders which many outsiders marvel at comes from a deeper place, a place of freedom. Those who don't wish to be there shouldn't be.

Harmony has nothing to do with coersion and control, it has to do with affinity, or perhaps a stronger word, love.

We have an individual purpose in life which is sacred, and anyone who puts us unjustly in prison or tries to kill us for their own end or entraps us in some way, is blocking us from that path. They are holding back Creation in us, damming up the river of life, with, of course, untold ecological damage to themselves and others.

There is an old expression "No one tells a Micmac what to do," and with many people this is literally true, especially an elder. If an elder is in a burning building and you try to drag him or her out, yelling, "Get out of there, now," the elder might say, "Nobody tells me what to do!"

You might be better off saying, "Elder, the house is burning and there's no water, and the roof is about to fall. You seem to be in that house, what would you like to do?"

Most elders would thank you, and step outside. But part of the general Algonquin view includes the idea that people don't need to be told what to do very often; they have some smarts. They are each directed by the Creator.

When a group of Micmacs came to New York for the first time, I was to be their tour guide, or so I thought. I soon found out differently.

I said, "I've scheduled a reception for you tonight. There's some people I'd like you all to meet."

"Okay, you do it," was the response. "We'll stay here, maybe take a walk in the woods, get a look at what kind of trees you have here."

I hadn't actually invited the elders — I'd merely scheduled them.

The next day, I said, "I have scheduled a luncheon for you at two o'clock. We'd better get going now if we're going to get there on time."

One of my guests answered, "What's the hurry?" The elders just walked away and did something else. They were not angry, I was addressing it as a statement, not as a question, which it should have been. They were answering in a way that was appropriate for them. It was a teaching, which is why they were there.

A unifying creed you will hear from most Algonquin traditionals is that anywhere you stand should be sacred because the entire earth is sacred. You don't need to go to a temple or church to see God, God is all around us. You don't need any kind of building or book to worship God, because the open air of nature is the highest and most sacred place to find God. Clearly this is different from mainstream Christianity, but not necessarily different from the pre-Mosaic Hebrews who were nomadic people as well.

141

NO PROMISES

Another aspect of Micmac individualism is the absence of promises, or the need for them. On one hand, because people take honesty and truthfulness so seriously, any sensible Micmac would be very reluctant to make a promise he or she might not be able to keep. My elders usually respond by saying, "We'll see." Promises are not in the now, they usually involve time.

A promise is an obligation which can encroach on one's

freedom — one never knows to what extent. When taken seriously, a promise is a loving form of debt, a burden which one goes into willingly. So even if we were asked to make a promise we can keep, we might choose to work out some other arrangement so that we could better respond to the inevitable changes life brings, and be free to "follow the spirit," as it moves us, to include spirit as a third partner in all transactions.

Geezoolgh never asks us to make a promise to It. On the other hand, the people, *ulnuq*, no matter how independent they wish to be, depend on each other from time to time for survival and support. Promises are saved — and kept — for times like these. When the people come to a point where a promise is necessary, they might pack the pipe together over it, asking the pipe and the Creator to help them keep their promises to one another. In a European context, a native person might simply say, "I'll do my best to be there, God willing." What more can we promise?

FREEDOM TO BE UNIQUE

Balancing the bold individualism of the Micmac is the principle of *nen-djak*, or "family." People on the medicine path are told to go to the elder and ask permission for everything, but the elder generally says "okay" and then gives them advice. The elder too is part of a subtle "institution of the family" that holds Micmac life together as it did in Chinese society during the Confucian era. There is a social structure which dictates everything invisibly, and that institution knits the native world together into a cohesive community where no one is left out, everyone belongs and has a job to do. This reality strikes a balance with the rugged individualism of Micmac philosophy, which is quite pronounced. Men go off hunting for months at a time and come back unannounced. (Today these could be job hunting trips.) People leave meetings when they want and come back when they want. People "follow the spirit" so much, it's hard to keep up with them, and you're not supposed to. These are "the Freedom People." They always fight for freedom, for themselves and others. On an interpersonal level, Micmac and other Wabanaki people are equally sensitive about "control issues," and I have learned some important personal lessons: communication works better than control most of the time, but it takes courage. Much of the pervasive dignity of the people comes from having the courage to claim these simple freedoms at every moment.

143

Fear and anger are one word in Micmac, *loo-weh-woo-dee*, and that word is also equivalent to evil, according to oral tradition. Courage with caution is the answer to evil, and to fear and anger as well.

Greed and destructive materialism come out of *loo-weh-woo-dee*, and courage is the answer here too. A fearless society is like a strong healthy body, it confronts its own weaknesses and heals its own confusion. We keep each other in balance through courage — when any member of the group surrenders under pressure to the control of another person, it makes life that much harder for the others in the group. It puts things out of balance. One of my favorite expressions has been attributed to Iowan Indian origins, but it could be Micmac as well: "A brave man dies but once, a coward many times."

If we try to do what the Creator wants of us at every

moment, where is there time to be controlled by others? Native life, as I have seen it, demonstrates that individualism and communal cooperation go hand in hand. The underlying oneness is already there. When the people are trusted with freedom in a healthy, supportive environment from birth, they choose voluntarily to work for the good of the whole. We are slaves to no man, but honoring the elders and deferring to them is in the nature of things, it comes from honoring God. It is part of that healthy balance between individualism and community, between being a lone wolf and running with the pack.

TAGS AND HANDLES

People and animals are given names which bull's-eye their unique qualities, or compare them with like creatures. Sometimes names are simile-like, but more often they are pure metaphor, and very effective. In many native languages, the word-cluster for rabbit translates as, "His Ears Are Close Together." Some dogs may have long ears, some rodents have large back haunches, but no other animal has ears so amazingly close together.

The Micmac are called the Squirrel People for reasons known to few. It is said that Micmacs are the descendants of squirrels, perhaps because they are so at home in the woodland forests. The word is *ahdoodooitch*, which means "He Comes Down (the tree) Head First," a unique quality of squirrels, though not of Micmacs I've observed.

The word for chipmunk is *abachbahamedch*. *Wabi* means white, *oo* means his/her, *bachem* is back, *baha* refers to fluffy fur, *edtj* is that person of (someone who). From this we might guess that the word was once *waboo-bach-ba-ha-medtch*, "That Person with the White Fluff on His Back." I've earned this nickname because my unique qualities are like the chipmunk, the way I wash every morning, the way I hold my mouth and my wrists. It fits, even though I don't have white fluff on my back. *Abachbahamedtch* is a humble servant, "Little Brother of the Squirrel People." The chipmunk is also the musician of the forest, his rhythmic sounds are very creative, and I do sing a number of traditional songs from time to time.

When Grandfather Turtle first came to the U.S., a large group of my friends came for the talking circle and to experience the sweat lodge. In the circle, I reminded Grandfather that when he gave me the name Chipmunk, he told me my job was to gather up the nuts for the eagles. I said, "Well, Eagle, I gathered up a real assortment of 'nuts!'" He was very happy. Later, in the sweat lodge, Grandfather threw an acorn at me playfully, saying, "Here's a gift for you, Chipmunk!"

That day was a gift for both of us, because we were both able to use our unique gifts in service to the whole of life.

145

ELDERS

The Cree say, "Never sit while your elders stand." Of course there is a lot more at stake than seating arrangements when we hold to tradition. It expresses a way of life in which experience and age are honored. Some have even called the Algonquin society a "gerontocracy," which means "governed by old men." This is not completely accurate, since middle-aged and young people are often encouraged to govern if that's what they do best — by elders who may be men or women. Most Algonquin societies were/are a "democracy," where the common people are wielders of political power. Respecting the elders is customary, and affects every part of life, including politics.

The elders are people who have walked the Red Road for a long time, and have been seeking real knowledge and insight during that whole time. The elders' job is to steer people away from the confusion of the tricksters in life, and there are many. "Good elders never ask anyone to be their follower and never give orders," to quote Maliseet writer Juanita Perley. They give you choices and ideas, and often they test you by giving you jobs to do. A Micmac healer and pipeman once told me, "The real Medicine Man is up there" (pointing to the sky). "That's who my Chief is."

In Asia we think of all-powerful masters with their humble followers, but in ancient times, this wasn't the case. The Taoist Chuang Tzu often wrote that there was no teacher or disciple, that all relationships should be an expression of the Great Tao. There was a time in India before the Aryans arrived when there were no *gurus* and no *chelas*, per se, but everything indicates that there must have been customary respect for elders. In Micmac language, there is no word or phrase that indicates a spiritual teacher and student relationship. You can't say it. However, you can ask someone, *"Geh-goo-noo-de-moo-ee?"* "Can you teach me something?" When it's specific, it's an action and doesn't imply an authority role. Just because you teach me something doesn't mean I can't teach you about something else.

We are all medicine for one another. The Sauk say, "Teachers not only teach, they also learn."

The concept of "chief" is a new one to Wabanaki people, only 500 years old. It is a French word indicating "captain" or someone in charge, and was first used to describe Wabanaki leaders; but Wabanaki leaders were elders who were stronger, wiser, and older. They won trust, not elections. They served the needs of the people or were not listened to. Today, there are governmental elections for chief for each tribe and you don't have to be an elder to win, but that's politics, not tradition.

CLOCKWISE

When you approach an elder, there is a way of watching and listening which shows respect. You approach an elder in a circular sort of way, never straight on, unless you are of equal age. I am not aware of any Algonquin taboo against looking directly at someone, but you shouldn't stare at an elder you don't know. While you are speaking, you can look, especially if s/he looks at you. There are times when you should look away. Trust your instincts.

If there is a group of elders, it is best to address and give a gift to the eldest of them first, and proceed backwards by age. If age is not clear, it is best to greet a circle of people clockwise. Once I was faced with a "farewell" situation where the elders happened to be seated counterclockwise by age! I was nervous but decided to honor the Creator above human age and greeted them clockwise. They looked a little surprised but I saved the last *"up-na-mool-tess"* for the high elder. *Upnamooltess* means, "I will see you again," and they responded with the same. There is no word in Micmac for "goodbye." In a world without time, everything is cyclical. Nothing is final.

The approach to an elder to ask a pointed question is a lot like that in hunting a moose. You circle around the elder, taking a lot of time, then circle around the question, poke at it a little, come back for more after giving it thought. Thoughtful practice of the art of conversation becomes more important when engaging a master of the art, which many elders are.

Wabanaki elders (and most Algonquins as far as I can tell) always move clockwise when turning, in ceremony and in everyday life. It keeps the flow of creation going. After working for several years with Wabanaki traditionals, doing anything counter-clockwise seems rude and unnatural, but I have not forgotten my first ceremony and all the confusion I caused! I felt like I was walking over land mines!

In ancient China and India, the clockwise flow was associated with the downward pull of creation, whereas the counter-clockwise flow was associated with pulling the energy of life back into the higher *chakras*, both equally important. Under Buddhist influence, this counter-clockwise flow became associated with liberating the practitioner from the grip of illusion, a basic Buddhist virtue. At that time, the clockwise motion seems to have fallen into disuse in China. In Wabanaki philosophy, the inward and outward journeys are equally important, but in practice, they always honor Creation, and the sun, *neesgam,* by moving clockwise. It is a life-affirming gesture.[30]

It is an ironic footnote that this most honored path of the sun is at the core of what time means for both native and non-native people. It's good to remember that even in Western society, the essence of time is not a clock, it is the relationship between planets, moons, and stars and how they tug on one another gravitationally as they waltz through space. Perhaps the distance between the two worlds is not so great after all.

Algonquin people don't speak of *chakras* but are aware of the *kundalini* energy as a natural force of Creation that comes up from the earth and then through the body, linking spirit with matter.

It has been stated that the "Shepherd's Crook" in Judaic and later in Christian symbolism represents the course of the *kundalini* from the spine to the thymus to the crown *chakra* and down to the pineal gland below the crown. The most sacred symbol of the Woodland Indians is the scroll (or fiddlehead) fern, and it is similar to the Shepherd's Crook.

The eagle flag, or eagle staff, which is brought into the circle to open the powwow, echoes the shape of the sacred fern. Could it be that the Woodland Indians, of whom the Wabanaki are a major branch, have always been aware of the path of the *kundalini*?

149

TEACHING BY EMBARRASSMENT

◆

I n my experience, elders teach situationally. They don't presume your ignorance by lecturing. They wait for you to make mistakes and then correct you. That way you don't forget. If you can't bear making mistakes, don't show up. Usually, they are very forgiving and compassionate; however, sometimes I felt especially honored by having my ignorance dramatically demonstrated and corrected by the elders. I consider it special training, like being called forward to play at a master class in music. Needless to say, big egos don't last very long in this school.

It can be a time-consuming way to do things in the short run, but the elders are in no hurry. They look at the big picture. When I first arranged a sweat lodge for my elders here in the U.S., they didn't tell me anything in advance but waited to see if I'd remember. I did terribly or wonderfully, depending on your point of view.

Right before the sweat lodge, the elder said, "Where's the pail? We can't have a water pouring ceremony without a pail."

I drove several miles to the nearest town and came back with a shiny new pail while everyone waited. The elder took the pail and said, "Where are the berries? We can't do a Bear Lodge without the berries. The Grandfather Bear won't be very happy!"

A friend and I got back in the car, drove several miles to the nearest town, and came back with some blueberries. "There's not enough water in the jugs," the elder said.

"I have some in my car," someone offered.

We waited for the water to come. Meanwhile people were milling around, waiting for the lodge.

We carried the water to the lodge site. The elder looked at the stones that had been gathered by a friend of mine, and then looked at me. "Some of these are not the right kind of stones," he said. "These porous ones can explode in the lodge. Why don't you look for a few more in the woods there?"

I went off to gather stones. Meanwhile, a few of my friends gave up on the sweat lodge and went home. But in the end we had a great sweat and I never forgot the berries again!

For several years I organized ceremonial gatherings in the U.S. and acted as a bridge between the elders and various friends who didn't know what to do. My job was to prepare them as much as possible for the inevitable "situational teaching," but occasionally I would slip up. At one gathering, I forgot to tell the people when to present the tobacco to the elders and the visiting Cree elder, as he began the talking circle, had plenty to say about that! One of my co-organizers jumped up in panic and cried, "I'll get some, I'll get some!"

"No, you stay here and listen!" he replied and went on reprimanding a while longer about the importance of offering the elder tobacco before the ceremony. When he finally said, "I guess you'd better go get your tobacco now..." the room cleared in seconds. None of them will ever forget: tobacco first, ceremony after.

OLD ONES

There is a subtle teaching among certain Algonquin people that the flow of human events comes out of the original moment of Creation, and that older things are closer to Creation than the newer. Elders are closer to Creation than their sons and daughters, so they are closer to the sacred. *Sagukayg* means "long ago." *Sa'an* means "old." The Great Spirit in Micmac is literally *Sa'an Otchitchahaumitchoh* which means "the oldest spirit." Great Spirit is the first creation of the Creator, so It is oldest. The twelve levels of heaven are the next oldest (reminiscent of the twelve Hindu *loks* or planes of reality) then the sky was created (which has twelve levels of clouds), then the earth, (with twelve levels of rocks), then the plants then fish then animals. The various spirits and grandfathers are of varying ages.

Man is farther from the Creation than the animals, so he honors them. The rocks are revered for this reason. The rocks have been here for many thousands of winters, and have been sitting there, seeing everything and becoming very wise. That is why "stone people" can be so helpful to us. They are closer to Creation, they are older than almost anything else we can touch. They too are called grandfathers.

When meeting an old woman, it is complimentary to call her Noogamee, which is the grandmother in the Micmac Creation story. It is good to compliment her on how long she has lived, and is polite to ask, "And how many winters have you been walking on the surface of this, the mother earth?" Everything is measured in winters, because at times it has been quite a feat to survive a "hunger moon" at the end of winter when the wood has run out. We call it "February." When only the strong survive, the oldest are distinguished and ennobled by their great age. Children who say loudly to a white-haired old woman, "Gee, you must be really old!" are not hushed but encouraged.

DREAMS OF MY ANCESTORS

◆

I t was the first night of my first vision quest. As I lay in the bed, I was visited in the spirit world by a large moose. He passed by in the woods and turned to look at me. I knew there was some connection between the Micmacs and the moose, but this was the first time I'd ever dreamed of one.

I was starting to dream in Micmac.

My friend Stephen had already told me about how in the old times, a young man of fifteen would go out and hunt a moose. If he killed the moose and brought it home, he was then considered an adult with full voting rights and privileges. That moose was his initiator into manhood. But what did this moose mean to me?

I woke up from the moose dream with a start. I thought about it, scratching my head. I had no idea what to make of it, but it seemed important and auspicious. I fell back to sleep.

Next I dreamed of my old house at 2016 Peabody Street, where I had lived from the age of two till the age of twenty-three. I dreamed of that place often, it represented my internal house, my mind and emotions. But here there was another startling difference, and new kind of dream language, that of the Micmacs.

Gazing out from what must have been the back porch door, I looked at the clothesline that used to stretch across the back lawn years ago, but instead of clothes, there were human skulls dangling in a row along that line. It was a little frightening at first, but something reminded me that I was no longer in my old frame of reference. Calm down and observe. Knowing will come.

153

The line of skulls went half-way down the clothesline, and I looked at the last one to the right. It was not speaking to me.

Then I looked at the next to last skull from the right. It seemed to hover and vibrate as if wanting to speak to me. It swung up suddenly and jumped off the clothesline and began flying in the air right toward me, so fast I couldn't get out of the way. It got larger and larger and zoomed right through me.

I woke up in a sweat. I was shocked into an altered state of consciousness. What did it mean?

I sat there again, wondering what was going on. I was prepared, or so I thought, to be fearless in the face of danger in order to complete this mission for my family, but now I was having second thoughts. Skulls? It was a little like something from a horror movie, yet I felt unthreatened. Perhaps it was some sort of ally.

I went back to sleep.

Ben appeared in my dream. He said, "Evan? Evan?"

I looked at him, but didn't answer. I didn't know what to say.

I finally got to sleep around four in the morning, and slept pretty late, as I recall.

When Ben came in to see how I was doing, I was glad to see him. I told him I had crazy dreams all night. I told him about the moose.

"I saw a moose. What does a moose do?"

Ben answered, "That's the ancestors. That's how they come. It could be one of your grandfathers, or a moose spirit. Maybe he talked to the moose when he was alive. When he was alive, he could communicate with a moose, and that's why his spirit comes as a moose. Maybe your grandfather is saying, 'This is how I was. I could really talk to this moose when I was alive.'"

He continued: "When a creature comes to you like that, you can say, 'What kind of spirit are you?' You watch what he does, and that will tell you something about him. He's there for a reason. We call that one *Dee-yam!*"

I went back in my mind to where that moose stood, and to my surprise he was still there. As soon as I thought the words, "What kind of spirit are you, *Deeyam?*" he reminded me of the initiation ritual of the traditional times.

He showed me how I had already been initiated into the inner community of the Micmac lodge that wintry day on the beach at fifteen when I took the name Seagull, or *Gwylan*. The moose told me that name had been given to me by my ancestors through the inner channels, and that I had passed successfully into manhood at that time. He told me that the initiation of the fifteenth year was by no means the final one. There should have been another at about my thirtieth year, and should be another one at my fortieth year, making me an elder, though not yet a grandfather.

The Moose told me that the name Seagull was no longer an appropriate name for me, that I had to move on, and I was overdue, in that I was now thirty-four. The moose seemed to say that this man could initiate me into that next stage and the next name.

This all transpired in a flash, and I opened my eyes and looked at Ben. He was still standing there, waiting for me to respond. I told him my realization, and explained how I used to be called Seagull and that I was ready for the next initiation, and a new name.

He said the word for seagull was *gloh-chun-dee-aitch-heh*, and that the seagull was very common up here, and not as highly

155

respected as were the eagles.

"They're scavengers, and steal from other birds. They are clever like cats, but don't have a lot of medicine teachings like the eagles do. Maybe in the sweat lodge, the spirit will give you another name. We'll see."

I had no idea what name he might find for me — Great White Medicine Bird, Blue Eagle, White Bear? Who was I kidding? The other of his Micmac students would be pretty upset if I got a more flashy name than they did, and rightly so. I was the neophyte. I should have a humble name.

Then I asked him about the skulls in a line. What did that dream mean?

He just looked at me, and I heard him say telepathically, "That was your ancestors!"

I repeated it out loud before he had a chance to speak. "They were my ancestors!"

He nodded in approval.

"I understand now." It all made sense. All the puzzle pieces were falling together. I'd asked the Great Spirit who it was that was teaching me, and had forgotten the question.

"That clothesline represents the Micmac blood line in my family, and the skulls represent the ones in that line who have already gone into the spirit world. The last one to die in that line was... my grandfather! But that wasn't the skull that rushed through me. It was the next to last one... my great-grandfather Bill. He's the one!"

"Maybe he was the moose too! He was coming to look at you," Ben added insightfully.

"So it's Bill, not my grandfather, that brought me here."

"I think you're right," answered Ben.

"This is his birthplace. It all makes sense."

"Some day, when you become a pipe carrier, and you fast for your pipe," he told me, "maybe that ancestor will come and work through your pipe and awaken it."

HE DREAMS

Spiritual names capture the essence of the person, that which makes them unique. Powwow is an old Algonquin name which meant "He Dreams." He was an old, old man who had dreams of such power, he could tell the future of the tribe, give healing advice, and awaken others to the walking of the Red Road. Soon Powwow became a title for the strongest medicine men who would hold mystical healing gatherings where teachings and prophecies were given and the people were healed. These meetings were also eventually called powwows, all referring back to the essence of that original old elder. Today that essence has been lost but the people are trying to return once again to having the old-style gatherings as they were once led by "He Dreams."

Each reservation among the Micmac people now has a powwow at least once a year, each on a different weekend, and they often involve sweat lodges, eagle dances, honor dances, sacred songs, and many powerful speeches. At one such powwow, I saw an eagle feather drop from the regalia of a medicine man, and the dance was halted. A lengthy ceremony, including special dances and offerings, was conducted in order to restore the sacredness to the ceremony and to atone for the disrespect that was paid to the eagle feather. This is how serious the Algonquin are about restoring the original meaning of Powwow and restoring the sacred manner of their ancestors.

On a hunting trip, or other excursion, there is a kind of pecking order, and the elder chooses the highest bedding place, the best food, and the others fall into age order behind him. There are traces of this type of gerontocracy even today. The older one is, the closer to Creation he is.

In Lao Tzu's teachings, some of the wisest teachings known to world history, he often makes references to the old ones who were the real sages, men who walked the earth millennia before him, men before whom he always humbles himself. We can only imagine who these men were. In the *True Men*, Chuang Tzu says, "The men of old... were not afraid....These are the ones we call 'true men.'" This phrase reminds me very much of "real people," of the old ones, the ancestors. This phrase "real people" comes up in numerous Algonquin languages, *Lenni Lenape, ulnuq, Alnubak*, etcetera. We honor our elders because they are closer to the old ones than ourselves.

Ironically, children are closer to their own (re-)creation, and therefore closer to the Creator in a different way. The Algonquin honor children most highly because spirit moves strong in them, as anyone can see. When people speak from their hearts, the young ones know it. When grownups start talking nonsense, children sometimes leave or interrupt. When children are laughing out loud at a serious gathering, you might hear the speaker excuse them, saying, "That's a good sign. It means that the Great Spirit is in that place, and joy is about, even if it makes it hard to hear."

Most Algonquin people (but not all) believe in past lives, and those who teach the medicine wheel teachings, teach that we keep coming back as different people in order to complete the wheel, from young soul to old soul. Wabanaki believe that they come back into the same area and live again as Wabanaki. Apparently it takes more than one or two tries to master this way of life from the spiritual point of view. We come back many times, although not as many as in the Hindu belief where we must be reborn 8,400,000 times onto the wheel of the *Bhavachakra*, [31] the Vedic "Medicine Wheel."

There is a certain type of *sa-ga-maugh* or wise, respected elder the old ones called "the snow plow" (a loose translation). He forges a path of healing in the world, clockwise around the medicine wheel, the way one might plow through deep snow in the winter. It is not easy, and there are many obstacles. He proceeds slowly, followed by his helpers and his novitiates (my choice of words), who are followed by the people seeking their answers. Of course, there are no leaders and followers, but sometimes it happens that a *Bpoo-ohin*, or "spiritually gifted elder," helps people in their struggle to complete their own journey around the circle from birth to youth to old age to death. He waits on them, serves them, and makes the way easier for them in this manner.

159

OLD HIGH SPEECH

Between gestures, circularness, and subtlety, the speech of the old *geezeegool-djeedjq* is hard to understand. Some use words so old that they have no equivalents in English or modern Micmac. Often they speak by inference, and instead of telling you what to do they might make a statement. Instead of, "It's time for you to go," they might say, "The door (behind you) is open." Behind you is gestured, of course. You are supposed to take the hint, but you have to be pretty quick on your feet. Such statements often imply opposites at once, which is something difficult in normal English speech. "The door is open," depending on the facial gesture, probably means, "It is open for you to leave, NOW," perhaps even, "Get out of here." But it can also mean, "It is also open for you to come back later when you've given more thought to what I just said...." All that can be expressed with two Micmac words: *ga'chun benadooee.* "Door open."

Literal expressions seem flat by comparison.

Speech between elders can become like a game of poetic chess, where long silences are punctuated by puffs on the pipe, and short baffling enigmas of native expression approaching Zen *koans* or the Baul's "twilight speech" in their complexity of meaning. The Federal Express fax-it-to-me-now world has no time for this Algonquin art of speaking. It takes too much patience.

160

WHEN LIFE WAS FULL THERE WAS NO HISTORY

Here is a quotation from long ago: "In the age when life on earth was full, no one paid any special attention to worthy men, nor did they single out the man of ability. Rulers were simply the highest branches on the tree, and the people were like deer in the woods. They were honest and righteous, without realizing that they were 'doing their duty.' They loved each other and did not know that this was 'love of neighbor.' They deceived no one, yet they did not know that they were 'men to be trusted.' They were reliable and did not know that this was 'good faith.' They lived freely together giving and taking, and did not know that they were generous. For this reason their deeds have not been narrated. They made no history."

Are these the words of the Micmac grand chief and *saga-maugh* Membertou? I feel they could have been. But these words are attributed to Chuang Tzu of ancient China. The wisdom of earth-based peoples is timeless.

ANIMALS ARE EQUAL

Most Algonquin people I've met don't "just adore" animals, they treat them as equals. They don't pamper them, they interact and communicate with them. They don't pat them on the head, they learn from them. Many Algonquin people hunt, some for a living, and many seem to have a fascination with taxidermy. They make jewelry and art out of bones, fur, leather, and other animal parts, but they treat a living animal with dignity. Death is not so much the issue as far as I can see; life is the real issue, the quality of life for both humans and animals.

When the New Hampshire colony declared their independence from England before any other colony and proclaimed the words "Live Free or Die," they were expressing the same fierce sense of freedom by which their Abenaki citizens, ancestors, and neighbors lived. It is the same sense of dignity which wild animals fight for, which whales beach themselves for (as far as we can tell), and which hunted mammals chew off their own entrapped leg for. Native people respect that spirit in animals and will set a pet free in the woods rather than put the creature "to sleep." Better to heal or die in dignity in the natural world at the hand of the Creator than to be "put to sleep" in a cold, white room.

It is true that when traditional Native Americans kill an animal they use every part of it, either as food, clothing, or art. I even know a native friend who gathers bones from game processing shops to utilize as part of her nativist art so that none of those parts would be wasted.

162

Many Micmac people use bear grease when it is available. I've been told that one bear carcass provides not only fur and food but gallons of bear grease, which keeps you warm in the winter, keeps bugs away in the summer, and is used as medicine for skin problems. Once when I got a burn on my arm, the elders gave me a whole jar of it to use as a salve with bandages. I used aloe vera slices as well, just to be on the safe side.

My Great-Aunt Helen raised hundreds of animals at a time and bought and sold them. What the people did with them after they were bought was out of her hands. If they died, it didn't seem to be her lot to worry too much about it. But one thing she could do was to see that they had a great time while they were living with her, and they did. At various times she raised flying birds who didn't live in cages but who roamed free and came back every day at suppertime. Her animals were exceptionally healthy, and few ever ran away.

If animals feel respected they seem to open up greater lines of communication with humans, and Helen's ability to "talk" to animals was legendary throughout the state of Maine. But she wasn't the only one. Grandfather Turtle seemed to talk to animals somehow, too.

THE MAN WHO TALKED TO ANIMALS

I t was my first day with Ben Payson and already I started to notice things about him. We were sitting together in an open cabin in the woods. A dragonfly came into the room and positioned himself in front of Grandfather's face, seeming to stare at him. He brushed the creature aside with a gesture — I guess he wasn't in the mood to talk. The dragonfly circled around the room and came back again to the same position. Grandfather gave his old friend a beady eye and said very deliberately, "Go away." The dragonfly jumped back an inch as if startled, stared at him in disbelief for a second, and then turned and shot out the open door.

163

Grandfather seems to draw animals to him, which never ceases to amaze me. It doesn't seem to matter where we are. I arranged to have him give a talk at a state historic site in the city of Beacon, New York, at a place where Lenape people had once traded. He chose to gather the people outside on the porch, against a beautiful backdrop of grass and trees, and began to speak.

He said, "Creation is happening now. We are a part of it. Everywhere we walk is sacred."

As he was speaking in this way, a deer and a fox walked up near the crowded porch as if to hear, and an eagle circled overhead. Other animals passed through as well. I pointed silently for the others to see what was happening, but a few were too spellbound by his words to notice.

A few days later, we were walking along a trail that ran next to a series of wooden fences toward the sweat lodge site in the woods, and a bluebird, a rare visitor to southern New York, led him along the trial, hopping to the next fencepost and waiting for him to draw near, then hopping to the next one. The bird led him clockwise around the perimeter of the horse pasture and into the woods to the site of the sweat lodge, then flew away.

At that lodge there were two visitors who had the word "wolf" in their name. Grandfather told them a story about a healing circle he'd held in northern Ontario with some native people.

He explained that the Creator always sends him a pair of wolves to warn him of danger. "Through the window I watched two wolves coming over the hill. Within a few minutes, a fight had broken out among the people, but I was ready to handle it, thanks to the warning."

He was especially generous and helpful to the two "wolf" people at the lodge. One of them was helped with a life-threatening illness, and is well today. Later that night he told me to be careful at the next lodge. Sure enough, the gathering a few days later was nothing but trouble! But he came well rested and prepared, and everyone got what they needed. Everyone was safe, including my family, who attended that gathering.

The moose, *dee-yam*, is the king of the forest, just as *bu-t'p* the whale, is king of the ocean. The Micmac say they are related. They are both *ess-boo-dek*, "superior to us." Their species are very old. Some Micmac people from up towards Labrador say their meat tastes the same and that they are closely related.

In the old days, a Micmac boy would kill a moose as part of his initiation into manhood. While many Micmac people still hunt moose and other wild game, it is for food only. If you hunt for sport, you should really make a fair sport out of it and go "tagging" instead.

Tagging is a highly esteemed sport where you track the wild animal and then walk up to it face to face and tag it with your hand. Few can do this any more. Grandfather Turtle once told me this story:

"In Old Town, Maine (a Penobscot reservation), there was an old Micmac man from Nova Scotia. A Penobscot elder showed him a traditional Micmac Indian outfit they had there, which they tell me is over a hundred years old. There was a moose over across the way and the elder told the man, 'If you're a Micmac, you can go over there and touch that moose without it running away. If you can do that, we'll give you this outfit. It belongs to the Micmac.'

"And this man was so strong in the Micmac way, he walked over to that moose. He walked, and walked, gently, and touched that moose! He walked back and the elders held up the jacket and said, 'Here, take it. It's yours. Take it back to the Micmacs!'

"And that man is wearing that jacket today!"

The bear, the moose, the whale, the squirrel are all important neighbors to the Micmac — some believe the squirrel is the cousin of the Micmac people. But the most important creature is probably the eagle, *geetpoo*. The stories surrounding the eagles and their powers are endless, but I'll share just one example.

Grandfather Turtle says, "Years ago, when there were no telephones, the elders used 'eagle holes.' They put their ears in this hole and they could talk to the other elders. (The hole is dug in the ground. Often, tobacco is put in the hole.) Nowadays, where there is a telephone we use it, but where there is none, we use the pipe and the messenger — the eagle — because there is only one bird who can see so far away and fly so high."

Animals are not known to discuss the metaphysics of God, but they are closer to perfection in the things they do than we can hope to be in ours.

THE LAND AND THE PEOPLE ARE ONE

My great-grandfather was born on the banks of the Miramichi River, and was led by economic conditions and perhaps political aspirations to move to the United States. My grandfather (his son), always said, "Before I die, I'm going back to the Miramichi! That's where we're from. That's our home." He said this to my mother many times, but died of a heart attack before he could make the pilgrimage.

I met Grandfather Turtle by the banks of the Miramichi River. The water there is blue much of the time and there is a lush stretch of deep green sweetgrass growing at the edge of the water just to the north. The Micmac people have always gone eel fishing there and fish jump out of the water now and then.

The rolling hills of the region are very gentle and often covered with pine and fir. Dirt roads are everywhere.

It is windy year-round and, although you do find occasional windless days in the summer, for the most part, it is breezy. During the long winter months, it snows quite a bit, and there are several words in Micmac for snow, including *hwa-sto*, and *pess-ach*, "it is snowing." A common word for rain is *git-pess-ach*, or "snow, but melted," which goes to show you how much snow they're used to seeing.

They get so used to cold in Micmac country that the cold doesn't bother them much. They remain one with the land in winter too. Once during the dead of winter I was having a long distance phone conversation with a girl who worked at the Band Office. I asked her how the weather was.

She answered, "Oh, about thirty-five below."

I said, "Do you get much snow?"

She said, "It's snowing pretty hard right now."

I started to tell her what the weather in New York was like. "It's about zero here, and sort of breezy..."

She listened patiently and then said, "I don't want to interrupt, but I'm at a pay phone right now and I'd sort of like to go inside now, it's getting cold."

I don't want to imply that Micmac people don't ever get cold but I think she was just bored with my conversation, and wanted to get on to her other calls. I'll never know.

The Micmac still live on the lands of their ancestors and they are proud of it, in rain or shine. For the most part they take care of it and keep it beautiful because it takes care of them.

Grandfather told me, "Every place you stop on mother earth, no matter where you are, that's your sacred area."

Here is a morning prayer, quoted from Albert Ward (from *Micmac Words and Phrases*) translated directly from Micmac:

"I am very grateful today to see the sunlight and to see the mother earth, to see the medicine in the trees, all the beautiful things You gave us, and the medicine that is everyplace. Each time I move my feet, I'm on the mother earth. The ground is soft as I lie on the mother. I fall asleep on the ground and wake up happy. I go with the mother earth into the spirit world. I go into the woods and feel the spirit all around me. I watch the animals. Mother earth gives me strength as I sit on it, or walk upon it. I love the mother earth and I take care of the land which holds up my feet."

THE RED ROAD

168

The Algonquin way of life, its customs, speech, medicine, philosopy, and spirituality are all part of one thing. They are all interrelated. Many refer to the whole of it as "the Red Road."

No two Native American tribes or nations share exactly the same customs or beliefs, and there are at least 255 in North America today. Each is unique. Yet there is an earth way which all native North Americans hold in common — the Red Road, which some also call the Beauty Road.

The Wabanaki people often wear red strips of cloth around their heads during ceremonies. This represents the Red Road and also honors the mother earth. It in itself is a sacred hoop, and fends off unbeneficial energies. Other native people wear headbands, or strips of cloth, and may use different colors, such as white or purple, depending on many factors. Many Taoists, Tai Chi masters and Japanese traditional people also wear red strips of cloth around their heads.

Recently, I completed an arduous four-day *sooneywen* "pipe fast" alone in the woods to "earn my feathers" as a healer within a certain circle. When I emerged from the woods after four days of storm, rain, and wind, holding a broken feather in my hand, I was covered with ashes from the windblown fire. I looked at the elder's glowing face and admired that clean red headband he had always worn. I told him I never felt hunger the whole time, until the last few hours. The elder said, "I know that. You did a real good fast. You can have anything you want."

"Anything? I'd really like to have that red headband!" I said without hesitation, as I pointed to it. I'd been thinking about it for days.

He lifted his legendary red bandana from his head, then took my broken feather and attached it to the leather thong that was tied around the bandana. He placed it on my head, giving me the teaching about what it meant to the Micmac people, and taught me about the Red Road, as his long white hair blew freely in the wind. Then he reached into his medicine bag and pulled out a new red headband, identical to the one I now had, and put it on his own head.

"I came prepared today," was all he said.

I always wonder how he knew what I would ask for.

169

RISING SUN

According to the "Red Record" (a translation of the *Wallum Olum*, the Lenape bible) the pre-Algonquian people came from central China, traveling east to find "where the sun wakes up." The Japanese also originated in central China and, possibly on their own quest to find "where the sun wakes up," took the southern route, becoming the "people of the rising sun."

The Wabanaki are the "Rising Sun" people of North America. They live where the sun wakes up, in the easternmost part of Turtle Island. In the time of the ancestors, *Niskam*, the sun (Our Creator) would rise up during the morning prayer and pipe ceremony (some say with help from the prayers of the people) and show itself *abachtuq*, "way out on the ocean," blessing the people with its light. It would lay out a long red mystical road along the top of the waters that a person could almost walk upon, right into the heart of the Creator.

AGLAMZ

Many native people talk of a Red Road and try to walk the Red Road toward the Creator all the time, every moment of their lives, but this Red Road is not visible except to the eyes of the soul. It is also called the Path of Beauty, or the Rainbow Path. They are basically the same.

The Red Road is the sacred path, the Tao, the Way, the

natural order of things in the universe. "It is the way heaven intends things to be," to quote the *Tao Te Ching*, a book whose title literally means "The Way Life Changes."

Red is the color of life. The word *Te* in *Tao Te Ching* also means life. The word for Red Road in Micmac is *Mayguayg Outee. Mayguayg* means "the color of your blood," the color of life. Many comparisons exist between the Tao and the Red Road. The Red Road that can be spoken of is not the way.

The Micmac word *a-glamz*, or *a-gu-lamz* relates to the Red Road. The word is translated by different people different ways but it refers to the innate intelligence in the universe. Some say *aglamz* is a profound understanding. Some say it means truth, the true way — how things should be, the way they are, the natural way. For lack of an English word, I equate it with *dharma*, a Sanskrit word referring to the cosmic principle behind everything. It is finding one's place in a wise and animate universe. It is a principle which is hard to think about, but easy to resonate and walk in balance with when we keep on the Red Road of our ancestors.

In Micmac we say, "*Mah-wee-da-djik*," or "Things fall together." In old Sanskrit, *dharma* means that which sustains and holds things together. It holds everyone in their right place, in the web of life. When we feel a part of *aglamz*, in Micmac we say, "My heart is in place."

Aglamz and *dharma* suggest that there is a great circle of life and that we participate, we each play a part. Our part is determined not merely by what we want, but by what we are destined to do. *Dharma* is the Way of the Indic people, their Red Road, their foundation, and is one thing that all Indic schools hold in common, including Buddhism. It is an over-arching principle that unites all the myriad Hindu teachings.

Similarly (according to Taoists at least), the concept of the Tao is one thing that all ancient schools of thought throughout the vast sub-continent of China had in common, and there were many. Everyone spoke of the unspeakable Tao. The Zen word for *dharma* is "*ho*," a common Native American exclamation. (In Algonquin, *daho* or *taho* is the common form.)

Underlying all these principles is the fundamental truth of life as a circle of being, a sacred hoop, which interconnects all of us. This I believe to be the foundation of Native American spirituality both historically and forever. It is the Tao that can't be spoken of, it is the "Way" or *Dharma* of India, which must be realized only through inner illumination. It is a spiritual principle which was known before there was a China, an India, an America. It goes back to Creation. This "way" is the Way of the Wabanaki. *A-glamz* is perhaps the essence of that way and it doesn't translate. You have to walk the Red Road to find it.

172

GEEZOOLGH

The Algonquin people as a whole are not atheists, nor are they pantheists. The Algonquin view is inclusive, and it "includes" a supreme being, which in Micmac is called Geezoolgh. This word relates to the word *gesalk*, or love. The love we feel for God is like that we might feel for a loved one here on earth, it is that strong. There is a great invisible divine presence of love one can feel "out in the woods" which is so real you can almost touch it. If you live in *a-glamz*, i.e. "live your truth," you can see it from time to time.

The Mesquaki say, "When you have learned about love, you have learned about God."

To the Algonquin, the pine forests are God-built cathedrals where one can witness the presence of God, which the Micmac call Geezoolgh, the greatest power in the universe. It is there one can drink of its medicine directly and experience the whole big light in its purity. Fasting in the forest opens the eyes to this truth and to this light.

Wabanaki people have the greatest reverence for the sun, which is called *Neesgam*, "where you come from." Although Geezoolgh is the Creator of the universe and the Creator of the sun, we speak of Grandfather Sun as the creator too, of our own world. Algonquin people do not "worship the sun," as European visitors may have first thought. They merely are thankful. Early Europeans knew this and, in isolated pockets such as the Frisian Islands, earth-based Europeans today still give thanks in their prayers to the sun, which gives life.

The sun is the closest thing in the visible world to the nature of the One who created the universe, so we speak of it reverently. It embodies many of the qualities of the Creator. It heals us, warms us, and gives us life with its "whole big light." In the mystical journey and at death, we may travel through twelve layers in the sky and fly through the sun as if on eagle's wings, to enter into the afterworld. Even *Nagooset*, "the one who walks/shines during the day," is the messenger of the Creator, and the Wabanaki honor it constantly, in song, ceremony, and story. However, when Creation ends, the sun will be no more, yet Geezoolgh will still live on, throughout eternity.

WAITING FOR GOD

When you walk the Red Road, you allow yourself to be the tool of the Creator. It is foolish to simply take from the universe, but you can partake of the universe in a fair exchange, giving of yourself to empower Creation to continue. By doing this you become the moving hand of Geezoolgh, Its tool.

During my first *sooneywen* or "vision quest" with Grandfather Turtle, I had many dreams and visions. At one point, I saw Grandfather in the spirit world, and he said, "*Eloogoq Neesgam*! I am the tool of the Creator. I work for Geezoolgh, the Supreme Being. What It says, I do!" I could see It in him — how he stood, how he waited. He seemed perched on the tip of Now, waiting for the moment Creation would need him again.

I wanted to try it too, as an experiment. I opened my heart to Geezoolgh and asked It to tell me what to do, so that I could serve as Its vehicle. As I lay there in bed, a bit dizzy from a hard fast without food or water, I found myself out of my body, moving across Canada, flying like an eagle over trees and houses. I came to a small, square house, a strange bright shade of blue. A middle-aged man came out and waved at me, a man I had never seen before. I knew I had to find that house somewhere in the vast expanse that is Canada. I didn't know why, but I was sure it had something to do with my experiment in being the tool of the Creator. When the *sooneywen* was completed, it was soon time to go and use what I had learned. Wait on God, wait for a signal, then act upon it.

A FAIR EXCHANGE

◆ was tooling around all day in *noo-ta-ba-g'n*, "my car/my toboggan," heading south for the Maine border, seeing several houses painted this shade of blue, but none of them the same design. It was a tough test of recall and inner perception — I would pause in front of each house and wait until I received a nudge to move on.

I was driving at least fifty-five with no intentions of slowing, when I passed a little yard sale off the highway and the voice within said, "Go to that yard sale."

Geezoolgh usually speaks to us in a friendly, chatty, manner, and so I answered back, casually, "I don't do yard sales."

A little farther down the road, the voice urged me again, "Go to that yard sale," a little stronger this time.

I thought, "There wasn't that much there to buy, I'll pass. I can't stop at every dog and pony show. I've got to get to New York!"

I drove another quarter mile or so when I saw the blue house I'd dreamed about on my right, and then my inner knowing was opened up. I saw the whole life of that man at the yard sale unfold before me. I saw how strong he had been and how impoverished he was now. He was selling everything he had right down to the carpet tacks to keep food on the table.

I saw that his bad luck came from health problems and that the Creator loved this man very much. Then I saw all the gold coins — Canadian Goose Dollars — that were in my pocket. There was a lot of it and I was just going to have to trade it in at the border a few miles ahead and lose a good chunk on the exchange. It meant nothing to me, but so much to him. I was shown how I could do good work with the Creator for this man and it brought humble tears to my eyes.

I made a U-turn, took another look at the blue house, and drove back to the little yard sale: a couple of planks propped up on cement buckets, laden down with household trinkets. I swerved in. The man was smiling and showing the other people around. He seemed in good spirits. Then I noticed that the people left without buying anything. I looked around: hubcaps, bottles, books, Elvis memorials: nothing. But he seemed so happy. Was the voice wrong?

I tried to start up a conversation. "So you're retired, eh?"

"Yeah, but not for long. I hope to go back to work soon."

I asked him what happened and that's when he told me the whole story, just as I had seen it. He had been an industrious worker, and then came bacterial meningitis. While recovering, he suffered a stroke and went back to the hospital. Along the way he lost everything but his life. He said the yard sale did pretty well, but I could see otherwise.

I pulled out all the change from my pocket and started to sort it all out into stacks. There were seven gold dollars, and other coins adding up to $11.75.

I said, "I'm heading for the U.S.; I won't be needing this change. It's just an extra burden to lug around. I don't suppose you'd want to be burdened with it, would you?"

He said, "I sure would," but he made it clear that he wasn't seeking a handout and would like me to buy something with that money. I understood the feeling — there's a thin line between compassion and pity. Everything is *saseeay-whye*, a fair exchange.

I looked around for a long time. I finally bought some old matchbox toy cars and a cheese slicer. It barely came to half that, but I told him, "Keep the change."

It occurred to me that $11.75 was not going to do much to change this man's life, so I asked Geezoolgh what I could do to bring him *el-la-ba-doo Neesgam*, "the blessings of the Creator." Then I remembered the blue house.

I asked, "Who lives in that blue house down the road?"

"That's old Ernie. He runs half the town. He's a real impressive guy. A nice guy too."

I said, "Maybe he can help you. Have you ever told him your situation and asked for some kind of help?"

He said, "No, but maybe you're right. He might help. He's a good man."

I knew that if "Ernie" could see me while I was dream traveling, he must be a tool of the Creator too. I reminded him to call Ernie and gave him a "good luck" handshake, and left.

I never found out what happened with Ernie, but a few days later, I was renovating an old farm house and, while pulling down a ceiling that had been collecting dust since 1910, I found a hidden jar with ten U.S. dollars in it. It fell literally into my hands. Holding the old bills in my fingers, I realized it was more than the American equivalent of $11.75 Canadian money. It was a *saseeay-hwye*, "a fair exchange."

SEVEN LEVELS OF CREATION

First of all was Geezoolgh, or God. What Geezoolgh refers to is not quite like the God of Abraham, but more like the "Absolute I Am" of the Hindu, "Aham Brahman Asmi." It is the Supreme Being, a being of love. [32] (Geezoolgh's name has been used in vain, unfortunately, as has God's, but that's free will for you!)

Second was *Neesgam*, the sun, embodiment of the creator, then came the rocks, the third generation. Fourth came the elements: the wind, fire, water.

Fifth came the plants, including the trees and the sweetgrass and all of our medicine and food. Next was the generation of animals and birds, which included every creature but ourselves, all the hawks, crows, eagles, deer, porcupines, whales, and snakes. We are the seventh generation from Geezoolgh, so if we don't think of the seventh generation of our own kindred, why should Geezoolgh think of us? We are the last branch on that tree. The other creatures all came before us and they are our elders. We need to listen to these elders.

178

THE SEVENTH GENERATION

What is the significance of seven generations in Native American life? It is truly endless.

When we say "*nogomaq*" in the Micmac language, we are saying "all my relations," which is a native blessing. This brings to mind those we love. First is the mother and father, then the children, then the sisters and brothers, then the aunts and uncles, then the grandparents, then the grandchildren to come, and on and on to all the cousins and second cousins, to the clan or tribe, and to the nation itself, circles within circles of relations.

When we pass through the door, kneeling, into the sacred sweat lodge, we say *"nogomaq!"* so that we remember and honor where our teachings came from, and to whom we must pass on these teachings. We remember that all those around us are affected by what we do and that our blessings come from those around us, for we are all related.

Yet beyond the hoop of the Wabanaki people, we are related to all people. Every community everywhere on earth, every nation, has a unique reason for being here and we are all part of the web. Yet we have other relations that are just as important. We are related to the eagle who brings the message, related to the moose who is the elder of the forest, related to the squirrel who is the cousin of the Micmac, related to the bear who initiates us, and to all the animals and birds. We don't look down on *wee-sees*, the animals, at all. They are also our cousins and elders and we are not separate from them. We are honored to be among them that walk so close with our Creator.

Beyond the hoop of the animals, there are the tree people, the stone people, the fire, and the air and all manner of living things. Even the sky and earth are our family for they are our father and mother and we love them and take care of them. The Great Spirit lives through every thing both seen and unseen and all of these things come directly from the Grandfather. We are all grandchildren in relationship to the oldest spirit, which we call Geezoolgh.

The way I see it, the human being is the seventh generation in the chain of creation from Geezoolgh. When Glooskap was created, everything else was already here, so we are the babies of the universe. When a man is old, he has learned much. When he has reached *geezeegodwit,* which means "he is so old that he is bent over like an old pine tree ready to fall," then he has experienced just about everything and has the eagle's eye view.

In traditional times, the generations were close together. People often had children while in their teens. Women could marry and bear a child as soon as they were past the *ebeedess* stage — a sensitive and poetic word which implies "she can bear children, but probably shouldn't."

When a man was *geezeegodwit* he had known his great-grandfather, grandfather, father, brothers and sisters, sons, grandsons, and great-grandsons — seven whole generations, which is as many relations as a man can know in the span of one life. When a man has seen seven generations, he has the whole picture and can share with others all that he has learned. By the time he has seen the impact of his great-grandfather's actions on seven generations, he knows that all of his actions will affect seven as well.

The problem is that the great-grandfather is now too old to do anything about it, so he must talk to the young people who are willing to listen. He must use the teaching stories of Creation, of Glooskap's trials and errors, of lessons in his own journey, and also his visions from the Creator. He must gently persuade the younger ones to realize the things they do today will affect all their relations for seven generations, and to be mindful of every living thing.

My Great-Aunt Helen, who has been my mentor in the

Woodland ways of her Micmac people, personally knew seven generations of her own Micmac lineage, stretching across time from her grandmother Roseanna, survivor of the Julian Tribe, to my own son.

When she was a child, she lived with the fierce black-haired traditional Micmac elder Roseanna, who was not easy to live with. She knew in turn her grandmother, her famous father Bill Mewer, brother Clinton and other siblings, her son and daughter and their children and grandchildren, and also me and my son, all of whom have in some manner honored the Micmac way of life, sometimes at great risk. She, among all of us, knew the importance of what our ancestors knew and constantly prodded us to keep learning about it, keep passing on the stories. It was a constant obsession with her. She was my living link with the Julian Tribe until August of 1994 when she passed on at the age of ninety. She has seen the effects of her elders' actions upon seven generations and, after all was said and done, she valued the Native American life most highly of all.

Of course, our actions may affect the lives of our descendants many generations beyond seven, but few have lived long enough to know of their own experience and see with their own eyes if this is true or not. Seven is enough for now.

181

REBIRTH

The elders talk about being reborn after the *sooneywen* and within the lodge, but that doesn't mean we don't also experience rebirth in the literal sense. As in all things, no one is expected to take anything on faith. You have to see it to believe it, yet how do you experience the truth of reincarnation without dying? I had such a proof after my first *sooneywen.*

I left my body during the first day of the fast and fell asleep and dreamed I was a young Micmac boy. I fell into the Miramichi River and was rescued by some Scottish settlers. It was a cool day and I was soaked to the skin. They asked me if I would like to come to their cabin and have some soup. I agreed, but was scared.

I did get sick and lay under the woman's quilt for three days before I felt better. I stayed with them a while longer, sharing their interesting tools, and learning about them. I wandered out the next day to play in the woods and my grandfather stepped out from behind a tree and held my hand firmly. He looked angry. I was in trouble again!

He said, "Where have you been?"

I answered, "The people who live here rescued me when I fell in the river. They saved my life and brought me back to health."

He looked displeased and said, "That's no place for an Indian. You can't go back there. If you stay around those folks, you get dependent on their way of doing things. Sooner or later, you become weak in your traditional ways."

I went home, but asked the Great Spirit to show me a way to honor my Scottish helpers. Soon, the answer came into my head. I imagined myself planting a tree of peace, a sugar maple.

I found a sprout of a sugar maple and dug it up. I went to their cabin, showed it to them and smiled. I stood beside the door to the cabin, and said, "I'll always be thankful in my heart."

Then I walked a hundred giant paces toward the east and began digging with a digging tool I had brought with me.

I planted the maple and said in the best English I could put together, "You have been my helpers. I plant this tree to be a reminder of peace between our families. As it grows tall, let our friendship grow as well, and may the sweetness of our friendship be like the sweetness of the sap of this tree, which you may enjoy always."

I took one more look at the tree and left before my tears got the best of me.

I blinked and found myself in Grandfather Turtle's sweat lodge, just waking up. It was all a dream.

I felt as if I knew right where I had been, many miles south along the river, although I'd never been to that place in my whole life. The stern grandfather... it was Ben! Wait till I tell him! He really *is* my grandfather!

Then a disturbing thought struck me. What if I was able to *find* the spot I'd dreamt of? Would I find traces of a cabin? At that moment, I felt confident I could find it blindfolded.

Several days later, vision quest completed, I was on the highway towards America still expecting to see that spot at any time. I saw an old house along the road next to a field and something nudged me to stop. I made a u-turn and circled back. I turned onto a dirt track that led into the woods, stopped the engine, and looked around.

A big yard was on my left, some kids playing in the distance. A little boy came away from that distant farmhouse and walked toward me. His sister was still at the bottom of the long, sloping hill, standing in front of a line of pine trees. The girl called out to the young boy, who was obviously her brother. She waved her right arm slowly, dramatically, in the air, calling from the distance as if a voice from the past, "E-vaannn! O-ver h-e-e-r-e! E-vaannn! O-ver he-e-r-e!"

I thought, "What a coincidence. Her brother's name is Evan, just like mine." But the hair on the back of my neck was bristling, as if to say, "Listen with your whole body. Something is happening here."

I squinted to see the girl. She looked like my sister? ... my mother? My great-grandmother? This was no coincidence. Someone in the spirit world was going through a lot of trouble to tell me something, but what?

I stood frozen, surveying the scene, listening. "E-vaannnn!" Her ghost-like voice wafted across the distance, her arm waving like an old, slow windmill, drifting in the summer wind. "Over he-e-ere!"

"Oh my God! The cabin! The cabin is over there!" I thought. I was certain of it. A wave of chills ran up my back.

I looked at the line of pine trees again. They ran alongside the road I was now standing on, and curved all the way downhill and around the field, circling behind her. The path of reddish clay would take me there. I walked down the road, ignoring the No Trespassing signs.

I came to the point in the line of trees behind where the little girl had stood and saw a simple shed. Green grass grew everywhere, nicely mowed, except for one square area which was completely overgrown. Why?

I approached. There under the cover of wild field grass, I found what I was looking for — the foundation of the cabin. I located the doorway to the foundation and entered. I stood in the middle of the cabin floor, now overgrown with weeds, and looked down the hill to the Miramichi River and the rolling hills beyond, just as I'd dreamt it, and I cried. I was home at last.

I got on my hands and knees and dug in the dirt. Most of the foundation stones were still in place, even some flat floor stones, although covered with dirt and grass. I laughed with joy as I cried with gratitude.

I settled peacefully on those old stones, relaxing in the summer sunshine. I was sure my own Scottish ancestors had built this house a hundred and fifty years ago, and were visited by a young Micmac boy whom they wanted to raise as their son. He did become their son, their great-great-great grandson, in a future life. That boy gave them a great gift; the good will of the Micmac people, and a tree, a sugar maple...one hundred paces due east!

I jumped up out of the tall grass and looked due east. When I saw it I exclaimed, "Oh my God!" and ran toward it, my heart racing.

There, a hundred paces due east was a cluster of great old trees that had seen many a winter and, hidden in the middle of them, the oldest tree of all, an old sugar maple.

I exclaimed, "I remember planting this tree! It's all still here!"

I simply stood for a moment, as all the parts of my life and other lives fell together and tied themselves in a bow. That boy had come back home, home to find his grandfather, his land, his language, and his people, as well as his tree. He had come full circle.

EARTH-BASED SPIRITUALITY

The basis of Algonquin spirituality is the earth, *oositg-amoo*. In the beginning, the earth mother which the Creator gave us, had everything that we needed to be happy and healthy. We never had to spend a dime for anything at all; we just had to hunt, or gather, and listen to the elders. We had time to learn from experience and, most importantly, to listen to the earth. The earth talks to us if we know how to listen. The Micmac say, "You are stepping on your own medicine." As builders encroach on Micmac land, this is becoming even more true and urgent. Every time an office building goes up, a hundred different types of healing herbs are killed.

186

I once fasted for four days without food or water in a place where the earth was fresh and strong. The trees and plants began to look enlivened and "magical" as the fast went on, and the earth began to speak to me, not in words, but direct communion. Everything I wanted came to me from the earth. During that four-day ordeal, I never felt hunger or pain or dizziness, the earth's energy was so strong.

The Algonquin have a great reverence for the mother earth and put that reverence into practice. Tobacco is offered before a hole is dug into the earth and digging is only done when necessary, such as for a sacred ceremony, a burial, or other traditional purpose. Some Western Algonquins practiced "sky burials" for this reason. (The body is placed on a wooden platform where the vultures can feast on it.) Whenever a bulldozer disturbs the surface of our mother, the Algonquin feel that disturbance deep within their own body. That is one reason why the early people didn't have highways and basements. It was too painful to make them. Many Asian cultures share the same view. [33]

PROPHECY

The history of the Algonquin people is filled with prophets and prophecies, secret medicine societies, and visions of the distant past. Some of these were written in pictographs on remote rock faces in the mountains where few ever go. Others were handed down from one strong elder to another. Many tell of the coming of the white visitors and how the beloved *oositgamoo*, the great earth mother at the center of Algonquin daily life, would become sick and fall away from misuse. Stories tell of the return of Glooskap, the coming together of the tribes, and the rebirth of the ancient ones, all at the same time.

187

But the stories also tell of the white visitors coming back to the earth wisdom and sharing in the Red Road at the time when the sun changes its appearance and the earth is falling away. The sun looks different now, just as the ancient Algonquin prophecies predicted it would, because of the changes in the atmosphere. The earth's biosphere is falling away, starting with the ozone. The air is the mother's breath, but we have polluted it. The water is the mother's blood but we have poisoned it. The trees are the mother's arms, but they have gone limp and weak. The grasses are the mother's hair, but they are becoming brittle and gray with lack of good nutrition.

Is it too late? Many Algonquin people believe it is. However, some say if two white deer, a male and female, are seen roaming free in the woods together, it means the earth will come back and the human race will survive the earth changes. In a similar way, many believe the birth of a white buffalo calf (a divine symbol for Plains Indians) at the Heider Buffalo Ranch in Wisconsin in 1994 is a sign of hope for all Native Americans, for Turtle Island, and for the earth.

There is a beautiful photograph of two white deer, a male and female, roaming free in the woods, and you can see it for yourself. It's on the wall in the men's bathroom at the State Line rest stop gas station on route 90 West near West Stockbridge, Massachusetts, the last rest stop in the state.

SPIRITUAL HEALING

W hy do some native people talk about "the medicine" with such reverence? As a child I thought medicine was pills you had to swallow and foul-tasting liquids on a tablespoon. Medicine was shots from a hypodermic needle in a cold doctor's office. What's so sacred about that?

M-pe-son is a word generally translated as "medicine," which is similar (cognative) in most Algonquin languages. It could refer to the herbs which grow everywhere on the earth and are medicine for the body. They can be eaten directly, brewed as a tea, cooked with food, dried and powdered, mixed and made into a paste for poltices. Clay from the earth can be used for the poltice to help cure us. That is part of why the elders say, "You are standing on your own medicine."

Eg-tji-m-pe-son, the great medicine, is a mixture of seven healing substances which restore wholeness to the body, bringing it back into balance when nothing else will work. According to Micmac oral tradition, it includes alum bark, hornbeam, beech, wild willow, wild black cherry, ground hemlock, and red spruce.

The sweat lodge is medicine because it purifies the body to help it become whole and balanced again, but also because it is healing to the person's spirit as well. It brings our being back to a place of wholeness, a kind of spiritual healing. Praying to the four directions is medicine because it centers us in a balance of the extremes where we can find ourselves.

A vision quest or fast is medicine too, for it heals our lives and brings us back into alignment with our original instructions, what we came here to do; to complete; to make whole; or to bring into balance in the world. It helps us become medicine for others as well as ourselves. Any moment of realization or enlightenment, any opening of the heart to the Creator, is a healing, for it restores us to our original state of oneness with all life, and it's the wholeness that's holy.

189

CREATION AS IT REALLY HAPPENED

Accoring to Micmac author Ruth Holmes Whitehead, the Micmacs possess the deepest body of mythology in the world, with over 3,000 separate myths. The Micmac people trace their ancestry to the Red

Ochre people (circa 7,000 B.C.) as well as to the central Algonquin, and many date their traceable origins back 11,000 years, to the end of the last Ice Age in the region, although scholars debate specifics. In any case, the Micmacs have somehow become the inheritors of an incredibly ancient body of knowledge, and their language is considered to be close to proto-Algonquin at its core. It has many variables and alternate terms, which also indicates great age. Some call them the "Grandfather Tribe," whereas the Lenape are sometimes called the "Grandmother Tribe."

It is a delicate thing to shorten the Creation story, but after Glooskap is created, he wanders Turtle Island in the four directions and comes across Noo-ga-mi, his grandmother. "Where did you come from?" he asks. She says she came from a stone. "In the morning, when the dew lays over the rocks, I was a rock on the ground. It wasn't till noon, when Neesgam is at his strongest, that he gave me power and strength and human form. I arrived as an old woman, already wise and knowledgeable."

Likewise, Glooskap meets Nedawansum, his nephew, who was created by the sun's rays on the foam that clung to the sweetgrass by the water, and then meets Neeganaganimq(oo)zeesq, his woman, who was born from a leaf that fell on the ground and collected dew until the sun came to warm it with its rays.

Each meeting on his shamanic journey is celebrated with a feast of some sort. He honors Noogami with a feast, when a pine martin that emerges from the water agrees to be eaten. He honors Nedawansum with salmon and other fish, and honors Neeganaganimqoozeesq with nuts and herbs.

When the co-author of the *Introductory Guide to Micmac Words and Phrases,* [34] Stephen Augustine, was selected by

Parliament to represent all Canadian Native Americans in authoring the First Nations chapter of the *Unity Pact Referendum of 1993*, he brought the book with him as he met with the elders of every single nation and reserve in Canada, and told them the Creation story as it appeared there. As I understand it, each of the peoples he contacted acknowledged having a similar Creation story, although not always well known. Each of the Algonquin peoples recognized the story as their own, although Glooskap's name is sometimes Sacajaweeya, Nadabozo, Mistapeo, or Gluskabee or another name. The geographical location of his creation seems to change from one tribe to another. This Creation story became a basis for Canadian aboriginal cultural unity, although that story is just unfolding now.

Given the above, it may be one of the oldest and most widespread Creation stories on earth.

191

It is for this reason alone that I withhold judgment concerning the Bering-Strait-land-bridge theory, in spite of overwhelming evidence to support it. There is more to the story. We can only conjecture, but the people who were there have it different. It would be interesting to talk to the elders of the Eastern Siberian region and find out how Creation happened to them. Perhaps they say they came from the South, or the East, or from a "Turtle Island" where their first man was created by lightning bolts. Perhaps where Creation occurred is not important.

The implications about several "stages" of creation — the animals from the water, the nephew from the foam, and the grandmother and young woman from the dew — are mysterious to me, but the elders who taught me the Micmac stories of Creation say they are not "myths" or "legends" in the conventional sense, that they are truth and really happened, inaccuracies in translation into modern Micmac and English aside.

This insistence on literal interpretation baffled me until I read about the work scientist Louis Lerman is doing at Berkelee Labs. His "bubble theory" of biogeneration proposes that life on earth found its origin from dew and foam. For all we know, the Micmac creation story may be scientifically corroborated within a few years. I spoke with him and sent him copies of the stories and am waiting to hear from him.

According to the order of events in the story, first life came from the geosphere, then in the next stage animals came from the water. In the next stage, life came from foam on the ocean. In the next stage life came from the leaves that fell off the trees.

The order is important. The Algonquin use the maple leaf's seven points as a visual aid to help remember the order of the creation and this ancient mystical tradition is the origination of the maple leaf on the Canadian flag.

The sun is the single most important element in Micmac spirituality and is always involved in every aspect of creation. Neesgam means sun, the Creator, grandfather, and literally means "where you came from." It figures prominently in the preparation of any traditional medicine or in the performance of a ceremony of any kind. Therefore, sunlight should not be overlooked in any scientific interpretation of Micmac creation. Either ultraviolet rays or infrared light contributed the missing ingredient to the first life forms, if the Micmac stories are any indication. [35]

The Creation story is very sacred. I have been told that at one time there were no actual fixed nouns in Micmac, except those used in the Creation story. Most nouns are encoded sentence-like descriptions in which the syllables could change order, but not all those used in the Creation story.

The fact that the Creation story is more fixed than other speech possibly indicates an effort to pass on exact information in an oral tradition.

THE COLORS OF THE WHEEL

Each Algonquin nation, and even each nation within the Wabanaki circle seems to have its own color attributions for the medicine wheel. In the Micmac wheel, the East is red, the South is white, the West is yellow, and the North is black. The red represents the sun coming up in the East. The South is where there is bright summer sun. Yellow is the color of the setting sun (actually orange) and the North is black because there is so little sun there in the winter time. In the Maliseet tradition, the East is yellow, the south is red, the West is black, and the North is white (for the snow, I believe).

193

There is a wheel in which the east is red because the red-skinned people came from the East, the South is black because the dark-skinned people come from the South, the West is yellow because that is the direction the Mongolians came from — across the Bering strait, and the North is white because that is where the white-skinned Celtic and Viking people came from (see appendix).

If the native people were isolated from the rest of the world all these centuries, how would they know where all the races came from? Well, in the first place, there was no isolation. People from all over the world have visited the Micmacs over the years and have intermarried with them. One story tells of an intrepid group of Basque fishermen who arrived on Micmac shores in the early 1500s and were greeted by a Micmac elder. He called out to them first in Latin, which they could not understand. Then he tried French, and then Norse (or Old English), then Breton, then Welsh. His last attempt at communication was in the Basque language. Upon finding themselves greeted in their own mother tongue, they eagerly engaged him in conversation in Basque and never got around to finding out in how many additional languages this man could hold forth.

I believe it was these same fishermen or yet earlier visitors who were taken to a quarantine area — basically a customs house — immediately upon arrival for observation. If Columbus discovered America in 1492, how did they know so much about intercontinental travel procedures in 1498? [36]

194

WISDOM OF THE WABANAKI

Once you have grasped some part of the great teaching, it's yours. You earned it. It may be something of the ancient teaching that you see clearly and can show others how to find, or it may be something new that no one else is teaching. Either way, share it with others who seem ready. With anything living, there is always new growth and you are part of the growth of the medicine teaching. Still, there is never a need to discard any of the ancient teaching; it is there for you to build on. The *mess-keeg*, the wholeness, or universe, is big enough for all truth. We don't have to destroy someone else's to make room for our own.

When you speak your truth without demanding anything of others, you gain respect, and people start to listen to you. It doesn't mean they should do as you say, but they will be changed by being in the presence of truth and begin to seek out their own truths. If you can help people find their own truths, you will be well loved and people will "listen on the edge of their seats."

Gay-da-ch'n is knowledge, and knowing is a truly spiritual state of being. As Grandfather Turtle put it, "People can see this in you and respect it." It comes from thinking deeply and thinking big thoughts. It comes from living the good way of life and honoring the earth. It is a gift from the Creator that comes to those who have offered themselves in exchange for it. It is a knowledge that can't be written down in a book. You have to walk that path of beauty "in your own mocassins," as they say, to find it.

195

Wisdom, *unkeedasee wach'n* in Micmac, means "the state of thinking big thoughts." It means you see the greater scope of things, how it all falls together, how we are all linked together in a very wide hoop.

Confusion is the absence of wisdom. When the spirit leaves, the people become confused. When people are allowed to become confused, the spirit is driven away. The trickster enjoys that confusion so much, (s)he will work hard to keep it going. When the teachers are teaching the Wabanaki way, you often hear this word as something to notice and question. When they speak, you begin to feel the confusion leave you. Then you start to see farther and understand how things fall together. In the words of a Maliseet elder, "As the confusion leaves, our Creator will take your heart and fill it with the light of his love. Once again, this depends on you as an individual. Only you can ask for this." Cultivating *unkeedasee wach'n* is at the heart of the Red Road.

NESSTADOOLTEE-EK

esstadooltee-ek means "we all understand one another." It is a philosophical kinship Algonquin people often feel (and sometimes don't feel) when meeting one another for the first time. It is how I feel when I talk with elders who are strong in their traditional ways. *Abeydan-idtch dan-wey-daik* is a popular phrase that brings the people together into unity, which means "going back to traditional ways" (literally: the past). But *nesstadooltee-ek* transcends this, for even native people who have taken to the cities to contribute to the world of politics or business or music and who may have translated their belief system into very untraditional ways, can still meet another native person on the street and feel *nesstadooltee-ek*.

When I meet a stranger and feel a certain profound *nesstadooltee-ek* with them I will sometimes begin to teach them about the Micmac language without really thinking about why. Five times in the past two years these people, all of whom have been successful professionals living in lower New York (far away from Acadia) have later had it revealed to them by various means that they have Micmac ancestry, but only after learning about the Micmac language. One case even involved the dramatic family revelation, "It's time we told you — you were adopted!"

Nesstadooltee-ek can be very specific like that, but it can also be general and far-reaching. Anyone who lives an earth-oriented lifestyle and honors the cycles of nature in daily life can share in this greater "we all understand one another" spirit with the Wabanaki people, whether they are Celtic, Slavic, Sephardic, Breton, Congolese, Kurdish, Indonesian, Tuscan, Baltic, Frisian, or any other ethnic group. We all have a place on the wheel, we just have to accept ourselves for who we really are and understand ourselves; then we can understand one another.

WABANAKI THOUGHT

◆

I f I were to refer to the Way of the Wabanaki as a "philosophy," I would be using the term literally. It means "love of wisdom," which seems to hit the mark. But in modern English, it has a connotation of something theoretical and speculative. I might occasionally indulge in this kind of philosophical musing, but not the Wabanaki. The Wabanaki are not theoretical. Everything is tested by experience, through trial and error. With that kind of procedure, you can't go too far wrong.

197

The Way of the Wabanaki is not liberal or conservative, but a mixture of both. They are liberal in that they believe in sharing the wealth communally. They believe in weak central government and much civil liberty (an Algonquin concept which was new to Europe in the 1700s). However they are not into quick-fix programs that are based on an idealistic theory. Things are handled on an individual basis. The Wabanaki could just as easily be described as conservative. The elders usually choose only the tried and true; they test everything, and go slow, to make sure it really works. They profess working for what you receive, and they maintain respect for tradition.

The Wabanaki philosophy is, "Don't throw out the old, build on it." Although conservative, traditional leaders are not inclined to abuse power, invent monarchies, or indulge in an us-over-them attitude. *Unk-kee-das-seen* is to think — not harder, but bigger — more expansively. When your scope of thought is big, you can slowly begin to see how everything relates, how things should relate, and where they don't quite yet. Everything that is here belongs here, but there are certainly improvements we can make. That's one way of being a co-creator.

The Wabanaki are generally neither pro-Christian nor anti-Christian, though sentiments differ greatly. Most elders respect Jesus and talk of the white prophet who walked across this land a long time ago, but have a mistrust of any church or institution where there are lots of rules.

198

The Wabanaki have a gift for thinking big thoughts, but are not frontal-cortex oriented, in my observation. They tend to have more trust in the central brain processes, which are more intuitive, holistic, and non-linear.

Thoughts are acted out and this prevents mistakes. For example, if a meeting was to be held three days from now, the runners would hold three sticks and destroy one for each day that passed. In this way, time was made visible and no mistakes were made.

Sociologists have been wondering why depression statistics double every five years in urban and suburban areas, and why depression and anxiety are absent among the Mayori and most other hunting and gathering peoples around the world. Perhaps it is their practice of acting everything out; perhaps it is the practice of thinking big thoughts in order to put things in perspective; perhaps it is a sense of community and meaningful context. And perhaps it is simply that in such countries, there's no word for time.

WAMPUM

Micmac and other Algonquin people traded in shell beads, called *wap-pa-bee-el*, or "wampum," for centuries before contact with Europe. Wampum was used for jewelry but I gather wearing wampum was not just fun and games. Wampum was hard currency, and the Pequotanog of Connecticut (and other native people of Long Island Sound), whose local shells were considered the most valuable, became very wealthy in a native context. The financial success enjoyed by the Pequot today is traditional for them. They are walking in the way of their ancestors.

199

The Micmac people were always aggressive traders, with a large non-military population to sustain. During the 1500s and on into the end of the seventeenth century, Micmacs acquired control of the fur industry in the Northeast and were involved in heavy trading throughout the area. Trappers from Europe had to learn the Micmac language to really succeed, and Micmacs were prosperous.

Today, most Micmac people are eager to *sasee-eh-whyn,* or exchange goods with people; however, money has taken on a bad name (as it has with many Native Americans). Money has never been fairly distributed among the "white" and "red" people in America and has led to much corruption, as has the desire for permanent control of property.

Most Wabanaki people are not shy about asking for money for goods if no trade seems likely, but are extremely careful in discussing money in the context of tradition or "medicine." Money is not sacred. Money does not come from God and does not go back to God, but your sincere effort in acquiring it does count for a lot. Tobacco is a proper gift for the spirit and for the Creator.

Many Micmac people are successful in business as was my Micmac great-grandfather, yet I have noticed a startling difference in the use of money between traditional Wabanaki people and modern, or non-traditional people. The Wabanaki do not use money as a security blanket or cushion against loss. Money is like food, something to be spent (or not spent) in a way that nurtures the spirit and the body. To the traditional Micmac, money is like fish: you get a little every day and stay happy. You pile it up in a secret place and something starts to stink. You can't hoard fish, but you know where to find it and how to get it when you need to.

The modern person spends money for bodily or emotional comfort, thinks always of tomorrow, "retirement," the mortgage, etc., and spends according to how much is in the bank as opposed to finding what he or she really wants and acquiring the means to get it, through trade or exchange of money, or perhaps through ritual. While the modern person worries about the future, the traditional elder only exists in the now. This is why some traditional elders don't have bank accounts; their money is only in the now too.

STILL THE SAME

The Algonquin people still live the same way as they did hundreds of years ago, only, being an adaptable and open-minded people and being unusually sensitive and attuned to their environment, they have adapted their customs to modern times without losing their essence. Instead of trading wampum and quillwork for furs, an Algonquin man may trade an old van for a serviceable motorcycle, or a hind of deer for a couple of good tools. Instead of wandering on foot from season to season across the Maritimes following the herds, the modern Micmac provider may wander in a van from Texas to California to Alberta, following the craft shows and pow-wows. Today's Algonquin woman may work an office job gathering a paycheck instead of herbs, but she would at least request a leave of absence if her elder or mother or father got sick and needed her healing attention, as would a man in the same position. The family is the basic institution of native life and no other comes before it. The reverence for one's elders is still as strong as ever — the eldest is offered the best first and almost always chooses to share with others according to their wisdom. The elders are well taken care of, for such a store of experience and wisdom is a rare and precious thing. By that time, they have seen seven generations and know what will be best for the future of all the people.

NO WORD FOR PROGRESS

Although the ancient Greeks understood the body-mind-spirit connection, Western sciences are just now beginning to figure out how things work through rationalism. As the information boom happens and one breakthrough rapidly leads to another, they are slowly coming closer to a picture of the world which the Algonquin people knew a thousand years ago, judging by the language. It is now trendy for psychologists to talk about the "body-mind-spirit" continuum, because it is shown that the healthy person is able to integrate all three, that the boundaries between the body and the mind are impossible to locate, as are the boundaries between the mind and the spirit. This new emerging picture is the science of "holism." The thousands-year-old Micmac word for body-mind-spirit is *uch-tup*. *Unk-tup* on the other hand means "the thing I use to think with," which is specific to the brain-mind functions. The word for holism is *op-set-go-weh*, which means "everything together" or "the all-in-all," another word thousands of years old.

I have found that most of the crazy ideas held by the Micmacs over thousands of years are now becoming more reasonable. For example, in Micmac language and culture, everything is always relative, time is always relative, good and bad are relative. The language was a study in botanical ecology long before Earth Day.

For example, there is no Micmac word equivalent to "earth," in the English sense, although the word earth is always used several times in any pseudo-Indian prayer. In Micmac you must

202

distinguish between *mahamaygo* (the geosphere) and *oositgamoo* (the biosphere). There is also Noogami, the grandmother of the earth (of stones), and there is Gidjou, the mother, whose trees and colorful flowers of the biosphere we enjoy. The rock mantle is "grandmother," while the biosphere is "mother earth" according to the Micmac language. Native people realize that the layers of rock far beneath the earth are much older than those near the surface, and this is one reason why pipestone and certain other kinds of rocks are more sacred than others, because they were created first and are older.

The more I understand Micmac words the less I understand the meaning of the English word "progress."

THE SACRED PIPE

The sacred pipe was given to the native people by White Buffalo Calf Woman thousands of years ago, along with an oral tradition of teaching. This teaching and the pipe itself help keep native society intact and connected with the Creator.

The Chippewa Medicine Society has been underground a hundred years, but its modern counterpart still passes down the medicine teaching today. It is very important that it remain an oral teaching. Anthropologists are not generally allowed to share this information because of its uniquely personal nature. It is not for sale and not for study.

As a pipe carrier I consider myself very fortunate. I carry the pipe basically for my family and loved ones and speak of it seldom. Those who know how to ask for help in a traditional manner will not be turned away, and no charge is demanded.

One cannot write about the pipe. One can only write about what the pipe is not. It is not ever intended for smoking marijuana or other illicit drugs. It is not meant to be boasted about or taken up without initiation and training. It is not meant to be used in anger. It is not meant to be used to make money, or other selfish goals. It is not a souvenir. It is simply to connect the person with their heart and their people, and to connect the heart with heaven and earth in a sacred manner.

THE NEXT STEP ON THE JOURNEY

204

As with all journeys, there is always another step to take, but the sincere elders will usually take you one step at a time beyond the place where you are and no further. They are not interested in wowing the wandering thrillseeker with miracles and mind-blowing ideas, and prefer to wait until the right question is asked. Since I am often asked about the Red Road, I have written about what is easiest to understand. But in order to do justice to the subject, I have to mention that there is much more to it than simply honoring the four directions of the wheel, for the teaching goes beyond the wheel as it is lived on this physical plane, and beyond the sky and the earth. There is a seventh direction and it is invisible.

The teaching of the Micmac medicine wheel begins in the East, with the awakening of all life at sunrise, a time when the birds begin their songful praying in thanks to the Creator for the splendor of creation. But the medicine wheel also ends in the East as well, and the gateway of the East is also the gateway of death, which invites the separation of the spirit from the physical body, the lone journey of the individual spirit back to God of which it is a radiant part. There are many elders in any tribe or nation who can help one prepare for this journey but these teachers can only take you so far. Becoming as one with Geezoolgh, the Great Mystery, is an individual experience. It is a journey one must enter into with purity and humility, alone, surrounded only by Geezoolgh's influence, and no other. No other person can enter with you into a place where there is no separation, and in that place there is only one being to begin with and always has been. What changes is only the realization of it and no one can give you a realization.

While the spiritual teachers speak of honoring Creation and all four directions, they know that we are here for only a short time, to fulfill our tasks and be done, but that God is eternal and a person's spirit goes on forever; that the Red Road is a path of beauty in this physical world, but that there is a greater path to which it leads — the path through the stars, the world beyond the sun.

The four directions are equal, but the eastern door leads to other wheels and other worlds, which will outlast this one as a maple tree outlasts its leaves. This is why the *sooneywen* (You Humble Yourself) fasting, or vision quest, is so important. When you reach the eastern door, it is time to let go of the things of the physical world, to forget food and water and become a ghost to this world so that you enter into the spirit world through that door. Then you can be reborn from out of that world with your eyes opened to what is really happening here. The spirit world is many times greater than this earth. Even though we cherish the mother with all our heart, the spirit world is at the heart of what reality is, *dellia'o-weh*, of things as they are, both here and in the *hwa-so'q*, the Whole Big Light of Heaven.

The elders tell us to slow down our thinking, to drop the "fast mind," so that spirit can catch up to us. They tell us not to think so hard, not to worry so much about tomorrow, and to trust and become more childlike instead. This humbling of the self is "turning toward the East." In order to see things of the spirit world and see where that Red Road is taking us, we need to turn toward the East once in a while and turn away from the physical self, entrusting its concerns to the arms of the loving mother.

206

CULTURAL COMPARISONS

As I was growing up, I was aware that I possessed Micmac Indian ancestry but was not clear as to what that meant. Like many young men, I was looking for a value system, a spiritual path that fit me, but was told that the Micmac people were extinct and their way of life wiped from man's memory. I was also told that the Native American lifestyle was no longer relevant or possible on this earth; that it had, like an old dog, had its day. I actually believed this... but wondered.

I probably explored every major religion in the world for pieces of the truth that rang true to my nature. When I finally made contact with the living tradition of the Wabanaki people,

I found it not only very lively, but full of wisdom as well and very relevant to these times of ecologic rethinking. I also found parallels between Wabanaki belief and those of peoples elsewhere in the world which had interested me in the past. Some elders discourage any parallels, saying truthfully that all cultures are unique. But we are all human and humanity is a mystery yet to be solved, so I have pointed out these remarkable parallels, in case it adds a piece to the world mosaic of cultural diversity before it gets lost in the monoculture of mass media. Parallels between Asian and Native American traditions do not prove that they are of common origin, nor of origin in Asia, and comparisons do not imply a value judgement on my part.

For those who are interested, here are a few more comparisons.

207

FIRE AND THE SUN

In northwest India, before there were the Vedas, there were aboriginal pre-Aryan people, Dravidian people living a native lifestyle. The Aryans entered the region and, though some say there was no great battle, the Dravidian culture was totally absorbed. The Vedas were a later mixing of Aryan and Dravidian wisdom as it had survived. If you believe in a second, more recent migration across the Bering Strait, there is this possibility of a cultural link between the Indic people and the Algonquins, as well as other early tribal people of Asia we know little about.

In the most ancient Vedic hymns, there is an indication that the cosmos proceeds out of ritual sacrifice, *Rta*. The first hymn in the Vedas was to *Agni*, fire, the messenger of the Gods. *Ghee* (liquefied butter) and certain grains, were sacrificed into the fire, as part of the ongoing process of Creation, echoing the beginning of the universe. The importance of fire lessened greatly in most later Brahminic schools, but Agni Yoga, as taught by Nicholas Roerich and others, preserves the spirit of the early teachings. The fire ceremony is used today for marriages and funeral services, as well as the cremation itself, but it is of a social-ceremonial nature.

Early Indic people honored the sun as it rode on its chariot of fire around the world. Vishnu is a name for the solar deity, but this too, along with the fire ceremony, has been lost during the last two millennia. There are many hymns to the dawn and many ragas specific to dawn, and there are parallels to the sunrise pipe ceremonies and songs of the Wabanaki, but these are only natural, due to the tendency of people living outdoors to awaken at dawn.

Zoroastrianism, Mithraism, and related beliefs honor the sun above all and maintain the fire ceremony as a central part of ritual practice. This tradition seems more closely parallel to the Wabanaki reverence to the sun and to fire, and may itself be linked to the practices of the earliest Asian peoples. The early Celts shared with the Zoroastrians a special sense of significance of the sun on a hill, and set beacon fires on hilltops to invoke the powers of the sun. Both are linked by Indo-European origins.

I found in my own experience through fasting and keeping the fire, that the fire spirit is best evoked from the east, the direction of the sun. They are essentially the same spirit. In Micmac traditional teaching, the sun is also a messenger, as is

208

fire, and brings the message at dawn which relates to the questions of the previous dawning. The Wabanaki offering of tobacco is made into the fire, lovingly, with great care. The fire is a messenger (as it is elsewhere in the world), and the smoke goes up to the Medicine Man who is "up there," The grandfather spirit, Niskam, who hears our prayers and helps us.

In Theravadan Buddhism, the Buddha is often depicted in statues lying on his left side, the side of the heart, with his head propped on his elbows, contemplating. This is an ancient traditional position of healing, prayer, and contemplation which may survive from pre-Buddhist or even prehistoric times. Thousands of miles away, among the Wabanaki people of the Maritimes, fasters are instructed to stay in the lodge after the sweat and lie on their left side with their head propped up, in the same position to better speak as one with the Creator. Is it that the human body is best relaxed in this position? Is it spiritually optimal to have the heart at the lowest point of gravity? If so, where is the European equivalent in sacred lore?

209

THE SACRED CIRCLE

T he Vedic traditions have honored the circle as sacred for thousands of years. Their word for circle is mandala, but this word has taken on many layers of new meaning through the millennia. Some Vedic books of hymns were called mandalas, as were some dances. In ancient times the early Vedic Brahmins would draw a simple circle around themselves to create a sacred space. As the Rig Veda developed, this cosmological space was broken off into smaller and smaller parts until it became a complex pattern like today's visually arresting mandalas. All this breaking up into parts is associated with Tantra, the living of life, and symbolically at least honors diversity and the "ten thousand things" as it is described in Taoism. This side of life is very much in harmony with native teaching.

There are many parallels between Wabanaki Indians and Asian Indians, but any common link must have been long ago before the arrival of the Aryans into the Indus Valley. I'm sure most Micmacs today would not be happy at all being Hindus in any Brahminic system. Modern Hinduism has developed in a very different direction from the Wabanaki way and from their own Dravidian roots as well.

In Tibetan Bonpo tradition, which is part of an ancient Siberian culture, there are circles and elaborate mandalas like the Hindu, but the directions have color attributes, as do Chinese and most Native American traditions.

Whatever the colors, each Native American family knows in the depth of their being the sacredness of the circle. Eggs, nests, ponds, holes, tree trunks, all are circles. The sun is a circle, and the grandmother moon at her height is a circle too. The wheel of life, from birth, to youth, to adulthood, to old age, to death and rebirth is a circle. The wheel of the year is a circle too. Our eyes have circles, our nostrils are circles, our ears contain spirals; circles are everywhere.

The troubled native person may spread tobacco in a thin line while chanting, making a circle around himself that unwanted spirits cannot go past. Native people meet in sacred circles, talking feather circles, medicine wheel circles, or council circles. Wigwams and sweat lodges make a circle on the earth. Fires create circles in the grass.

Creating a sacred space with a circle of some kind is one of the most universal rites in mankind's history, [37] but each time the Wabanaki traditional person creates that sacred space, it is the first time. It is real. It is powerful.

The five sacred rites of yoga, as practiced in the remote regions of the north of India today, are based on spiraling motions, the circle in the context of time and space. The Wabanaki don't have a yoga system of exercise, but as they do their hard daily work, they always move in a clockwise spiral, which honors the path of the sun and keeps them moving in a spiral or circle during the course of the day. In a sense, each activity becomes a poem, an ode to the sun, our grandfather.

211

THE FOUR DIRECTIONS

According to Carl Jung, the oldest known mandala was a paleolithic "sun wheel" found in Rhodesia and, like the medicine wheel of today, it too expressed the "fourness" of things. This fourness is expressed by a single Micmac word, *naul-ql*, literally "four of anything" or "fourness."

The Wabanaki taught me to pray and give thanks to the four directions, without explaining a million reasons why, but I've found that it keeps life in balance. There are different directions we need to go in life, but we can't think about them all at the same time any more than we can face the moon and the sun at the same time. When we go around the wheel, we are induced into honoring the variety of the world and of ourselves. I've noticed that the spiritual direction in life — going alone to the Creator and withdrawing from relationships and daily goals — is opposite to the direction of relationships — love, community, reaching out to others. You can't focus on both at once, but you need both, and are both part of the same wheel. Likewise, there is a direction in life of thought and planning ahead and an opposite direction of mystery and surrender. There is a direction of celebration and making things and one of diving into the darkness of meditation, of "sitting in your chair and going somewhere," leaving the body and journeying within. We need both, but in order to do a good job, we need to use one-pointed attention. The medicine wheel shows us how to do this.

During the ancient Micmac *sooneywen*, or vision quest, as some call it, the quester is treated as one who has died. Those who see him do not look. He is not touched by anyone, even the elders. He fasts to destroy the little ego self to "speak as one" with the Great Spirit. He contacts the wise spirit of the South, the grandfather eagle, on the first day. The color is white. On the second day he contacts the spirit of the West, the loving grandmother who brings the healing. Her color is yellow. On the third day he contacts the strong bear of the North, of the lodge and the ancestors. His color is black. On the fourth day, he contacts the grandfather spirit of the East, Neesgam, the Creator. Its color is red. There are four gatekeepers, one for each of these directions as well. [38]

If the quester does this, he will earn the wisdom and the answers he is looking for. He will be reborn in the spirit. In the Micmac wheel, East is fire, South is air, West is water, and North is earth, which corresponds exactly with the ancient *Fu-Hsi* trigrams of the *I Ching*.

Most Native American medicine people say that each person has a soul, called a "spirit," which survives death. This soul concept in Wabanaki culture is more akin to the Hindu *atman* than the Buddhist concept of no-self. In Micmac, the soul is called *uch-ji-ja-cha-mitj,* which means "shadow." There is also a "blood soul," which isn't spoken of today too much, but which was important long ago.

According to Carl Jung, many cultures speak of a shadow soul and a body soul. Jung equates this with his "animus" and "anima" theory and notes the same existing in ancient Chinese culture. In Chinese, *hun* is the light soul, which is yang, whereas *po* is the dark soul, the shadow soul, which is yin.

The Wabanaki belief is that people come back to progress along the medicine wheel over many lifetimes, but this is a joyous dance, not a curse. When one comes back as a pure being, one may reach the age of fifteen and not experience any loss of innocence, but continue till death with a childlike heart. That is the last lifetime, unless he or she chooses to come back to help the native people, as Glooskap our ancestor does.

213

TOOLS OF THE CREATOR

At the end of the Bhagavad Gita, Krishna teaches Arjuna, "You are merely an instrument of the divine." Rumi later took this up in his Masnavi, "the Reed of God." In Micmac we say "*Eloogoq Neesgam,*" "(I am) the tool of the Creator."

In the ancient Bhakti tradition in India, Bhaga is a share in the food of the gods as it has been sacrificed to the fire. The

Bhakti devotee is one who shares in the Godhead, an intimate participation in the absolute beginning, by sharing the Bhaga. Again this goes back to sacrifice as the act of Creation. Later Bhaktis elaborated on this theme. It is the Bhagavan who possesses bhaga, and each of these are ones who are filled with love and devotion to the One. They are instruments of that One, and of their "elders" (the guru). They are "tools of the Creator" in a way that is right for their people. Among these Bhakti devotees were Baul singers, those who were divinely inspired to walk through the village singing songs in honor of the tribal deities of India.

In a comparable fashion, the medicine people of the Red Road are filled with love and devotion to the One, the great circle of life. They are given tobacco to sacrifice to the fire to cause Creation to continue, yet they are allowed to share in the offering, to smoke it in their own pipe. They participate with the ongoing process of life, and yet are only the instrument, *Eloogoq Neesgam*. They honor the sun in everything they do, and work for the good of all the people.

Both the Bhakti singer and the pipe carrier teach that we are all tools of the Creator; to be conscious of it every moment and try to demonstrate that way of life by example: "Walk what you talk," to put it in native terms.

There is some dispute as to the history of the Wabanaki pipe carrier tradition, but I've been told that the Western Cree, the Algonquin allies and western neighbors of the Wabanaki, were given the pipe by White Buffalo Calf Woman at the same time as the Lakota. In the old days, the Cree pipe carrier, like the Baul singer, went from place to place letting his hair grow long, offering teaching to anyone who asked for it, hoping but never asking for anything for himself. Of course, the people of India realized that it was up to them to feed the Baul singer, for the Bhakti renunciate was at the mercy of God and would not provide for himself, but relied on the love of all the people. Likewise, the Wabanaki people took care of their pipe carriers, offering them gifts and food and shelter wherever they went.

When the communal tradition of taking in holy beggars dies, part of Indian wisdom will die with it, for then the teachings will have to be traded for money or disappear. When this happens, the teachings become a commodity and go to the highest bidder. But the needs of the Bhakti *sadhu* or holy man are so simple, even a simple family can provide them, as long as tradition is in place.

Today in the Native American world, there is unrest over the manner in which the pipe carriers conduct themselves. They are criticized by some for accepting travel and food money and the other expenses that go with living in America, but these same critics will not take pipe carriers into their homes and provide for them. It is a difficult time for all. I know two or three native teachers who do this in the United States and manage to keep teaching, living the mendicant life, and going from family to family, but it seems to have become a life more full of conflict than harmony. Most pipe carriers today try to balance out their spiritual healing work with their jobs and with family duties. Either way, the cost of cars, auto repairs, insurance, licenses, and phones seems to stand in the way of the Wabanaki pipe carrier.

MASTER OF THE HUNT

The Wabanaki are the descendants of hunting people. They have always revered animals and looked to them for wisdom. The Wabanaki are historically close to the roots of shamanism, a way of life in which communication with animal spirits is beneficial. Wabanaki animal lore is for Wabanaki people only. I don't consider it urgent to pass on, but it is extremely important for all human beings to respect animals and their ways. Most cultures have animal rites of some kind at their root, if you go far enough back in time.

Everyone associates Native Americans and the shamanic teachings with reverence and respect for the power of animals, but India's cosmology owes a lot to animals as well. Again, the farther back in time you go, the more in common each culture has with the Native American.

Twelve thousand years ago, the protector and spiritual guide of the paleolithic people of Europe was the Master of the Hunt. In Dravidian culture, over 4,000 years ago in what is now India, a whole mystery school developed around the Master of Animals later known as Pashupati, Lord of Beasts. Only after the Vedic period (1500 to 500 B.C.), Pashupati evolved into Siva himself, the grandfather of many subsequent religious figures. [39] These mystery schools taught people who knew from childhood the basics of well-grounded living: fundamental wandering in the woods, or Eye-Hand Coordination 101. The teacher who noticed the occasional initiate lacking in these skills took it upon himself to correct the situation before moving on to the esoteric lore we now associate with mystery schools, as well as certain animistic traditions. There was a shared foundation of natural understanding which they were able to build on. The Tibetan lamas call this "foundation practice."

Tibetan Buddhism still carries on both animistic and esoteric traditions, but when teaching novices of European descent, they wisely focus on what is called "foundation practice," centering on the breath, chanting, compassion, and humility.

Shamanism, which was spread via the Inuit around the Arctic Circle and southward to the native peoples of many lands, is based on communication with animal spirits and recognizes the "master of the hunt" in another form. It has been said, therefore, that animal spiritualism may be the basis of the world's religions, including Hinduism and Tibetan Buddhism. Zeus, Dionysus, Cernunnos, Hern, and other gods evolved from the Caucasus Master of the Hunt. The early mystery schools transcended, but never lost touch with the animal aspect of human life. It is the source of our energy, creativity, and will to live. Animals know how to be what they are. [40]

217

INDIVIDUAL CHOICES

Not every native person of Algonquin descent lives an exemplary life of what I call the "Way of the Algonquin" but each person seems to express certain aspects of these sacred teaching in his or her own way. I do not hold up these people, or any one person, as better than the people of other paths and cultures. However, I do not know of any belief system anywhere in the world that makes more sense, has more answers, or that is more artistically and emotionally satisfying than this one which comes down to us from neolithic times and beyond.

The flaws of the Algonquin people are individual and adaptive, they are their own. Yet according to the medicine teaching, there is no bad person, no crazy person; each person's flaws are part of the wheel of life, which is itself flawless. Each person's struggles are a great mystery to be revealed, each struggle becomes a story, each story becomes teaching, each teaching becomes medicine, and medicine makes the people whole and well in spirit.

NOT ALL SAINTS

218

From reading this little collection of thoughts on the native way of life, you may conclude that all native people are saintly and sweet and never have any problems. Actually, this may come as a shock, but even the Algonquin are not perfect!

What is so wonderful is the medicine teaching which has come down to us from the ancient ones. This is what is so precious. This is not different from the teachings that were handed down to other peoples elsewhere on earth, from the beginning of time, but many of these teachings were lost and replaced by spiritual theories which do not arise from the natural universe, they are from people's heads.

When people make mistakes, you can look and see if their mistakes come from the teachings, or if they come only from the people. Some teachings lead people to make mistakes. Algonquin tradition teaches a good way of life and what I have presented here is the way given the Wabanaki people. There are many Wabanaki people today who do not know this way of life or know it and choose not to follow it, perhaps a majority. That is their choice; it does not make them less Algonquin, because to be of "We the People" is to always know your own mind and follow your own path.

However, there are a growing number of people who follow the medicine path who are learning these ways and, for them, it is very powerful. Even among them, many mistakes are made, but those mistakes are their own and do not arise from errors in the teaching. Each mistake, each misunderstanding of natural law, becomes a step on the path of learning. Any person with native blood can see and speak with the great teachers from the times when everyone on this land followed the Red Road. Their spirits are still here. Many people see them, especially at this time, when the earth is calling the children back home.

I met a woman at a lecture who told me her brother was recently murdered by three Native Americans. I knew they weren't Wabanaki, but they could have been, so I didn't duck the question. It was a terrible thing to happen. If the native way is so good, why did these three people kill her crippled brother?

I reminded her that all people have free will and that any person can choose to turn his back on the Red Road. It's not the fault of the teaching. She admitted to feeling rage and anger against these three "brothers." I answered it was good for her to feel angry for now, but to be angry at those lost brothers, not at the teaching of their ancestors.

Then this woman, whose own blood contained native blood

219

too, answered her own question. In the circle we had, she had a vision of an ancient native teacher spirit, a strong elder, with large hands. He took her to the sky and showed her the silver-shining path of the river of life flowing on beneath her. The river of life flows ever on. You can dam it up for a while, but it always finds a way to return to the ocean. It is its destiny.

Later on, she found that her struggle was not with "Indians," but with the nature of humanity. The Native American murder suspects were found innocent, themselves victims of another man's treachery.

There is occasional unrest today on the reservations of the Wabanaki people. Their spirits have been dammed up for a long time. There is unhappiness with the government, there is occasional violence against white people. There are problems with drugs and alcohol and crime everywhere and yet the medicine way is growing by leaps and bounds. I discourage people from invading the privacy of the Wabanaki people without a personal contact and introduction. Some of the powwows and gatherings in the region are now closed. It is sad in a way, but it is a necessary stage, while the people find themselves again in a new light. I hope it is the birth pangs of a new great nation.

220

AFTERWORD

For me, writing is becoming. My books are teachers to me. Three summers and more have passed since *No Word for Time* was first published, yet still it teaches me. Ironically, my life became a very busy one almost as soon as the book was released, and time has become a point of discussion ever since, a contested boundary line between two worlds. I guess that is my offering as well as my lesson. How many ways can you find to remember that there's no "time" when so many want to borrow it? Not that I mind; spending time with people is my favorite pastime, next to spending time alone in the wilderness. I'm grateful that this message spoke to so many hearts. At the time I first wrote it, I only knew that the material spoke to my own heart.

Since the book's publication, I've driven over 120,000 miles, talking to people about Algonquin values and trying to find out how Micmac people such as myself fit into that immense cultural design called the Algonquin Civilization. On the way, I spent a lot of time in local libraries, history rooms, and used bookstores across the country. What I discovered was that, before Columbus ever got on a boat, a united states of Algonquin-speaking North America, a confederacy of self-governing hoops within hoops, once spanned the continent. This confederacy was united by kinship, stories, and language. Their population centers were the templates for our own: The regions of New York City, Philadelphia, and Detroit all had Algonquin populations in the tens of thousands in the 1500s. Their trails are now some of our major highways. Eleven of the

fifty states and three of Canada's thirteen provinces bear names
that refer to Algonquin people, places, and things. The new,
expanded Appendix B lists about four hundred of these
Algonquin-related subtribes, bands, and nations as well as what
they call themselves and how they are related. Yet this shows
only the faintest outline of what was cut down by disease and
the fires of war just as it was blossoming into its golden age,
inspired in part by the Algonquin's increasing contact with
white explorers, much as they had been inspired by contact
with their resourceful Cherokee, Iroquoian, Siouian, and
Muskegian neighbors in early times.

Where did all those Algonquin people go? Their children are
still here, but today we know them as individuals, not as face-
less digits on reservation rolls. That is as it should be. They contribute to every discipline and walk of life. I have compiled over
two hundred biographies of such Algonquin descendants. Some
are household names, some are not; some are among the living,
some are not; some are heroes, some are not. Among the better
known are Buffy Saint Marie (Cree), Winona La Duke
(Chippewa), Jim Thorpe (Sac and Fox), A's pitcher Chief
Charles Bender (Ojibway), Ben Nighthorse Campbell
(Northern Cheyenne), Wayne Newton (Powhatan), Mrs.
Woodrow Wilson (Edith Galt Wilson, Powhatan),
Pocahontas (Powhatan), Roy Rogers (Mesquakee), and Joe
Bruchac (Abenaki). Some important Algonquins are not yet
household names: Ingrid Washinawatok and Albert Lightning,
for example.

Many of the great war chiefs and peacemakers of the late
1700s and early 1800s were of the Algonquin nations: Pontiac
(Ottawa), Tecumseh (Shawnee), Black Hawk (Sac and Fox),

Teedyeskung (Lenape), Tamanend (Lenape), and Dull Knife (Cheyenne). The inventor of the potato chip, George Crum, was Mohican, and there is reason to believe that Clara Barton may have been the offspring of an adopted Algonquin.

Much has happened in the last three years. As I've mentioned above, I've deepened my knowledge of Algonquin civilization. I also have become a professor of Native American history, among other subjects, and have learned the deeper meaning of the word *deadline*, as I try to satisfy academic standards of clock-driven living. Over these same years, Grandfather Turtle has been able to open a healing retreat at his own reserve. His assistant has become involved with a number of projects, including the release of a successful CD of his own songs, and the writing of a book about his own journey, which is still in progress. When I read parts of his book, I was amazed at the ease with which he sidestepped many of the problems with which English-speaking writers such as myself struggle, by sticking close to his own natural manner of speaking and story-telling. It is a good book, one I hope to see published some day.

It wasn't until Grandfather Turtle's birthday that I was able to present him with the published edition of *No Word for Time*, and also give him a brightly beaded "Native American" wrist-watch, as a joke. I thanked him for introducing me to the world of no time and apologized for dragging him into a wrist-watch world of time where there were such things as birthdays. He thought it was pretty funny, and put the watch on his wrist. I doubt that he ever really "used" it or the book, but he seemed happy. I never saw either object again.

During the last three years, much has happened for my family as well. My sister has worked harder and closer than ever

223

before with native people of many nations and has earned a place of respect in countless hearts with her songs and her down-to-earth Micmac teachings and advice, which she gives freely and often, to her younger *en-tchee-ga-nam* (brother) in particular.

My parents both embrace the path of the Red Road now, and it has only made them better teachers for me. I know that because of this, we all embrace each other as a family more than before. Much to their surprise, they've also been adopted by a number of others as foster clan parents in recent years. A few years back when I led their fiftieth anniversary remarriage cere- mony Micmac style, many of their volunteer children and many old friends as well were standing in the circle. It was quite an experience for me. How many people get to join their own parents' hands in marriage, surrounded by so many broth- ers and sisters? Strong teachings have made us a stronger family.
        ****

I chose the title *No Word for Time* as a reference point for both linguistics and natural philosophy, but now people often ask me to speak about the nature of time, and what I've learned about it. It is hard to explain a "nothing" to an object-oriented society. Therefore I explain native time as a "thing" — actually two things: there's a natural time and a spiritual time, and we walk in balance between the two, just as we strive to walk in balance between heaven and earth. Natural time I describe as horizontal, and spiritual time I call vertical. At least it makes people think and scratch their heads. Horizontal time is the progression of moments from the past, forward toward the future. Vertical time progresses from the heart of the Creator through us, his children, and straight through us to the heart of

the Mother Earth. That is the path our dreams take and that is the "time" of now in which we really live, move, and have our being. One is internal, one external. Both are real, more or less.

What becomes less and less real is "clock" time. Indigenous people all over the world honor the rhythm of the seasons — cyclical time, and spiritual "dreamtime" as well, but that's not clock time. Confuse these two with clock time, or try to "rule" the others with the clock and you could lose your heart, and your mind could soon follow. If you decide you'll only live to your eightieth birthday and calculate the number of minutes left, you could go crazy. Just waiting helplessly in line at the grocery store as those miserable minutes, *your* minutes, tick away could be enough to send you over the edge. Better to live in the moment, or in a pace of time measured by "winters," "moons," and "suns" — things you can see and enjoy.

225

The seasons follow one another, but there is no specific time in which the fall becomes winter — when the creek first freezes. The Lenni Lenape say that the grandmothers and grandfathers of the four directions play dice all the time to determine the weather, and the timing of the seasons. Like us, they win a few and lose a few. That happens in horizontal time, but not clock time.

In the same way, instead of measuring your world in horizontal feet and inches, always on your way to somewhere else, try measuring it vertically for a change. Imagine yourself in a beam of sunlight and think of how far it is to the sun; its warmth radiates throughout your body, connecting you to it. Imagine the line of gravity that connects you to the center of the earth, pulling you toward the earth with its motherly love. Now imagine a spiritual beam of energy flowing from the

Creator into your heart, warming your heart with its love, then flowing on through you to the center of the earth's core. That's how spiritual time flows, and it's all happening now.

When we pull in all our thoughts and focus on the center of our being, on the verticalness of time and space, the outer flow of events seems to stop. When chronological time stops, metric space collapses, and everything is *neegeh ga'amee*, standing here and now. When everything is here and now, then all is truly interwoven, interconnected and ever present all at once. We experience the meaning of the saying, "Creation is happening now!" From that point we can taste what it is to be everywhere at once, know anything we need to know at once, and live our whole lives at once — within reason of course. Some, however, experience this vertical focusing as "nothing" and experience a loss of self, or no more self than a bug. Both are realistic accounts of what it feels like to stop time. Go into the moment, and it is as if a portal has opened up under our feet, and our visions and thoughts become powerful. Most importantly, when we stop time we can stop fear and anger. We can stop hate. We can even stop pain. I have tried this out on myself and have encouraged friends to try it when they were in serious pain, with great results. It works. When you are in the moment, you aren't obsessing about past pain, or having paranoid fantasies about future pain. And generally speaking, the pain we have right now is never more than we can bear, if we stop past-ing it and future-ing it.

Ritual helps stop the flow of horizontal time, and helps us get into that sacred space where the boundary line between real time and dreamtime becomes fluid. Sometimes the line between what we want to happen and what we foresee happen-

226

ing vanishes, and we can truly "speak as one with the Creator," *alsootomaee geezkook.*

In my travels I have met many Algonquin descendants who say that these tales I tell reinforce that sense of timelessness in their lives which they enjoy and which they miss when it is obscured. I can't tell you how many traditional indigenous people have said, "When I saw the title, I knew I had to read it!" At the same time, I have met many industrial-revolution people in those same travels who were completely confounded by the title, even outraged. One proper British woman said, "No *time*? How can they get any *work* done?"

People often ask me, "How can I experience that timelessness in my daily life? What steps can I take to get there?" I came to realize that these were important questions, signaling an urgent problem with societal, medical, and philosophical consequences. It seems to me that unless we are able to temporarily suspend the demands of clock time once in a while, all the reading in the world won't help us "walk in beauty" or even "walk gently upon the earth" as the ancestors suggested. We will stumble along the path instead, possibly hurting ourselves and others in the process.

Most people find it difficult to quiet the thousand beguiling charms of a time-clock society. They feel the need to *do* something to stop time. It's hard to talk in terms of doing something in order to stop doing, but there are things we can stop doing that will help restore the natural sense of time with which we were all born.

True, there are days when we just can't seem to slow down, because our anxiety with clock time has pulled us so far away from our own creative power. But there are certain exercises we

227

can do, and things we can avoid, at least for a few hours — to remind us of what we once knew. We can't all abandon our lifestyle overnight, but we can abandon the most harmful parts of it for at least one day.

If I were asked to sum up what I've learned since the publication of *No Word for Time*, I would have to say it's that a balance *can* be struck between the clock-crazy world and the native one, but finding that balance isn't easy. (Grandfather Turtle had warned me about this.) My return to New York City had caused me to lose the very connectedness I was coming back in order to express. Experiencing timelessness around nature is easy, but working a lecture schedule and a teaching job required that I develop specific ways of keeping time fluid while meeting the obligations of a rigid schedule. Here are seven steps I found helpful for addressing this problem.

First of all, stop thinking about clock time. Put away all of that machinery, all of those electronic devices that connect you with the wind-up world. You may want to spend a whole day away from machinery of all kinds, including your watch. Many people fast or abstain from sweets, alcohol, or fast foods for their health. Every once in a while, go on a fast from gizmos and gadgets. Try to avoid any sort of timepieces for one whole day. Focus on your anxiety (if you can find any) and try to identify what is causing it. Think simply and courageously. What's the most basic way to simplify your life? Do some drumming, sing a song without words. Pray. Make up poetry in your head. Ask yourself, ask Creator, "What should I do? Am I trying to do too much already?" or, "Am I wasting too much of my energy on things that don't bring me happiness?" Then stop worrying about it. This can work even if you live in a city

228

apartment. If you live near the woods, by all means, go out for a long walk in the woods. Nature is the greatest — perhaps the only — healer. All of the power in medicine comes from the earth. Walk in the woods and the trees will absorb your anger and balance you inside with their energy. You can't see or smell that tree energy, but if you go out when you are sick or angry or confused and walk among the trees, you will feel a change. Talk to them and tell them your problems. You never know what you might learn! By the end of the day, you should find it easier to slow your world down to a more human pace. In the spiritual life, as in almost any physical training, "the slower you go, the faster you grow."

Second, stop thinking about other people and what they think. If people-demands are worrying you, think of ways to make yourself less needy so that you can assert your rights. If people are getting the best of you, it's because there's something you can't let go of and they know it. Some elders go to great lengths to avoid people "getting to them." The Algonquin ancestors believed that every time you were forced to do something against your will, you lost a little bit of your spirit. Even in battle, when they were captured and tortured, they would sing rather than cry out in pain, because it was their choice and not someone else's. If they could do that, then surely we can choose to stop being annoyed at or afraid of someone who just had a bad day. Sing instead!

Third, stop thinking about money, at least for twenty-four hours. If you believe that time is money, then slowing down will always be a struggle. If time equals money, then the hour you spend with a child, a friend, or out in nature robs you of thirty bucks. Most Native Americans have trouble understanding this way of seeing. It is just as true to say that "Time is love," and it makes at least as much sense. Just as every moment holds financial potential, each moment also holds the potential for love and beauty. If for one day you could look at each moment as a golden opportunity to experience love and beauty, you might see that each moment you spend in greed, hate, anger, and fear is robbing you of a precious commodity that *you* could be spending as you see fit. It's a question of balance, for in these days we need both a little money and a little love. At the end of the day, ask yourself, "Is it better to be in it for the money, or would I rather be in it for the love?"

Fourth, stop thinking about getting things done. Take time to reexamine the relationship in your life between work, *lagoowach'n*, and play, *pop-oo-wach'n*. The two words are very similar in sound, and their meanings are related. *Pop-oo-wach'n* implies a state of playing with the universe as if it were a toy — it's all a joke. *Lagoowach'n* implies making things work in the literal sense: making things happen, putting the pieces together, getting them done. My understanding is that in Algonquin there is some considerable overlap between the two.

People in the old days used to sing while they worked, and sometimes made a game or sport out of it, even though the most important thing was to "get things done." The same people would also play games in which there was no immediate practical benefit but which would serve some long-term purpose. For example, lacrosse games were played on immense fields to develop strong runners who could be used as messengers. Many games young men played helped them in their future hunting skills. When we are at play, we don't think about how much time it is taking. We could care less. Imagine if life were like that. Imagine hunting for a job the way a Micmac boy would play at hunting for big game. I have heard that creative peak performance teams in the business world work together better if they can play together.

Fifth, stop taking in caffeine and other stimulants such as sugar. Don't wait for a health crisis to stop you. I have learned this the hard way; I started drinking colas *after* the book came out and I started lecturing more. I should have known better. The ubiquitous "highway" drinks such as coke and coffee can start you on a dance you can't stop dancing. Your body becomes dependent and you can go into debt to clock time by borrowing caffeine hours of wakefulness that may not be repaid for years. Candies, coffee, and sweet drinks all distort time.

Sixth, in order to have a genuine experience of timelessness or vertical time, of being totally in the moment, it is good to get out and run around. There's something that happens right *after* exercise that puts you in a different dimension when you sit down, pull inside yourself, and feel totally calm. Sink into that without rushing on to the next thing. Consider those moments as the gold medal; don't throw them away. You've earned that inner peace. Meditation, by the way, was part of ancient Algonquin spirituality — they just didn't call it that. They didn't call it anything to my knowledge, they just did it. *Unkee-da-see-wach'n* is "thinking big thoughts," but there's something about thinking no thoughts that is equally important. I associate it with *wunt-tak-tek*, or peacefulness. I also use light visualizations and encourage people to use the ones that work for them, to help them relax the body and connect to the spirit world.

Many Algonquins were great runners—Jim Thorpe, Louis

231

Sockalexis, and Chief Charles Bender, to name a few. Some still run today. They say you have to crawl before you can walk, and walk before you can run. I think you have to run before you can really "sit in your chair and go somewhere" totally without inner time or motion.

My *seventh* suggestion is to stop worrying, and focus on being unconditionally happy instead, no matter how much of a struggle it is. Letting go of time can certainly help you be happy, but it works the other way too. Being happy can help you let go of time. Even if you are engaged in a survival struggle, just think of happiness as a weapon, an impenetrable shield. Or think of it as the position you are struggling to defend.

232

If that doesn't work, take the opposite approach — abandon the fight. Leave it at the door as you go into that timeless place within yourself. Enter the heart of the Creator through the door of grieving. Lay yourself down as an offering before the Creator and say, "Have your way. I know nothing! Do what you want with me." These moments, which some call "zero moments" when we "burn to ashes" and become nothing, are often life-altering experiences. Time stops, and we glimpse a vision of truth. Gandhi, Nelson Mandela, and Martin Luther King, Jr., all reached zero moments that changed their lives. Algonquin elder William Commanda was sick and dying with cancer forty years ago, and he prayed for the Creator to take his life or do something useful with it. A bird came and sang to him at his window, and when he heard that song, time stopped, and tears came to his eyes. The anger he'd felt his whole life disappeared and never came back. Nine years later, he was made the carrier of the Seven Fires Prophecy wampum belts and a Wisdom

Keeper for Algonquin people. Now eighty-seven, he has traveled millions of miles in the course of being useful to the Creator, and has spoken to the leaders of the U.N. and many governments, but he seldom wears a watch or gives the impression of having anything to do. I can't think of anyone I've ever met who seems happier or more timeless than him.

Just by pondering these points, you may already have healed yourself a little bit from the "time" sickness. Perhaps the Algonquin tradition of natural living no longer seems to you like a thing of the distant past, but a present reality, a way of being that is good for your body, your mind, and your spirit. Of course, there's much more to traditional ways of life than this. What's been lost is a whole context that is difficult even for native people to reconstruct here in North America, their own homeland. But the context of natural time is a good place to start. It can benefit a person's life and the lives of those around them. I had to learn about time all over again — twice, first upon returning to the people of my ancestors and their traditional way of life, and second, upon going back into the mainstream industrial-revolution world to talk about it. The first part was fun (*pop-oo-wach'n*); the second part was hard work (*lag-oo-wach'n*). Together these experiences have induced me to think hard about what we can do as a society to reverse the "I want it yesterday" mentality.

Now, stop time. Enter into the timeless moment of "here and now." Step into the flow of vertical time. Let all horizontal events come to a stop. See how the echoes of the past are present "now." See how the seeds of all future events are present now also. Let all space revolve around the microcosm where you stand, at the center of the universe. Close your eyes and let

233

the pictures flow into the blankness that you see. Can you stop time? Can you bend space? Maybe not, but if you can just let go of the chatterbox mind and stop time for a moment, that's all that you need. Spend one moment beyond time, and the answer that you are looking for will come, maybe from your own intuition, maybe from outside of yourself; the opportunity you were waiting for will arise, the letter you were expecting will finally arrive, the vision you were seeking will manifest.

Spirit is waiting to help us. Spirit is looking over us all the time, but time can get in the way. Heart time moves slowly, but Spirit can move as fast as lightning once we stand still. The expression *tchee-tchan-kwee-wee* in Micmac (and many old Algonquin tongues) means "Spirit is watching over me." That's also a word for "living the spiritual life," because trusting and surrendering to Spirit is such an important key to being in the free flow of a happy spiritual life. We ourselves are small. The Creator is great, and full of love for all of us. Inviting Spirit to watch over you can open the door to many timeless moments, and to becoming part of that greatness. It allows you to stop sleeping with one eye open, stop watching the door, the clock, the purse, the TV, long enough that you can focus on seeing the river of timeless time that flows from the heart of the Creator through our hearts and into the heart of the earth.

When I received my first several copies of *No Word for Time* from the publisher three years ago, it was at the time of William Commanda's elders' gathering in Pitobig Mikan in Quebec near the Ottawa River. I didn't really know him very well, but my happiness opened up that door for Spirit, and I "got" that I was supposed to find him up there in Canada and give him the book. People had told me how hard it was to get

time with him when he was running the gathering, but I felt
certain that my steps would be guided. I made the ten-hour
drive overnight, and made all kinds of stops along the way the
day before, so there was no way to predict when I would arrive.
As I recall, I also had no directions. As it turned out, I drove
onto the property just at dawn, and a beautiful one it was! I
clutched one book, a bit nervous, perhaps, stuck another in my
coat pocket, and felt I should walk down to the edge of the lake
that lay just beyond the houses and down the grassy hill. I would
get a better view of the sunrise there, which was just beginning
to happen over to my left. Spirit guided my steps right to the
place where the elder was standing, all alone at the edge of the
lake, smoking his pipe and looking at the brightening sky. I gave
him the book, and we enjoyed the sunrise together. He looked at
the list of eighty-four nations of Algonquins, all of which recognize the Seven Fires Wampum Belt (which he had nearby) and
its prophecy, with great interest. He said, "I never knew there
were so many!" That was the dawn of a remarkable friendship,
and it is one that has helped confirm for me the importance and
viability of the Algonquin culture today.

235

Soon afterward, there was a sunrise pipe ceremony on the
point of land to the east and I stood in the circle and watched as
four pipe carriers, including William Commanda, conducted the
ceremony together. One of them reminded me of my first
Micmac teacher, Stephen, the person to whom *No Word for Time*
is dedicated (along with my great-grandfather, who is in the spirit world), and whom I had been trying to find again for years.
This man looked much older.

After the ceremony, I ran to talk to the man. He kept walking. I asked him his name, and he told me "Steve." I shook his

hand and said — now with a touch of humor — "My name is Evan." He took another look and said, "Yes, I remember you now. Your hair is longer. *Maydalain geezkook!*," he exclaimed. It was the first expression he had taught me, seven years earlier, one that launched the creation of a *Micmac Phrase Book* by us both, still in use on some Micmac reserves. It was that book which led him to be chosen by the Canadian government as a representative for native people in Canada during the discussions on the Unity Pact.

I said, "I wrote a book, and dedicated it to you, and it just came out yesterday. I've been looking for you all this time! I've researched everything you told me about the Algonquin people and found it all to be true. I wanted you to check it over before it was published, but you were nowhere to be found, so I had to go ahead and publish it."

236

He said, "Maybe it's better you did it your own way." I inscribed the second copy of the book and handed it to him. He looked very surprised when I gave him a bear hug, but I had always thought of him as an older brother. Later we went to the same spot by the lake where I'd met William, and he gave me some more teachings in Micmac language, translating some traditional songs for me, and continuing my education.

He handed me his business card. It said *Director of Native American Research, Canadian Museum of Civilization.* I thought back to the time when we first met. He was working as an office helper in the extension division of a community college, and few were taking his lofty ideas about Algonquin high culture very seriously. Now he's something of a celebrity in Canada, giving interviews on TV, testifying in government courtrooms on native rights and traditions, narrating in premieres of multimedia works by native composers, and consulting with authors and museums. It's not an easy life, but he's being useful to the Creator and sharing his great knowledge.

I realized that whether the book was to be a financial success or not, it was worth it just to hand it to him and let it say for me what I could not say for myself; how much it meant to me that he had taken the time to share with me the traditional teachings of his grandparents and great-grandparents those many years ago, and for giving me clues to help find Grandfather Turtle out there by the Miramichi River. Creator had worked out all the details. Grandfather Turtle had often said that when you are really touched by the Creator, tears may want to come. I started to feel that way.

I quickly said, "*Upnamoodtess*," or see you later, and went off by myself into the woods to be alone with the Creator. The ancient Algonquin civilization was alive and well. Its new day was beginning to dawn and I would live to see it. I was grateful beyond words.

237

THE MICMAC
NATIONAL ANTHEM

The birth and rebirth of nations often involves bloodshed, but I am hopeful for the Wabanaki rebirth. Perhaps this seems a naive hope but while many national anthems are filled with bloodshed and hate, the Micmac anthem, the largest nation of the Wabanaki people, is one of love and peace and communication. It is sung like this:

Geb-mee de deme nidj donn delee ulnootimq
Meegamooatch doh ohd mahwee danidj
Geb-mee de deme nidj donn badabeck sultig
Meegamooatch doh oh daba wun ma dool tin nidj
Daba wun ma dooltin idj donn Geezoolgh dellee gaaloog seeg,
oo laoo sitgamoo, wa hey-ya hey-yo!
Wey yo he hi ya ya wey yo hey yo hey yo weyhi ya
wey yo hey hi ya ya weh yo wey hi ya
wey yo hey hi ya wey yo weh hi ya ya wey yo hey hi ya hey yo!

Here is a rough translation:

> *Let us all think about how we the people*
> *are Micmacs, all related by blood.*
> *Let's all get together and remember*
> *how we bang the drum all night long;*
> *let's all help each other*
> *let's all help each other understand*
> *how (why) the Creator put us here*
> *on the surface of our mother earth.*

I hope that the Wabanaki people win the freedom to follow their own way of life and follow the Red Road again, even if it means each person walking it in solitude. I also hope that they heed the words of the honor song and help each other to understand why the Creator put us here on the surface of the mother earth. May they eventually find a way to help all those who come to them in friendship. May they find this understanding in themselves, in accordance with their own culture and teaching, and in the light and love of Gezoolgh who created us all and is in everything.

I would like to thank Stephen Augustine, Micmac historian, and all the elders and *bpoo-ohin*, who wish to remain anonymous, for sharing their teachings with me. The printed word cannot do justice to their speaking, thick with inflected meaning. May this *maskweegadayg'n*, "the thing I am writing on," only serve to prepare the reader for the oral teachings of the elders. I would also like to thank both Eric Huberman and Rick Jarow for their help and inspiration in gathering together the cross-cultural information. I'd also like to give thanks to Jean Campbell for the initial encouragement to "write it all down," and also to her late husband Joseph Campbell, for his inspirational example.

There is no goodbye, there is only *upnamoodtess*. I will see you again.

239

APPENDIX A

Some Speculation
On Micmac History

Although there are many plausible theories, most native people hold that their origins may still be completely unknown to the European. The Bering Strait may have been used as a land bridge, but which way? If native people originated on Turtle Island, where are the other higher primates? (There are spider monkeys in South America, but no apes.) Did the people of North America descend from Polynesian seafarers, island-hopping across the South Pacific, perhaps landing first in South America? Did their mysterious ancestors escape from some lost continent as it was sinking into the ocean? Were they deposited here by the Pliedians, or by gods? Or was the first ancestor created by a bolt of lightning out of the soil as oral tradition firmly maintains?

Native Americans are genetically Mongolian, with countless customs in common with Asia, so they must have some link with the people of northern China and Siberia. In *The Red Record*, David McCutcheon finds similarities between pictographic writing in Mongolia (Northern China) and in Algonquian pictographs. Micmac elders use similar hieroglyphic writing today, although most contend it was a system introduced by missionaries. No one knows the entire history of the Native American; there are many mysteries.

Likewise, no one knows the whole history of the Wabanaki

240

people. Many varying scenarios have been proposed. I have put together my own thumbnail sketch of its history from conversations with elders, native and non-native scholars, archaeologists, and other interested parties.

The Abenaki believe Gluskabe was created on an island in Lake Champlain. The Micmac believe that Glooskap, the singular ancestor of the people, may have been created near Kanawaga or Kanastaki near Montreal. Many ethnologists say the root Algonquian group left there 3,000 years ago. But other sources add up to a much more complex history, involving many waves of settlers over 11,000 years.

Conventional wisdom says the original group crossed the Bering Strait during the last Ice Age, 20,000 years ago, during the Pleistocene Era, and skirting the edge of the glaciers, went southward to follow game. Twelve thousand years ago, the ice receded northward, and the game and hunters followed.

The Naskapi of Labrador, the northernmost of the seven Wabanaki tribes described in this book, have held to the most ancient sacred rituals concerning hunting, gathering, and daily life. I have never visited the Naskapi, but their way of life is often compared by archeologists to the Clovis people who lived in what is now New Mexico 11,000 years ago, the oldest identifiable "Native Americans." It seems likely that the Wabanaki culture took root in the Maritime region during that same period, and the Naskapi, due to their remote location, were better able to hold to these traditions, which are the oldest Native American traditions known to outsiders. Most Wabanaki people today are, at the very least, kindred spirits to their Clovis-like ancestors, but those who have lived among Europeans have changed the forms which that spirit takes.

The Clovis-like ancestors of the Wabanaki arrived 11,000 years ago in the Maritime region, which must have then been geographically very different. These were probably Mongoloid people, Siberians with strong Asian characteristics. These people may have led a Spartan existence, and may have been few in number. Their cautious and deeply religious ways were apparently successful in inhabiting this cold region and they left some artifacts from that time which have been catalogued.

Micmac lore contains references to knowledge of large beavers, mastodons, large squirrels, and other animals from this period. (If Micmac people had developed archaeology, it could explain how they came to this knowledge, but Micmac beliefs discourage digging up the mother earth for any but the most sacred reasons.) That dozens of species became extinct during this time gives us an idea how hostile and rapidly changing that environment must have been. It is a testament to the power of the Way of the Wabanaki that it survived not only the onslaught of European culture which has penetrated every corner of the globe, but that it survived the end of the Ice Age, a period which saw massive extinctions of flora and fauna. I believe it is this rock-solid core of hunting-gathering spirituality which makes the Wabanaki so strong as a people. But there is more to the story.

According to some conventional wisdom, the sea-going Red Ochre people arrived in the Maritime area 7,000 years ago, radiating out from some central point to occupy the shores of Europe, Iceland, and America. I believe they were probably Neanderthal-like in appearance, and proud of their naturally red skin, which they made redder through the application of ochre. These fairly advanced "red people" settled all along the Atlantic

242

coast. The early settlers from Europe rarely mentioned red skin in their description of Native Americans. Apparently, it was not a trait universally inherited from the Red Ochre people, cropping up in some tribes and not others. Somehow, all native North Americans ended up with the name "redskin" at a much later date, and this has been the source of much confusion.

There are Micmacs today who have bright red skin. It is said by certain natives and non-natives alike that the red people are the survivors of Atlantis, and that some day the clues will be found on the bottom of the ocean which connect that doomed island with native North Americans. Micmac people today build modern *gwendjeegooum,* or European-style houses, on their reserves, complete with basements and plumbing, but when they dig the foundation and find Red Ochre burial sites (such as happened recently at the Red Bank reserve) they say, "These too are our ancestors!"

243

The now-extinct Beothuk people and their related neighbors are direct descendants of these Red Ochre people, as well as of the native-Mongolian stock. Both of these peoples were hunters, but the Red Ochre people were seafarers, whalers, seal hunters, and such. Today's Naskapi are also related to these Beothuk whalers, as are the Montagnais and the Micmac. Due to climate, the Naskapi's lives are not unlike that of modern Eskimos. Culturally, however, they are very different from Eskimos (who are not "Indians") and the two often have skirmishes over territory and other matters of survival.

Where the next waves of visitors came from is highly controversial. I can only mention some possibilities. Some may have come across the remaining land bridge, or in boats along the southern coast of the Bering Strait, possibly from central southeast Asia. Some may have been a cinnamon-brown skin group genetically related to the modern Thai (who came south from China thousands of years ago). They may be related to the "Hibernians," a black-haired people who occupied Europe before the Celts, and who spread all over the globe, or to ancient Polynesians, or all of the above. In any case, brownish-skinned people of a southern Asian climate came to Turtle Island long ago and became part of the Wabanaki heritage.

At the same time, there must have been a second Asian influx from an area somewhere in China, whose language was proto-Japanese, and whose culture was that which eventually became Hinduism and Taoism elsewhere. This group made a pilgrimmage eastward, leaving remnants of Algonquian culture from Alaska to Maine and the Maritimes as they trekked toward the rising sun over generations. The migration group split many times, before settling in the Kanastaki area, and developing as proper Algonquian. There is a story about how the fifty Algonquian tribes spread out as sparks from one central fire which seems to describe the radiation of Algonquian culture from a central point, the southeast branch becoming Lenape, the northeast group becoming ancestors of the Micmac.

The Algonquian culture may have arrived in the Maritimes as recently as 3,000 years ago, bringing their highly developed Algonquian language with them. The Algonquins are a relatively peaceful people, and it seems likely that any contact with remnants of the "red race" must have been friendly. One theory is that much of the red race was wiped out by disease by the time the Algonquins arrived — one archeological level shows little human habitation — so there would have been little conflict.

Again, all this is quite speculative, but interesting.

History indicates that the Algonquins as a group are a highly diplomatic people, open to new ideas, and somewhat generous to strangers. However, these same people have often resorted to violent and bitter acts of war, specifically toward the British. The Micmacs were even victorious in naval battles against the deadly British gunboats, a boast which the American colonies could not make. Algonquian vocabulary mainly allows for defensive thinking rather than offensive thinking, and one would have to conclude that there was something about British foreign policy which Algonquian individuals across North America found to be a basic threat to survival.

This Algonquian culture adopted many of the words of the local people, especially for nautical terms, and words for animals and geography that are unique to the region. The Micmac word *bu-tup,* or whale, is very likely borrowed from the Beothuk people, whose group name may have meant "whalers." Other terms adopted at this time may have been *abachtuq* ("ocean") and *go-beet* ("beaver"). It is interesting to hear Micmac people today use the word *Bu-tup* and realize the word may have been heard in the same region much the same way over 7,000 years ago, around the time when the Lascaux paintings were being made in France, 2,000 years before the oldest pyramids were built, and yet longer before the Tyrolean "Ice Man" walked the earth.

After the Algonquins arrived in the East at least 3,000 years ago, there were many more arrivals, some definite, some speculative. We know the white-skinned Vikings arrived in 996 A.D. and settled in various regions, bringing a strong European influence into the genetics of the Micmac people, and a few myths

245

and words. Some Micmac myths seem more Viking than
Native American, and a large number of Micmacs had white
skin at the time of contact with the first explorers. In the 1500s
they were described as having "auburn hair and hazel eyes." We
have no records of any war occurring to repel the Vikings, and
some stories indicate reverence for those who came in boats
from the East with teachings about life. There have always been
discussions of Celtic explorers exploring most of North America
before Columbus' arrival and leaving their mysterious traces
behind them, but the Ogham script they left behind has been
dated anywhere from 3000 B.C. to 500 A.D. There are
Micmac words which echo Celtic vocabulary, such as *cwmmdn*
for mountain, but this may be of recent origin.

246

The colors of the traditional medicine wheel are as follows:
red from the East, black from the South, yellow from the West,
and white from the North. Is it not interesting that the "yellow"
ancestors arrived in the Maritimes from the West, the "red"
ancestors arrived from the East, the dark-skinned ("black")
ancestors arrived from warm Southern regions, and the "white"
Viking explorers of 900 A.D. arrived from settlements in
Iceland and Greenland to the north? Could it be that the
Micmacs' unique choice of colors for the wheel retain a memory of who came from where?

Although the word "Micmac" is a French transliteration of
the Algonquian *meegamooatch* ("all-related-by-blood") it is
interesting to note the expression "micmac" in Canadian French
means "mix and match." Anyone who knows the Micmac people knows how Micmac children of the same "pure blood"
mother and father can come out in every color of the wheel,
but all Indian. Genes don't blend, they divide and mix.

A people with many genetic origins will contain pure throwbacks to their sources, as well as those whose faces contain a little of this and that, even if they are all one people at heart. Perhaps the Micmac people are a hint of what is to come for the whole human race as the trade winds continue to blow and people continue to fall in love. I hope those future people adapt to such a state of affairs as well as the Micmac have. I've never known a Micmac to be shunned by other Micmacs on account of his or her color, which could be anything from "black" to "white" to "yellow" to "red."

"White" people use terms like "full blooded this, a quarter that, an eighth blood of the other..." but native people don't believe much in numbers, especially when they divide (and subdivide) people. What's important is how you live and why. The Micmacs know who they are.

247

The story does not stop with the colors of the Micmac wheel. Around the same time the Vikings arrived there was an invasion which shook the roots of Algonquian life, and that was the invasion of the Haudenosuannee people, the People of the Long House, the "Iroquois."

I gather from talking to Iroquois people that their ancestors once cohabitated with the Pawnees in the lower Tennessee and Mississippi area. Both are descendants of the Mississippian culture, a highly advanced agricultural people who were proud of their warriors. There must have been some drought or famine in the area, because there was a civil war, and while the Pawnees remained, the other tribes charged north "with war clubs in their left hands," reaching as far as the Arctic Circle before being repelled by the Northern Cree. Those Iroquois warriors fought for that northern land down to the last man, but lost it.

The Mohawk were defeated and captured as slaves by the Ladirondiak people of New York, an Algonquian people who played a significant role in the American revolution, but who were then destroyed or assimilated into the Abenaki Nation along with Mohawks, Sokokis, and other native people. The Iroquois gathered in the Kanastaki area which was sacred to the Algonquins, and made their civilization there. They lived all along the Mohawk River from the Niagara to the Hudson, and south to Pennsylvania. Their centralized, highly socially organized way of life was much different from the Algonquin, who were more freewheeling and soft spoken. The Treaty of Peace and the forming of the Six Nations by the Peace Maker (as some call him) must have been around 1200 to 1400 A.D., although some say it was at the time of Christ. Today, the Algonquin and Iroquois stand side by side in political resistance against "outside" opposition, but historically, the influence of the Iroquois on most Algonquin people was as an outsider, or worthy opponent, and not as an internal force.

Other arrivals and explorations from the East have been suggested by Barry Fell and others, but not everyone is in agreement. Parallels between the early Celts and Micmacs abound — the early Celts had a sweat-lodge-like sauna under the ground, as did the Vikings.

The origin of the Micmac hieroglyphs, still in use today, is highly controversial. It may indeed indicate an early contact with explorers from the Dynastic era of Egypt, and Barry Fell claims them to be in some instances identical, but this is not generally accepted by Micmac people. The Siberian pictographs are a more likely cousin. The trade winds from Europe and Africa may have at one time led directly to Micmac shores, which might explain some of Fell's more stunning theories about visits by Libyans and Ethiopians in centuries past, but it's more wild speculation. It seems that the Micmac culture is the product of many layers of development, but each new layer has conformed to the strong original mold that is unique to the region, with a strong belief in the land, plus individual exchange and interaction with the Creator.

A UNIQUE PEOPLE

Defining what "pure Wabanaki" culture might be is a difficult thing. There is a core culture unaffected by the last 500 years of white European interaction, yet that culture has Viking, Celtic, Iroquois, Algonquin, Mongolian, and Red Ochre influences. Due to the great expanses of time the people had to adjust to these outside influences, they are each well digested and adapted to the Native American world view which they share in common with most Native American tribes. Therefore, regardless of these lesser influences, Wabanaki culture is just as "Native American" as any other, and should be regarded as such.

We have a different way of life today in America's cities and suburbs. In spite of the superficial comparisons listed above, the modern European must go far back into ancestral roots to find what could be called "native" in the Wabanaki sense. I often point out that the cultural gap between traditional Native Americans and Europeans is as wide as the Atlantic Ocean. Europeans never want to hear that — I always hear arguments based more on emotion than fact that "we are all one." Yes, we are, spiritually, but culturally we are not. Even full-blooded

Micmac people who have been raised in residency schools or white public schools are vividly aware of the cultural distance between themselves and their traditional grand- and great-grandparents. Much of it boils down to the difference between literate and oral cultures, the biggest chasm on earth, I believe.

In order to do my part to preserve what is left of that strand of oral tradition I have encountered, the Wabanaki, I choose to focus on the differences between the Wabanaki people and Asians and the rest of the world. In spite of all the similarities, the Wabanaki are not Siberians, Chinese, Japanese, or East Indians. They are not just like Americans or just like Canadians. They walk to the beat of a different drum, and follow it with dignity and purpose. They are the Wabanaki, and their ways are unique in the world.

ETIQUETTE TIPS FOR
NATIVE AMERICAN CEREMONIES

Speak from the heart rather than the mind in ceremony or circle.

Honor the elders, give gifts or greetings to the oldest elders first before giving to the younger ones.

Try to avoid rambling on in the lodge or circle just to control the situation. Get to the heart of it.

Listen rather than debate in the lodge.

Let other people cry, let yourself cry. (Some traditions discourage you from touching someone who is crying unless they ask for it.)

Move in a clockwise motion where possible, unless an elder instructs you otherwise.

Be helpful to others. (Actions speak louder than words.)

251

Really take care of the earth in every action. This is a serious point, not just a philosophical one.

Don't invoke entities from other cultures or address them in ceremony!

Don't put on airs like you know "all about Indians." (No one knows all about Indians.) Be careful when making parallels between native ways and Christian or other mystical traditions; it's best to pose these as questions if they come up.

Don't judge anyone's "Indianness" by the percentage of their blood. This is not a native concern. Native people recognize each other and don't entertain these debates which divide people.

Remember that the lodge is more mysterious than we can understand. The elders learn something new with each lodge.

Don't eat right before a lodge (for your own comfort).

Show respect during each step of the ceremony.

Your energy helps create what the lodge will be. Participate without trying to control. It is not a passive experience like TV or a lecture.

Don't monopolize the elders' time and attention, especially if someone else is waiting to speak. Don't expect answers immediately. Things take time.

Don't assume anything the elders say or do is not important.

Always ask the elder about problems or situations concerning the building of the lodge, the preparation of the fire, or other logistical matters.

There is no "time" in "Indian Time." The Great Spirit controls when things will happen. Don't rush things. Go one step at a time.

252

Don't leave a ceremonial circle to go to the bathroom unless it's desperate.

Don't stick your feet out toward the center of the circle in lodge or ceremony if possible.

Volunteer to help in setting up lodges, etc.

Take native culture seriously, without making it silly. If you feel silly, say so, but seriously.

Always say "thank you" and be grateful.

In ceremony, keep your mind focused on one or two simple questions, needs, problems, that you want help with. If there are more, save them for another ceremony.

Be creative, but responsible. What the Great Spirit moves you to do is probably right, even if it contradicts all of the above.

RESPECT FOR ALL LIFE
THE SEVEN POINTS OF RESPECT

The seven principles of respect are close to the heart of Native American wisdom and the art of speaking.

1. Respect for feelings, and for suffering. Always show compassion. Do not add to the suffering.
2. Respect for individual space. Practice non-interference and non-control. Don't use people. Respect each being's life, limb, land, privacy and property, including your own.
3. Respect for limitations as well as strengths. Honor both in yourself and others, and no one will be abused.
4. Respect for boundaries and individual differences. Take responsibility for your own choices and disentangle yourself from the choices of others.
5. Respect for truth. Show directness and integrity and speech and action.
6. Respect for the earth and for all paths, peoples, cultures, and customs growing here. All have a place in the hoop.
7. Respect for yourself, for all aspects, high or low. We all have bodies, hearts, minds, and spirits for a good reason. Spirituality is the relationship between each of them. Conduct your life fully, but with dignity.

253

CREE PLAINS
CENTRAL ALGONQUIN
(BLACKFOOT, BLOOD & PIEGAN)

CREE

BLACKFOOT

GROS VENTRE
WITH ARAPAHO

OJIE

CROW

MENOMIN

SIOUIAN

SAUK
FOX
KICKAPOO

NORTHERN
CHEYENNE

Continental Divide

ILLINOIS
CONFEDERACY

ARAPAHO
SOUTHERN
CHEYENNE

PAWNEE

MUSKOGE
(RELATE

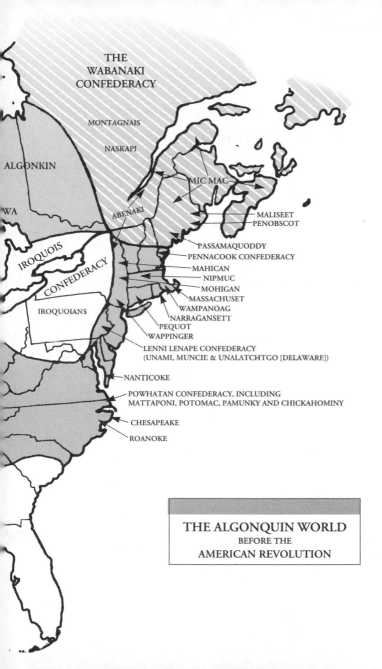

THE
WABANAKI
CONFEDERACY

MONTAGNAIS

NASKAPI

ALGONKIN

WA

MIC MAC

ABENAKI

MALISEET
PENOBSCOT

IROQUOIS

PASSAMAQUODDY
PENNACOOK CONFEDERACY

CONFEDERACY

MAHICAN
NIPMUC
MOHIGAN
MASSACHUSET
WAMPANOAG
NARRAGANSETT
PEQUOT
WAPPINGER

IROQUOIANS

LENNI LENAPE CONFEDERACY
(UNAMI, MUNCIE & UNALATCHTGO [DELAWARE])

NANTICOKE

POWHATAN CONFEDERACY, INCLUDING
MATTAPONI, POTOMAC, PAMUNKY AND CHICKAHOMINY

CHESAPEAKE

ROANOKE

255

THE ALGONQUIN WORLD
BEFORE THE
AMERICAN REVOLUTION

Appendix B

The Major Algonquin Nations Throughout North America and What They Call Themselves

The term "Algonquin" was apparently introduced to the world by Samuel de Champlain in 1603, typically, by mistake. He was referring to a specific group of Native Americans he had encountered at Tadoussac, which the Malecite had told him were "Elaegomogwik," which means either, "these people are our allies," or "the people on the other shore." Champlain mispronounced it "Algoumekin," which later became Algonquin, and this is the name still used today to refer to the nation of the Ottawa River. Those people call themselves "Anishnabek," which has been translated as "The True Men," or "The Good Men." They also call themselves "Mamawinini," or nomadic people, but one band of "Algonquins," the Kiche-sipi-rini" or "People of the Great River," were among the first of this ancient culture to settle down in one place, Allumette Island.

Allumette is the largest island in the Ottawa River, the river that forms the boundary between Ontario and Quebec. There is evidence of sedentary Algonquin settlements on the island going back at least 6,280 years, and occupation in the area dating back 7,000 years as it became inhabitable after the Ice Age. From this power base in the center of the Ottawa Valley trade route, the influence and language of the Algonquin spread throughout North America. Hence they have been called "The First People." Their relatives a few miles to the east who settled at Oka may be yet more ancient, and habitation in the Micmac region may go back 11,000 years, but all are of a common origin. Nonetheless, Allumette Island was a turning point in Algonquin civilization.

There is little doubt that the Algonquins of Allumette are the direct descendants of the so-called "Clovis" people, long considered the oldest group of Native Americans. Clovis points have been found close to the borders of Quebec — in Maine, Vermont, New York, Nova Scotia, and Ontario. Clovis roots date back at least to 14,000 years ago when the glaciers forced them to make present-day New Mexico their home. However, whether they came across the Bering Strait 20,000 years ago or came up from South America via Mexico is now being debated.

257

At the time of European contact, cousins of the Anishnabek language could be found from coast to coast and from the Arctic Circle to the Gulf of Mexico. This large and diverse cultural and linguistic group was termed "Algonquin" in 1891 by John Wesley Powell and the name stuck. It is taken to mean "The First People."

According to Captain John Smith and others, the term used by natives in the 1600s for the original root language was "Algonkeen" (Elaegomkeen?). Algon*quin* is probably a French spelling of that same word. The ending *kee* is a suffix in that root language which means "place" or "land" (short for *ha-kee*), though *keen* has no meaning in Algonquin tongues. "Anishnabi" would have been the term used further west.

The following is an outline of those languages and dialects as they were named and recorded by the first Europeans to write down their encounters with native people. The groupings in sevens are the author's own, based on oral histories and library research. The seven major hoops are Wabanaki (or Northeastern), New England, Lenni-Lenape (including Southeastern), Cree, Great Lakes, Prairie Nations (including Illinois), and Western Plains. This is an approximation, illustrating the ancient teaching that the Algonquin people were created by seven sparks emanating from seven fires (which emanated from the original fire as described in the Gluskap story). These seven sparks (nations) each gave birth to other sparks (nations). There are eighty-four major Algonquin nations that have played a significant role in history as we know it. Also listed here are some of the offspring hoops, or subnations, which are less well known. That this process still goes on today illustrates the old saying, "Creation is happening now!"

WABANAKI

Known as the "People of the Dawn," the Wabanaki are a hoop of seven great nations, each with its own subgroups. The formal Wabanaki Confederacy of the 1800s was short-lived and did not include each of these nations.

Micmac (from Meegamooatch) ("We Are All Related by Blood"/ "Allies"). The seven council districts are Gespegeoag, Sigenigeoag, Epegoitg ag Pigtogeoag, Gespogoitg (aka Souriquois), Segepenegatig, Esgigeoag, and Onamagi.

Maliseet ("They Talk Differently") aka "Etchemin," the people of the sandy berries.

Abenaki ("Dawn Land People"). The Abenaki Confederacy could be said to include seven bands: the Casco ("Muddy"), the Kennebec (aka Canabas, "Long Water Land"), the Norridgewock ("Where the Swift Water Descends"), the Pejepscot, the Saco ("Outflowing"), the Wawenock, and the Sokoki. The Ammonousucs, Arosaguntacooks, Kikomkwaks, and Nulheganocks were subtribes of the Sokoki. The Arosaguntacooks or Androscoggin ("Fish-Curing Place") were subtribes of Norridgewock. The Ossipee ("Rocky River") and the Pequaket were subtribes of the Saco.

Passamaquoddy ("Place Where Pollock Are Plentiful"), closely related to the Maliseet.

Penobscot ("Place Where the Rocks Widen" or "It Flows on White Rocks" or "White Water on the Rocks"), closely related to the eastern Abenaki.

Montagnais (French for "Mountain People"). They call themselves Innu. The Montagnais circle of nations include the Tadoussacien, the Kakouchak, the Chekoutimien, the Nekoubaniste, the Chomonchouaniste, the Oumatachinrini and possibly the Oupapinachiouek. The Naskapi hoop includes the Oukesestigouek, the Oukesestigouek, the Chisedech, the Bersiamites, the Ouneskapi, the Oumamiouek, the Outakouamiouek, the Attikiriniouetch, the Mouchaouaouastiiriniouek, and the Outabitibec.

259

Naskapi ("People from Where It [the Land] Disappears"). They also call themselves Innu people. The Innu language is closer to Cree than the other Wabanaki languages. One could say the Montagnais and Naskapi are one nation, the Innu, but then it is equally true that the Abenaki are made up of two nations, usually referred to as Western Abenaki and Eastern Abenaki. Either way, there are still seven Wabanaki nations.

NEW ENGLAND

There were seven great confederacies in the New England area south of the Wabanaki, which together formed one great hoop of related nations. These confederacies often exchanged member nations, or absorbed others as neighboring confederacies dispersed. This information has been influenced by several sources, particularly the book *Ninnuock (The People)* by Steven F. Johnson and Bert Salwen's dialect map, "Indians of Southern New England and Long Island, Early Period," published in *Handbook of North American Indians, Northeast*, vol. 15, edited by B. G. Trigger, Smithsonian Institution, Washington, DC, 1978.

Pennacook Confederacy ("L" dialect). Their seven nations were The Pennacook ("At the Foot of the Hill" or "Where the Path Is Narrow"), Concord, New Hampshire, area. Also called Merrimac ("Rapids"), the Agawam ("Lowland" or "Overflowed by Water"), the Amoskeag aka Namoskeag ("Fishing Place"), the Nashua ("Where the River Divides" or "The Land Between"), the Souhegan (Southwest, or variation on Squawkheag: "Watching to Spear Fish"), the Wamesit ("There Is Plenty of Room for All"), and the Winnipesaukee (possibly "Land of Fine Water" or "Land of Good Fishing Waters").

Johnson also includes the Naumkeag, ("Eel Place"), Agamenticus, Cocheco, Coos (Pine Trees), Naticook, Newichewannock, Ossipee, Pawtucket, Pemigewasset, Pentucket, Pequaket, Piscataqua, Saco, and Squaukheag as members of this group at some time.

Massachusett Confederacy ("N" dialect). Its now-scattered nations included the Massachusett ("Great Blue

Hill"). It is said that the hill, which is southeast of Boston, got its name because of all the blueberries that used to grow on it. In 1650, the noble and dignified Massachusett people were captured as slaves and sent to Jamaica, where they still exist as a cultural/ethnic group. Also included are Nahant, Nashoba ("Between the Rivers"), Neponset ("Early Summer"), Norwottuck ("Far from Us"), Punkapoag ("Shallow Fresh Water Pond"), Quabaug ("Red Fish Pond"), Saugus ("Outlet"), Shawmut ("He Goes There by Water"), Wachusett ("Little Hill Place"), Wessagusset ("At the Small [Hidden?] Salt Water Cove"), and Winnisemit ("Fine Spring"). There were twelve nations in all.

The Agawam and Nashua tribes went from the Pennacook to the Massachusett Confederacy during hard times for the Pennacook. The Pocumtuck ("A Narrow Swift Current") were also part of the Massachusett for a while. The Nonantum were an important Massachusett nation but are overlooked by most text books. Little is known of them.

Wampanoag Confederacy The Wampanoag ("People of the First Light" or "People of White Wampum"), aka Massasoit, after Chief Massasoit, spoke an "N" dialect, still spoken by those living in exile in the Bahamas. Also included in their numbers are the Pokanokets ("At or Near the Cleared Lands"), Nemaskets ("Fishing Place"), Munponsets, Pocassets ("Where the Stream Widens," similar to Paugasset), Sakonnets ("Abode of the Black Goose"), Patuxets (or Pawtuxets, "At the Little Falls" or "Place of the Round-footed Ones [Wolves]"). The Manamets ("A Place of Portage"), Masnipi, Mashpee ("Great Water"), Matachees, Nobsquassets ("At the Rock Ledge Cliff"), Monomoys ("Deep Black Mire"), Nausets ("At the Place

Between"), Sokones (part of Mashpees, could mean "Of the South"), Capawicks ("Enclosed Harbor" or "Place of Refuge"), Shawmut and Tommokomoth could also be included, bringing the number to eighteen.

Narragansett Confederacy The Narragansett ("On a Small Cape"/ "At a Small Narrow Point") spoke a variation of the "N" dialect. Also in the confederacy of seven were the Eastern Niantic (Rhode Island coast and Connecticut: "Point of Land on the Tidal Estuary" or "Tidal Land") who spoke a "Y/N" mixed dialect, Cowweset ("At the Pine Tree Place"), Manisses, Shawomet (possibly "Spring of Water"), Wabaquasset ("The Place We Make Mats for House Coverings"), and the Wunashowatuckoog ("Where the River Splits").

Pawtuxets were affiliated with both Narragansett and Wampanoag and spoke an "N" dialect. The Montauk ("A Fortified Place on High Land" or possibly "In the Island Country") were affiliated but spoke the "Y" dialect.

Pocumtuck Confederacy The Pocumtuck probably spoke the Nipmuk-type of the "L" dialect. Their allies included mostly those from other groupings, including Agawam (from Pennacook), Norwottuck (from Massachusett), Podunck (from Pequot), and Squawkheag (who were also affiliated with Pennacook and Sokoki). The Tunxis and Wangunk were also with the Pequot. The Pocumtuck tribal seat was in present-day Deerfield, Massachusetts.

Nipmuk Nations The Nipmuk speak an "L" dialect. This alliance included the Nipmuk ("People of the Freshwater Fishing Place"), Wachusett, and Quabaugs (from Massachusett), Nashuas (from Pennacook), Quinebaugs (from Pequot), Wabaquassets (from Narragansett), Hassanamissits ("Sandbar"),

Wunnashowatuckoogs ("Where the River Splits"),
Wusquowhannanawkits ("Pidgeon Country"), and Awashacom.

Pequot Confederacy (from Pequotenog, "The Killers of
Men," aka "The Destroyers"). The "Y" dialect Pequot language
group includes the Pequots, ("Destroyers") the Mohegans
("Wolf People"), who split off from Pequots in 1637, the
Montauk (from Narragansett), the Western Niantic (from
Narragansett), the Wunnashowatuckoog (Narragansett), the
Wusquowhannanawkit (from Nipmuk), and the Shinnecock.
Of these seven nations, only the Mohegan and Pequot were
part of the confederacy. The other five nations of the political
confederacy are associated with the "R" dialect of the
Mahican/Quiripi type: Quinebaug ("Long Pond"), Quinnipiac
("Where We Change Our Route"), Tunxis ("Fast-flowing
Stream"), Podunk ("A Swampy Place" aka "Where You Sink in
the Mire"), and Wangunk. The Mohegan assert that the Pequot
(and therefore themselves) are descendants of the "R" speaking
Mahicans as well, hence the choice of tribal name.

263

LENNI-LENAPE

("Ordinary Speakers," or "Real People")

According to some traditions, there were twelve clans in the
Lenape nations. The three major nations of the Lenape
Confederacy (aka "Delaware Confederacy") were of these
twelve, each with their own subtribes. The three lost boys of the
Lenape creation stories (who were rescued by Maysingway and
showed their future home when one of them was taken on a
ride in the sky) may have represented these three nations. The
homeland he showed them may have been Lenape-Hoking, the
middle Atlantic seaboard. The three powerful "Grandfather"

nations were — and still are, though their peoples are now mostly intermarried — Munsee, wolf totem (*ptuksi*, or "round foot"); Unami, turtle totem (*pakoango*, or "the crawler"); Unalatchtgo, turkey totem (*pullaeu*, or "he does not chew'). It is believed that the Lenape are the descendants of some of the oldest Algonquin groups.

Some scholars, such as Herbert C. Kraft, have stated that the association of the three grandfathers with the three animal clans (wolf, turtle, and turkey) are later additions. Most Lenape today, however, are familiar with them, and have various ways of explaining their meaning. Kraft also questioned the existence of a formal "Unalatchtgo" nation, but I think this is a technicality.

Munsee (Muncie or Monsey, wolf totem; literally, "The People of Stony Country"). The best known of the Munsee-speaking people are the Esopus, the Minisinks ("Island Place"), the Sinsinks ("A Stony Place"), and the so-called Manhattan Indians. Robert Grumet includes as Delaware speakers the Weckqueesgeeks ("People of the Birchbark"), the Rockaways ("Sandy Place"), and the Sanhikans ("Firemaking Place" or "Fire Drill"), even though there were skirmishes between them. If they were Munsee speakers, they were probably culturally and genetically Mahican, which some have supposed to be true of the Wappingers.

The *Esopus* had five sub-tribes: Waoranecks, Warranawon-kongs, Mamekotings, Wawarsinks, and Katskills.

The "*Manhattan*" Indians were also a Munsee subgroup. Their many bands included the Manahattin ("Hilly Island"), the Rechgawank ("Sandy Place," possibly related to the Haverstraw), the Tenkenas ("Wild Land"), the Rechewanis

("Sandy Place"), the Conykeekst ("Little Narrow Tract"), the Muscoota ("Place of Rushes"), the Ranachqua ("End Place"), the Sachwranung, the Quinnahung ("Long High Place"), the Schorankin, the Keskeskick ("Short Sharp Sedge Grass" or "Where the Grass Rustles"), the Shorakapkok ("A Cover"), the Paparinemin, the Kentipath, and the Acqueegecom ("Steep High Bank"). Some of these may be place names only.

I have also met members of a subtribe known as the Pochuck.

I have recently learned of the following Munsee subtribes but do not have complete information yet. They are (from www.dickshovel.com): Cashiehtunk, Lackawaxen, Marechkawieck (same as Gawanus, mentioned elsewhere), Meochkonck, Mengakonia, Mohickon, Outauninkin, Pakadasank, Papagonk, Peckwes, Shepinakonck, Waywayanda, Wildwyck (of Kingston, New York, probably same as Warranawongkongs), and Wysox.

Unami (turtle totem; literally, "The People Down River"). The Unami bands include the Hackensack, Mosilian (or Mosinan), the Raritan (some say these are the same as Sanhikan), the Navasink, the Axion (or Atsayonck, or Atsayogky), the Remkokes, (aka Ramcock, Ancocus, Rancocas, Rankoke, Rarncock, or Remahenonc), the Momakarongh, and the Assomoches. Most Canarsies probably spoke Unami, in addition to other dialects. The Rockaways have yet to be identified as Munsee-only or Unami-only speakers, and may have had close ties with the Mahican-speaking peoples of Long Island's Matouack Confederacy as well.

The seven *Hackinsack* bands included the Hackinsack ("Hooklike Mouth of the River Land" or "Place of Sharp

Ground"), the Ackkinkash, the Weehawken, the Hobokan ("Tobacco Pipe"), the Aressick, the Passaic ("Valley"), and the Watchogue ("Hilly Land"). There may have been a Harsimus band of Lenape in this area.

Seven major bands of the ***Western Unami*** include the Wyoming, the Tulpehochen ("Turtle Land"), the Shackamaxon, the Nittabakonck, the Playwicky, the Passayunk ("In the Valley"), and the Okehocking.

The ***Western Canarsie*** include the Canarsie ("the Fortified Place"), the Nyack ("Land at the Point," two settlements), the Gowanus ("Young Pine," from a chief's name aka Marechkawieck, which may be a subtribe of the Nyack), the Pagganck ("Place for Walnuts") /Kapsee ("Sharp Rocks in the Water"), the Rechtank/ Shepmoes, the Werpoes ("In the Thicket"), the Achwowongen ("Steep High Bank"), and the Rinneganconc ("Pleasant Land").

The ***Eastern Canarsie*** include the Makeop ("Open Field"), the Mocung ("Black Muddy Place"), the Narrioch ("Point of Land"), the Mannahaning ("Hilly Island"), the Shanscomacocke ("By the Ocean, Wholly Enclosed"), the Hoopaninak ("Enclosed Island"), and the Winippague. The Massabarkem ("Land by the Great Water") may have originally come from another area, but they borrowed land from the Canarsie. It should be noted that the term "Canarsie" in Dutch records refers to those near the King's Highway/Flatbush crossroads only, and not the others. However, convention has it that all of these peoples were linked together under the influence of the Canarsie. It is difficult to be sure that all Canarsies spoke Unami. Some, such as the Gowanus, spoke Munsee. Although the languages are mutually intelligible, they are, nonetheless, distinctly different. It is even possible that the Canarsie were a bilingual people, which would explain their ability to pick up distant languages in the course of maintaining their trade routes.

I have recently learned of the following Unami-speaking sub-tribes, but do not have complete information yet. They are (from www.dickshovel.com) Ahaimus, Aquackanonk, Armeomeck, Assunpink, Brotherton, Calcefar, Coacquannok, Coaxen, Communipaw (Gamaoenapa), Cranbury, Crosswick (Crossweeksung), Edgepilock (Indian Mills), Eriwonec (Armewamese, Armewamex, Erinoneck, Ermamex), Gweghkongh, Haverstraw (or Haverstroo, but they are well within Munsee territory), Hespatingh, Keskaechquerem (a band of the Canarsie region), Konekotay, Lehigh (Gach-wehnagechga), Hockanetcunk, Macock, Matanakon (Matikonghy), Matovancon, Mechgachkamic, Meggeckessou, Meletecunk (Metacunk), Momakarongk, Mooharmowikarun, Mookwungwahoki, Muhhowekaken, Muhkarmhukse, Muhkrentharne, Nittabonck (Nittabokonck), Neshamini, Meshannock, Paatquacktung, Pavonia, Pemickpacka, Pocopson (Poaetquissingh, Pocaupsing), Sawkin, Schuykill (near Philadelphia), Soupnapka, Tappan, Waoranec, Weepink, Welagamika, Wickquakonik (Wicoa), Wichquaquenscke, and Yacomanshaghking.

The Unami's neighbors to the north were the Unalimi, "The People Up River," a less historically significant Lenape band, with few if any subtribes.

Unalatchtgo (Turkey totem clan; literally, "People Near the Ocean"). Seven principal nations are the Armewamex, the Mantaes, the Naraticonck, the Little Siconese/Big Siconese

267

(Chiconesseck), the Sewapois, the Wicomiss, and the Kechemeches.

The dickshovel website list includes the following subtribes of the Unalatchtgo (or "Unalactigo" nation of southern New Jersey, northern Delaware and southeastern Pennsylvania — until 1682: Amimenipaty, Assomoche, Atayoneck, Chikohoki (Chihohock, Chilohoki), Cranbury, Hickory, Hopokohacking, Kahansu, Manta (Mantes), Memankitonna, Minguannan (Minguahanan, Minguarinari), Nantuxet, Naraticon (Maraticonck, Narraticong), Quenomysing (Quineomessingque), Roymount, Tirans, and Watcessit.

Also of the Lenni-Lenape culture are:

Mahican ("People of the Water That Flows Both Ways") wolf totem. There were nine tribes in the Mahican Confederacy. The Mahican lived along the Hudson River (or Mahicanituk) from Poughkeepsie northward on the eastern shore. The Wappingers lived along the eastern bank of the river from Poughkeepsie to Manhattan. On the western bank up to Catskill Creek were Munsee. North of this point were the Mahican up to Lake Champlain, and as far west as the crest of the Catskill Mountains. More than any other Algonquin culture, the Mahican were influenced by contact with the Iroquois.

Eastern Mahican The Mahican "R" dialect expanded quite a ways into New England during the early colonial period. The Quiripi dialect, which covers the western half of Connecticut, is also an "R" dialect and is hard to distinguish from Mahican. In fact, it may be Mahican in origin. Some "New England" nations' languages were closely linked with the Lenape through the "R" dialect, though they allied themselves with the Pequot and other confederations: Mahican, Schodac,

Stockbridge, Scatacooks, Housetonics ("Over the Mountain"), Wepawaugs, Pequamocks, Potatucks, Cupheags, Quinnipiacs, ("Where We Change Our Route") Paugusset ("Where the River Widens"), Pequannocks ("Battlefield" or "Slaughter-place"), Wangunks, Tunxis, and the Podunks.

The **Rockaway** subtribes included the Rechquaakee ("Sandy Land"), the Wandowenock ("They Dig Pits"), the Mespaeches, the Yameco aka Jamaica ("Place of the Beaver"), and the Equendito ("Cleared of Trees"). Little is known about these groups and their names may be mistranslated. When they left the area, some joined the Unami to the west, others joined the "R" dialect nations of the Matouac (Long Island) Confederacy to the east. Rechquaakee is thought to be a Delaware word, but an argument could be made that they were Mahican-Quiripi speakers and belong with the Matouac.

The **Siwanoy** were Mahican-Quiripi-"R" dialect-speaking people of the East Bronx area and part of the Matouac (Long Island) Confederacy. Their bands included the Conangungh, the Shippa, the Wanaqua, the Siwanoy, the Snakapins ("Between River and Water"), the Mishow, and the Asumsowis.

The **Western Matouac (or Southern Mahican)** include the Matinecock ("Good Hunting Place" or "Place of Rough Ground"), Massapequa ("Water from Here to There"), Seawanhakee ("At the Salty Place" or "Wampum Land"), and the Madnack. All of Queens and adjoining Long Island are Mahican-Quiripi, or "R" dialect speakers (which is clearly different from Munsee) of the Matouac Confederacy, and there is reason to believe they were rivals of the Munsee. Matinecock may be a Delaware word.

Wappingers (from Muwapinkus, or "Possum Clan").

There were nine tribes in the Wappinger Confederacy. They may have been related to the Mahicans by blood, but were apparently Munsee speakers. Muwapinkus means "he has no fur on his tail." They occupied parts of Dutchess, Putnam, and Westchester counties. However, the belief that they once had a much greater confederacy in the time of Chief Tamanend is now in doubt.

Nanticoke ("Tidewater"). A mixed group, closely r elated to Lenapes. Some joined the Iroquois Confederacy later on. Their seven bands included the Annemessex, the Assateagues, the Chicacones, the Choptanks, the Nanticokes, the Wicomicoes, and possibly the Pocomoke ("Dark Water").

Piscataway ("High Passable Bank around a Bend in the River"). Their many bands included the Anacostians, Chopticans, Kittamaqundis, Mattawomacs, Nanjemoys, Patuxents, Piscataways, Potomacs ("Where Tribute Is Brought"), Potopacs, and Taocomcoes, among others.

SOUTHEASTERN
(Relatives of the Lenni-Lenape)

Powhatan Alliance (after Chief Powhatan, "Falls of the River People"). During the time of Pocahontas, there were thirty-one small tribal groups and two hundred villages. The principal seven included:

Roanoke ("Northern People")

Pamunkey

Mattaponi

Chickahomini ("Pounded Corn People," aka "People of the Clearing"). Pocahontas and her famous father were of the Chickahomini nation.

Chesapeake ("Large Waters with Large Clams and Oysters"). Some were of the Hatteras-Powhatan group.

Pamlico of the Hatteras-Powhatan group. (Some believe Lumbees are descendants of Pamlicos.)

Smaller bands aligned with the Powhatan were the Cuttatawoman, the Taughanono, the Onawmaniet, the Sekakawon, the Wiccocomito, the Piankatank, the Chiskiac, the Kecoughtan, the Quiyoughcohannock, the Appamattuck, the Arrohateck, the Paspahegh, the Accomac, the Kisiack, the Occohannock, and the Opiscopank.

The Hatteras Algonquins of North Carolina were also aligned with the Powhatans, and the Hatteras language was also Lenni-Lenape in character. Their bands included the Warrashoyack, the Nansemon, the Weapemeoc, the Moratok, the Secotan, the Aquaseogoc, the Comokee, the Hatteras, the Ocracoke, the Pamlico, the Machapunga, the Pomeiok, and the "Noose" or Noosiak, also known as the Coharie. The Coharie were finally recognized by the state of North Carolina in 1971 and currently have four settlements in Sampson County. The Coree and the Croatan of the area may have been Algonquin as well. The Chawanoac also joined the Hatteras-Powhatan Confederacy at one time. The word Chawanoac resembles the Cherokee word for "salty," so there is some speculation on the origins of the Chawanoac, however most sources now indicate these were Shawnee.

CREE

Cree (from Kirishtinoo?) The meaning is uncertain and theories vary widely, though it may perhaps relate to those who were converted to Christianity. Although these tribes were highly migratory, certain groupings can be made.

East Main Cree, the largest group, has seven subtribes located at Waswanipi, Lake St. John, Chicoutimi, Tadoufsac, Escoumains, Oumamiouek, and Godoubt. The traditional band names include the Nisibourounik, the Pitchibourounik, the Gesseiriniouetch, the Opinagauiriniouetch, the Grand Mistassirini, and Le Petit Mistassirini. (The Bersimis, Papinachois, and Mistassini settlements in the region are affiliated with the Montagnais.)

West Main Cree, seven subtribes located at Moose-factory, Moosonee, Fort Albany, Attawapiskat, Weenusk, Severn Band, and Fort York. Traditional band names include the Alimibegouek, the Monsoni, the Attawapiskat, Washahoe (aka New Severn Indians), the Weenusk, the Penneswagewan, and Wappus ("Rabbit" Cree).

The other five nations of the Cree hoop might include:

Tete-de-Boule Cree, Abitibi, Timiscimi, Outoulibi, Piscoutagami, Outchichagamiouetch, and Gens des Terres general, plus Attikamek.

Woods Cree include La Barriere, Paun, Bois Fort, Prairies, L'eau Trouble, Cree de Lacs, Brochet, and Michinipicpoet Cree.

Also, the three Blackfoot nations:

Blackfoot (from Siksika, or "Black Moccasins")

Blood (Cree of the Northern Plains; they call themselves Kainah or "Many Chiefs.")

Piegan (perhaps from *pis'kun*, a corral at the foot of a cliff over which buffalo were driven. Other sources say this means "Small Robes.")

GREAT LAKES

Ojibwa Confederacy

The nations of the Ojibwa hoop call themselves Abishinabe people. At one time a formal confederacy was created with the Ojibwa, Ottawa, and Potawatomi, who were once one nation. The seven fire prophecies record their migration from the East back to the lands of their ancestors, about A.D. 1400.

Ottawa (Odawa or "Trading People"). The Ottawa River was the main trade route for thousands of years, hence the confusion of names.

Ojibwa/Chippewa ("People Who Draw on Birchbark"). The prophecies and visions of the elders were written on birchbark scrolls and on sand and rock as well.

Subgroups include the Outchiou (Ojibwa) Marameg, Noquet, and the Salteaux (northwestern band, pronounced "So-to"), and the Amikwa (Nez Pierce). The term Bungi refers to the Plains Ojibwa, the Mississauga Ojibwa-speaking people between Georgian Bay and Lake Ontario after the Huron Wars. They ceded much valuable land to the English in the middle to late 1700s. Lesser-known groups include Ouasouarini, Graisse Ours (aka Makoua), and Nameouilini.

Menominee ("Wild Rice People"). The word relates to the prophecy mentioned above. They were told to go west to the land where the food grows on the water — wild rice.

Algonkin ("The First People" or "Allies"). They call themselves Mamawinini ("Nomadic People") or Anishnabek ("True Men" or "Real Men"). Their seven main bands are the Kitchesipirini (Allumette/Morrison Islands, "People of the Great River"), the Weskarini (Petite Nation area), the Kinounchepirini (the Ottawa River area below Allumette

273

Island), the Matouweskarini (Madawaski River area), the Ottagoutowuemin (Ottawa River above Allumette), the Nipissing ("People of the Small Lake" north and south of the lake), and Nippean ("Where We Slept"). By 1785, these had become fourteen bands: the Barriere, the Baskatong, the Gatineau/Lievre River, the Mississipi/Chats River, the Madawaska/Bonnechere, the Mattawa, and the Nipissing. Also, the Temagami, the Saugeen, the Temiscamingue, the Long Point, the Wolf Lake/DuMoine, the Grand Lak, and the Ottawa River/Coulonge bands. The Algonkins of the eastern sector from Ottawa city to Oka had become Mission Christians by this time.

Potawatomi ("People of the Place of Fire," aka "The Fire Nation"). This may be a clue that they are linked directly to the central fire of the Creation story, which was moved from the Montreal area to the Detroit area, part of their ancestral land. They call themselves Neshnabek, "The People."

The **Mississauga** are often considered separate from the Ojibwa. The Nipissing are often considered separately from the Algonkin.

PRAIRIE NATIONS
Ohio Valley Confederacy
Shawnee ("People of the South"). A large influential group made up of many "septs." These "septs" are the Makujay, the Piqua, and the Kispoko/Kispotaka of the Lenni-Lenape root, the Chalgotha/Chillicothe of the Siberian root and the Telegwa/Ft. Ancient of the Mound Builder root. The Shawnee always speak of them as five septs, however, two are split, leaving seven groups. The Prairie Confederacy under Tecumseh was

called "The Seven Nations" by 1794, but the Shawnee did not play the dominant role.

Miami (Ohio area, related to Illinois, from Oumamik, "People of the Peninsula")

Piankashaw (related to Miami)

Sauk (from Osakiwug, "People of the Yellow Clay"), now in Iowa and Oklahoma.

Fox/Mesquaki ("People of the Red Clay"), now in Iowa and Oklahoma.

Kickapoo ("He Moves About, Standing Here and There"), now in Oklahoma, Kansas, and New Mexico. The Sauk, Fox/Mesquaki, and Kickapoo were Sac Tribes, as were the Mascouten ("Place of Rushes").

ILLINOIS CONFEDERACY

(Illinewek). Related to the Prairie Algonquins.

Illinois ("Ordinary Speakers"). From *ileniwe*, probably a mix of the French "il" + the Algonquin "lenni" + the Algonquin "weh" or "they" or the French ending *ois*, as in "Quebequois."

Peoria ("He Carries a Pack")

Moingwena ("Bear Lake People")

Michigamea ("People of the Great Waters")

Kaskaskian ("Where the Grass Rustles"?)

Cahokia ("People Who Live Near the Cahokia Mounds")

Tamaroa ("People Who Live Near the Tamaroa Mounds")

WESTERN PLAINS

Arapaho ("Wolf People"). Arapaho is a Crow word for

"Enemy with Many Skins." It also may be a Pawnee word for "He Who Trades." The Arapaho traditionally call themselves Kananavich or "Bison Path People." Originally from Minnesota, the Kananavich were the first Algonquins to move west. They are now divided into northern and southern bands. The southern are called Siksika.

Gros Ventre (from French for "Big Belly People"), a western branch of the Arapaho.

There were three other Arapaho bands, the Woodlodge People, the Rock People, and the South People.

Cheyenne (from a Lakota word for "they speak unintelligibly"). They call themselves Tsitsista, or "The People." Ten bands.

Sutai (closely related to Cheyenne)

Arapaho and Cheyenne are not closely related, but are the only western Algonquins today.

ALGONQUIN-RELATED LANGUAGES AND BANDS OF THE PACIFIC NORTHWEST

(* indicates acknowledged links to Algonquin languages; others in its grouping would presumably also be linked)

SALISHAN

Plateau, Northern Interior Salish: Shuswap (aka Sexwepemx), Thompson (aka Nl'akapamux), Lillooet (aka St'at'imx)

South Interior Salish:* Coeur d'Alene*, Flathead* (aka Selish), Kalispel*, Spokan*, Colville (aka Sweelpoo), Okanagan*, Lake, Sanpoil, Nespelem, Methow, Columbia (aka

Sinkiuse) Wenatchee, Chelan, Entiat

Coast Salishan:* Northern Salishan*: Bella Coola* (aka Nuxalk)

Central Salishan: Comox*, Pentlatch, Sechelt, Squamish*, Halkomelem (including Cowichan, Musqueam, Chilliwack) Nooksack, Lushootseed (aka Puget), Twana

Straits Salishan: Lummi, Songish (aka Lkungen), Sooke, Klallam (aka S'klallam)

Tsamosan Salish:* Quinault, Chehails*, Cowlitz*

Southern Salish:* Tillamook*

Salishan Isolates: Haida (includes Kaigani, Masset, Skidegate) and Tsimshian (includes Coast, Southern, Niska, and Gitksan) Pend-d'Oreilles* (Salish?) Nisqualli* (Salish?)

WAKASHAN*

Nootkan:* Includes Makah, Nitinat, Nootka* (aka Nuuchanuth)

Kwakiutlan:* Northern Kwakiutlan: Bella Bella (aka Heiltsuk), Xai Xais, Owikeno, Haisla (aka Kitimat)

Southern Kwakiutlan: Kwakiutl* (aka Kwakwaka'wakw)

ISOLATES

Yachi, Kutenai,* Ritwan,* (includes Wiyot,* and Yurok,* and related to Yukian. Yukian includes Yuki, Coast, Huchnom, and Wappo). These 65 western bands combined with the roughly 464 Algonquin bands brings the number of Algonquin-related peoples on this list to 529. There may be more.

Three Ancient Civilizations

ALGONQUIN

The ancient world of the Algonquin probably covered most of North America. That territory today would include the lower provinces of Canada from Newfoundland to the Rockies, and the United States from Maine south to Florida, west to the Mississippi Delta and northwest along the Arkansas River and the Continental Divide to Alberta and possibly parts of British Columbia.

SIOUIAN

The Siouian-speaking nations originated long ago in the southeast, possibly South Carolina, where they would have been allies of the Algonquins. (The Catawaba of North Carolina are Siouian-speakers.) Many of their word roots have been traced to Algonquin origins.They journeyed far south and then migrated north through the less populated Great Plains, dividing the western Algonquins as far north as Canada. The Crow (a Siouxan Nation) then migrated westward to the Rockies, dividing the Arapaho and Cheyenne peoples. Siouian nations often allied themselves with some Algonquin nations while warring with others. There are seven Teton Sioux nations today.

MISSISSIPPIAN

The Mississippian culture of the southeast was subdued by DeSoto in 1539, but the descendants of the Mississippian Mound Builders are many, and represent the most diverse cultural group east of the Rockies after the Algonquin and Sioux. Their descendants include the Caddo (Pawnee, Wichita, Waco, Caddo, Kachai, Arikara), the Iroquois (Mohawk, Oneida, Onondaga, Cayuga, Seneca) and Iroquoian nations (Susquehanna and Erie, etc.), the Seven Cherokee nations, and the seven Muskegian nations (Choctaw, Chickasaw, Creeks, Natchez, Apalachee, Timucua and Calusa). Various Muskegian and Creek peoples later formed the Seminole colony in Florida.

The Muskegan language is closely related to the Algonquin (the word means "marsh") but Muskegan people are Mississippian. The Cherokee and related nations are closer cousins of the Iroquois. They settled in the Smoky Mountains and surrounding areas, where many still reside. Related nations occupied Florida until removal in the 1800s.

279

NOTES

Introduction

i. The original presentation was based completely on first-hand experience, which I was later able to substantiate to some degree by reading the work of others. It is still more or less a collection of oral transmissions from native and non-native sources.

ii. Helen Perley ran the White Animal Farm for over fifty years and is the subject of several stories which recently appeared in *Reader's Digest*, plus the children's book *Mrs. Perley's People*. According to the book *The Julian Tribe*, King John Julian used his wits to overcome British legalistic efforts to take vast stretches of Micmac ancestral land away from them during the establishment of the Provinces in the mid-1700s. King George III was so impressed with his tenacity, John was summoned to the Royal Palace in London, whereupon John declared himself "King" of his people and of equal treaty status to George III. Without his audacity, the Micmac people might not still live on ancestral land today (nineteen reserves, most of them from that time). In fact, it is a rare circumstance in the Northeast for a native people to live on their ancestral land.

iii. The Wabanaki Confederacy, which existed between the mid-eighteenth century and the late nineteenth century, consisted of many nations (most notably the Abenaki) which have become five modern Native American Nations: Micmac, Maliseet, Passamaquoddy, Penobscot, and Abenaki. However, certain oral traditions hold that there have always been seven tribes in each of the great hoops of Algonquin peoples, and that the Northern Montagnais and Naskapi people are now and have always been the sixth and seventh tribes of this Wabanaki hoop.

The Penobscot, then a leading Abenaki group, withdrew from the Confederacy in 1862, which led to its eventual dissolution.

iv. The talking feather circle is a ceremony in which a feather is passed clockwise and only the one holding the feather may speak. It may have originated (at least in its present form) by the Cherokee years ago, but has long been used by the Wabanaki with a "talking stick" or a feather.

v. See iii. Although classified as subarctic, I understand that the languages and customs of the Montagnais (Inu — or "We the People") and Naskapi are closely related to Micmac. Plus, the Naskapi are equally as "eastern" as the Micmac and see the dawn of Labrador at the same time as the Micmac see it in Nova Scotia, thus being "children of the dawn" as well. (In 1970, the Canadian census recorded 6,000 Montagnais and 400 Naskapi people.)

vi. See *North American Native Authors Catalog*, 50 pp., Greenfield Review Press, P.O. Box 308, 2 Middle Grove Rd., Greenfield Center, NY 12833; (518) 583-9741.

vii. ... and exploiters: read Jack Weatherford's *Indian Givers* for the grim details.

viii. Informal estimate from private conversations with anthropologist Jack Weatherford.

ix. Abbe Museum, Bar Harbor, Maine. Joseph Polis was Thoreau's guide on his trip into the Maine Woods, but earlier exposure to Algonquin thought seems likely.

281

x. *Indian Givers*, by Jack Weatherford. (The Iroquois Constitution also uses this term.)

xi. I'm not aware of current books that overtly denegrate Native Americans; however, since I occasionally travel around and speak about the subject — and stereotypes is one of my favorite topics — I listen to outcries and statements about Indians that seem rather erroneous, at least to me. I try to engage detractors (who are often close friends) in rational discussion, which is one of the principles of the Wabanaki free society.

xii. Many linguistic historians believe that all languages derived from one source. Don Ringe, Jr., of the University of Pennsylvania believes that Algonquin, one of the world's major language groups, diverged from other languages less than 10,000 years ago, and places the breakup of an original language over 40,000 years ago, several ice ages back! Joseph Greenberg, Stanford University, believes that almost all Native American languages are of one family.

xiii. This term is Lenape but has counterparts in Wampanog and Wabanaki. We were all originally one people not too long ago.

Text

1. Of the 1600 Native American languages that have existed, only one-third still exist today, according to a recent documentary, "In Search of a First Language." I have read that there were approximately one hundred Algonquin languages at the time of the Plymouth Colony.

The least-spoken of the seven Wabanaki languages is probably Abenaki, one of the most difficult. However, Abenaki speakers such as Elie Joubert are quite in demand as teachers of the language and have many students, including those in Elie's classes at SUNY, Albany. Joseph Bruchac has popularized many Abenaki stories and the Bruchac family produced a musical CD, "Ulnubak," with lyrics mostly in Abenaki. Although not recognized by the U.S. government for political reasons, the Abenaki part of the wheel is well on its way to rejuvenation.

2. Herbert Kelly once commented, "If you can't be with God in a pigpen, you're out of luck!" (this via Madeleine L'Engle).

3. Buddha referred to it as "the Great Mystery." The same in Abenaki is too-see-noo-ahsk.

4. In concert with this is the Aramaic expression *hamartia,* "the arrow that misses the mark," used by Jesus, which has been retranslated along the way as "evil" (M. L'Engle).

5. Published by Station Hill Press, Barrytown, NY 12507.

6. Manichaeism, a Persian/Christian philosophy taught openly from the third through the seventh centuries A.D., equated the soul with good, God, and light; the body with Satan, darkness, and evil. This dualistic view was absorbed into Christianity and various mystical European teachings in myriad and complex ways.

   Although not all Europeans believe this by any means, I feel it is very important in understanding the separation between the Christian view of the world and the predominant indigenous view. Although the Wabanaki teachings revere light as divine and holy, Manichaeism and Wabanaki philosophies are worlds apart.

7. Taoism in particular.

8. Also spelled *pigsa't,* the softer b and d are the pronunciation I have heard. The Micmac lexicon lists *mglu'tyew* as smoke from a fire, a logical word-construction; however, I have never heard any word but *bigsod* or *busk-oo-sod* used to refer to smudge smoke.

9. *Bpoo-ohin* refers to "an elder with extraordinary spiritual powers." "Medicine man" is a term in much dispute, but is used frequently to refer to healers, seers, and those who work with spirit helpers, all of which are very much a part of Wabanaki shamanic tradition. The dispute comes in as to what part of that practice today has been influenced by the Lakota "medicine" teachings.

Equally disputed is whether the "medicine wheel" of the Western Algonquin people, the Cree, etc., is native to the Wabanaki. I sense that it is. In that the Lakota migrated from South Carolina (Walker) and are of proto-Algonquin stock, with some linguistic roots in common, I suspect that the medicine wheel teachings are quite close to ancient Wabanaki knowledge. As to what degree, there is little chance of proving it. According to *A Concise Dictionary of Indian Tribes* by Barbara Leitch, most Abenaki, Penobscot, and other Wabanaki tribes had a domed sweat lodge in every village.

10. In ancient Rome, February was the last month of the year (as it is in many cultures) and the word February derives from "the rites of purification" which itself derives from the root word *dhwes* — "to fumigate or smoke." (Our Valentine's Day was the eve of the new year, which would make December "the tenth month" as its name implies.) The use of incense in church, the burning of frankincense and myrrh, and the incense used in India, may all be rem-

nants of smudging practices.

11. Animal sacrifices were very common among Vedic Brahmins at the time of Buddha, and in Mongolia and the Middle East, but unknown in Wabanaki history. Offerings are based on giving what you yourself possess, and the idea of having possession of an animal is something of which the Wabanaki are wary. It is not customary to "put an animal to sleep"; it is believed they are better off in the woods. Hunting animals for food is a very different story. In the subarctic areas frequented by Micmac, Montagnais, Naskapi, and other Wabanaki hunters, it is necessary for human survival.

12. From the Latin *lei*: "to pour out"; the ritual of pouring out wine or oil on the ground as a sacrifice to a god.

13. R is the seventh letter of the Sanskrit alphabet. *Rta* is the Indic root word of rite and ritual, which is an aspect of its meaning. When we speak of "Native American ritual," we are using the derivative of *Rta* to refer to it.

285

14. Popular Hindu festivals are sacred dramas for the people who attend them, people who don't read the Vedas, but who know the stories of Siva and know the meanings of each highly stylized gesture and dance. Not unlike Wabanaki culture today, popular Indian culture is a complex integration of folk, pop, and traditional influences, one which is constantly evolving as an oral tradition.

15. Dance has a sacred history all around the world, even in Europe, where the Manichaean influence on Christianity did it serious damage. To find out how other cultures shared the Wabanaki practice of sacred dance, read Havelock Ellis' book, *The Sacred Dance*, in which he reveals, among other things, that the Catholic Mass includ-

ed dances as part of ceremony until the Middle Ages.

16. Psychologist Virginia Satir, after studying a number of cultures including Native American cultures, came up with four universal "coping stances" which people use when confronted with stress and anger. They are "the Placater," "the Super-Reasonable Man," "the Blamer," and "the Irrelevant One." There is also a fifth stance, the only one that doesn't eventually lead to more anger and conflict, and that is "the Congruent Stance." It is open and well balanced; this is the stance of the artist of life and also the stance of the *geenap* or strong elder.

17. There is another handshake I've heard of but never seen which is with held wrists. This gesture of greeting is probably from the south of the region.

18. In Tai Chi, schools of motion derive their names from the movement of animals, as do the movements themselves; Crane, Tiger, Snake. One of my favorite Tai Chi terms is "Grasping Sparrow's Tail."

19. According to Blofeld, "the body takes part [in the spiritual process] through prostrations, offerings, and mudras" in Tibetan religious practice.

20. Swami Chetananda. From *Parabola* article, 1993.

21. The plural ending *q(oo)* is silent in this case.

22. *Tao Te Ching*: Thomas Merton translation.

22a. The popular Pan-Indian trickster, Kaioki (or *Hey-yo-ka* in Lakota) is one who goes contrary to the natural way of things. Some say it means "coyote," a close relative of the wolf. According to Thomas Parkhill, Malsum (Maliseet for wolf) is largely an invention of Sylas Rand, an early missionary. Lahks is not a brother of Glooskap, but Rand described Malsum as Glooskap's brother. The Abenaki had a trickster referred to as the Raccoon.

23. There are enough parallels between the Sami and the Micmacs to construct a separate book, if there isn't one already. Currently, there are over one hundred Micmac people living with the Sami in Lapland. The original group left Canada in the 1960s to seek cultural and political freedom.

24. According to many accounts, a number of tribes of the Pacific Northwest north of Vancouver Island still speak Algonquin-related languages; Kutenai, Salish, Flathead Coeur d'Alene, Kalispel, Spokan, Okinagan, Pend-d'Oreilles, Ritwàn, Yurok, Wiyot, Nootka, Kwakiutl, Coast Salish, Chehalis, Nisqualli, Cowlitz, Squamish, Comox, Tillamook, Bella Coola are all related to Algonquin.

25. Peter Nabokov, *The Indian Running Book*. Although it doesn't mention the Wabanaki people, it mentions similar nations who have extensive running traditions, complete with stories, myths, and heroes.

26. Parabola, "Oral Traditions," 1993. According to Thomas Coligan (*Art and Politics*, Jan. 1995), King Ammon (from Plato's *Phaedrus*) believed that, by reading, people would cease to exercise their memory and grow forgetful.

27. Spontaneous overflow of affection and love is central to the Bhakti tradition. The Bhaktis known as Sahajiyas demonstrate sincerity and affection through spontaneity.

28. The Wabanaki of Maine and the Maritimes tell us that the old word for that waterfall meant "fish ladder," and it was the place where the salmon climbed up the falls as if on a ladder. If you like the taste of salmon, that's a good thing to know.

29. These are the Micmac terms. In Maliseet-Passamaquoddy they would be pronounced *neeloon* and *geeloon* — usually spelled *nilun* and *kilun,* respectively.

    In Micmac, there are singular, dual, and plural forms to most words, so it is not surprising that there is a dual "we" and a plural "we" as well.

30. In *The Secret of the Golden Flower*, a Taoist text, the clockwise flow is the downward, life-manifesting flow of spirit into matter. It is Creation becoming manifest. "The way leads from the sacrum upward in a backward-flowing way to the summit of the Creative and on through the house of the Creative; then it sinks through the two stories in a direct downward-flowing way into the solar plexus, and warms."

31. Literally, "the Wheel of Being" in Sanskrit.

32. Surprisingly, God is not literally a "God of love" in Hindu tradition. *Ananda,* or bliss, is an aspect of God which is a bit more undirected, less personal. However, the Hindu devotee can experience *Prema,* the divine love for God, within himself or herself.

33. In Confucian times in China and Tibet, it was not permitted to dig into the ground for any reason. Those people respected the earth that much.

34. Co-authored with this writer, Evan Pritchard. Published by Resonance Communications, P.O. Box 215, Beacon NY 12508.

35. The sun plays an important part in many Creation stories around the world. In the Mahabharata, Krishna says, "I taught this undying discipline to the shining sun, first of all mortals, who told it to Manu, the progenitor of Man.

Manu told it to the Solar King Ikshvaku."

36. These stories were told to me by Marge Bruchac, an Abenaki. However I have heard similar accounts from Stephen Augustine. They have been published elsewhere.

37. Early European spirituality is well known for its use of circles, both for honoring spirit, and for self-defense. When Jesus was in the desert, some believe he protected himself from Satan with a drawn circle.

38. In the *Bardo Thodol* of Tibet, actual death is described as a very similar journey to fasting, with similar attention to directions:

The first day after death, one sees Vairocana, in white light. The element is space. This is the Buddha of Dharma and Wisdom.

The second day, one sees the Lord Dorje Sempra (also called Vajrasattva), a being of mirror-like wisdom. The color is blue, the direction is East, the element is water.

On the third day, one encounters Rinchen Jungne, a being of great equanimity. He is of the South, the element of earth. The color is yellow.

On the fourth day, the departed meets Amitaba, a being of wisdom and compassion. He is in the West, the direction of Dewa-chen. His is the red light of the fire element. One sees rainbows everywhere.

On the fifth day, one meets Amoghasiddhi, the Lord of Air, in the North. The color is green.

On the sixth day, the departed sees all five Buddhas together. Then appear the Protectors of the Four Directions. They are the "doorkeepers" of the Mandala, or "gatekeepers."

On this day all forty-two deities appear, and one has an

opportunity to attain enlightenment for all time. These deities and all the four directions emerge from your own heart. This is the center of man, the center of the heart. The primordial Buddha, Kuntuzangpo, and his consort Kuntuzangmo, appear. All are essences of your own higher self.

On the seventh day, all the knowledge-holding deities shine their lights to you, creating a rainbow of many colors. According to the great lamas, you must reach the pure land by the end of the seventh day or suffer hell realms and eventual reincarnation.

(Compare with *The Woodcarver* by Chuang Tzu describing a seven-day fast.)

39. Though Siva was never a Vedic god, he remained a god to the indigenous people. Pashupati should not be confused with Prajapati, Lord of Humans, who later became Brahma.

40. It is interesting that Chuang Tzu often used animals in his own storytelling to speak for him. This shows a reverence for the wisdom of animals and nature that goes beyond a literary device which may have been prevalent at the time. Perhaps animals really did speak to him in some way.